TO A

SHOOT STRAIGHT,

AND SPEAK

THE TRUTH

TO RIDE,

SHOOT STRAIGHT,

AND SPEAK

THE TRUTH

KIRCHNER

JEFF COOPER

Paladin Press · Boulder, Colorado

Also by Jeff Cooper:

The Art of the Rifle
Fireworks: A Gunsite Anthology
Principles of Personal Defense

To Ride, Shoot Straight, and Speak the Truth
by Jeff Cooper

Copyright © 1998 by Gunsite Training Center

ISBN 0-87364-973-7
Printed in the United States of America

Published by Paladin Press, a division of
Paladin Enterprises, Inc., P.O. Box 1307,
Boulder, Colorado 80306, USA.
(303) 443-7250

Published in association with:
> Gunsite Training Center
> P.O. Box 700
> Paulden, AZ 86334

Direct inquiries and/or orders to the above address.

PALADIN, PALADIN PRESS, and the "horse head" design
are trademarks belonging to Paladin Enterprises and
registered in United States Patent and Trademark Office.

All rights reserved. Except for use in a review, no
portion of this book may be reproduced in any form
without the express written permission of the publisher.

Neither the author nor the publisher assumes
any responsibility for the use or misuse of
information contained in this book.

Cover illustration by Paul Kirchner

Visit our Web site at www.paladin-press.com

FOR

JANELLE

CONTENTS

III. The Rifleman

IV. The Hunter

V. The Past

ACKNOWLEDGEMENTS

Several of the chapters in this book have been previously published in the periodicals of Petersen Publications, to whom the author owes thanks for permission to include them in this collection.

I wish to thank my client and friend, Paul Kirchner, for the various appropriate drawings he contributed to this work, and my niece, Austeene Cooper II, for the frontispiece.

And I wish gratefully to acknowledge the expert assistance of Nancy Tappan, who put the project together.

FOREWORD

"Delightful task! to rear the tender thought, to teach the young idea how to shoot."

James Thompson
1700-1748
The Seasons, Spring

Fighting Handguns was published in 1955. In it are pictures of the author, a young Marine named Jeff Cooper, demonstrating what was at that time the proper stance for pistol combat: knees bent in a "combat crouch," gun held in one hand below the belt line, eyes on the target. Viewing that photograph today evokes the same embarrassed amusement as seeing one's own baby pictures. Yet it tells an important story.

Jeff Cooper is famous as a soldier, writer, handgunner, rifleman, philosopher, and scholar, but most of all, as a teacher — a guru. His impact on the theory and practice of handgunning is immeasurable. It is probably safe to say that, were it not for Jeff Cooper, there would be no International Practical Shooting Confederation. If it were not for Jeff Cooper and his American Pistol Institute, we would still be shooting one-handed from a "combat crouch," and missing. But for Jeff Cooper, we would spend our weekends at the range shooting 38 Special wadcutters from a one-handed "target" stance, with the off-hand in the trousers pocket — and thinking we were adequately prepared to defend ourselves.

Psychologists define "learning" as "a change in behavior." If you see current photographs of Jeff Cooper's contemporaries, men of the same age and background, you will note that they still shoot one-handed from the hip. Only he was open-minded enough to try new and different ideas, until he eventually developed the Modern Technique of the Pistol. These days, it is generally acknowledged that the correct way to use a pistol is with both hands, at eye-level. (There are still a few die-hards, of course, but there is still a Flat Earth Society, too.) And so it turns out that the acknowledged world's greatest *teacher* of pistolcraft is actually the world's greatest *learner* of pistolcraft.

Jeff Cooper has written many books since 1955. *Cooper On Handguns* is the basic text on the subject, and *Principles of Personal Defense* should be required reading for anyone who proposes to call himself an intelligent adult. In his *Fireworks* anthology, Cooper proved himself to be a fine writer,

ix

instead of merely a "gun-writer." With subjects like automobile racing, and bullfighting, and love, and nature, he displayed his astonishing skill at storytelling.

I remember a night when we "solved the problems of the world" in front of his fireplace. We discussed politics, history, guns, the meaning of life, and other topics suitable to what the Spaniards call a *tertulia*. For our entertainment, he recited W.W. Jacobs' *The Monkey's Paw*. Though I had heard it many times, my hair stood on end. You will see what I mean when you read his account of a German soldier's escape from a Russian P.O.W. camp. If that one doesn't set your blood afire, then you need to check your vital signs.

This new collection will delight those who thought *Fireworks* "didn't have enough gun stuff." There is gun stuff galore in these pages, and the ideas are new, and thought-provoking, and exciting. Naturally, they are also beautifully written.

Mark Moritz
April, 1988

THE TITLE

"To Ride, Shoot Straight, and Speak the Truth. This was the ancient law of youth." These lines were cherished by Theodore Roosevelt, one of America's two greatest presidents and her dozen or so great men. I thought the verse was American in origin until I went into the matter and discovered its ultimate source in Herodotus.

According to "The Father of History" the precept originated at the court of the great kings of Persia, where wealth and power were so concentrated as to produce a style of life conspicuously unsuited to the upbringing of a young nobleman. Luxury and authority are not good for a young man, and if he enjoys such things in his adolescence he is most unlikely to develop into a man of character.

Therefore, as soon as the sons of the great were old enough to do for themselves, they were farmed out to the households of minor chiefs on the frontiers of the empire. Their masters were told that the boys were to know no soft beds, no fine raiment, no rich food or wine, no philosophical complexities, no slave girls, and no money. What they were to learn was to ride like Cheiron, to shoot like Apollo, and above all to speak only the truth. With these three attributes they were deemed fit to return to court at the age of eighteen. What else they needed to know in order to become princes could then be imparted easily and quickly by their seniors.

This is certainly an antique notion, but what is newer is not necessarily better — nor, looking around us, even usually so.

There is little in this book about riding, but there is a lot about various aspects of shooting, an art which has been notably diminished in this twentieth century in which it has become most needful. By my great good fortune I happen to know much about shooting, both technically and tactically, and in what follows I speak the absolute truth about it, insofar as God has granted me the ability to do so.

This book, therefore, is not for the trepid, the faint of heart, the soft, nor the overcivilized. It is, on the contrary, for those who aspire to command of the unruly environment in which they now find themselves.

Jeff Cooper

Gunsite, July 1988

I. THE PRESENT

To Ride, Shoot Straight, and Speak the Truth

·KIRCHNER·

2

HOLD! ENOUGH!

"Is life so sweet, or peace so dear, as to be purchased at the price of chains and slavery? Forbid it, Almighty God!"

Patrick Henry

Why do you suppose the creeps of the world have declared open season on Americans? Are we not the posterity of Patrick Henry and George Washington and Nathan Hale and Buck Travis and George Custer and Teddy Roosevelt and George Patton?

How do they dare?

We seem to have changed, and not for the better. The Fathers won the country with sweat and blood. The sons seem to think that gives them a free ticket to the fat life — a life without fighting. Now where do you suppose the idea arose that a man can make it without fighting? It was certainly not prevalent in the 1920's or 1930's. It is new, but it is now almost universal. And it is *sick*. It delivers up the soft to the wicked. It makes the American the laughing stock of the age.

The issue is "hijacking" — air piracy. It is now intolerable, and it promises to get worse. We wring our hands. We look for "solutions" in concepts and gadgets, but what we need is *will*.

The goblins do not hijack El Al. Not any more. If the Shi'ites wanted their people back from the Israeli P.O.W. camps, their obvious target was an Israeli airplane — one might suppose. But they hit T.W.A. instead. Why? Because they believe — correctly — that Americans will not fight, and that — also correctly — Americans will grovel at the possibility that other Americans may be killed. And they further believe that by savaging a prisoner to death they will intimidate, rather than enrage, the American public.

3

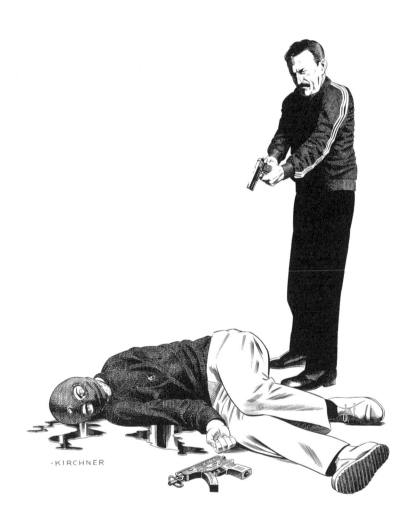

No, they did not try El Al. As cowards, they fear the Israelis. But they do not fear the Americans. They know the Americans will not do anything but whimper.

How in the name of John Hancock did we come to this disgusting pass!

For whatever my opinion is worth, the root of the problem is the demise of the nuclear family. Morals and ethics are taught at the mother's knee, and consolidated around the family dinner table. When mother is otherwise occupied in the marketplace, and dinner is taken in front of the tube, there can be no inculcation of righteousness in a developing personality.

See, now, over the portals of our academies are engraved the words: "Duty. Honor. Country." How many people under the age of forty can you name who can even define those words? As generation follows generation this situation degenerates. If Daddy has no idea of what honor means, how can he explain it to Junior, even if circumstances lend themselves to it — which, in most cases, they no longer do.

The press, academe, and the law enforcement establishment preach: Do not fight back! On the street, in your home, on the airplane, on the high seas, anywhere, anytime. Do not fight back! You may be hurt.

Of course you may be hurt. You may be killed. As my daughter put it just last week: "Big deal. You expect to live forever?"

The only honorable response to violence is counterviolence. To surrender to extortion is a greater sin than extortion, in that it breeds and feeds the very act it seeks to avoid.

Fifty years ago young people were made to understand —around the dinner table — that strife was part of life, and that they might well encounter it, and that it would then be their duty to face it without blinking — ready, willing, and able to use force quickly and expertly if necessary. Boys were taught to shoot and use their hands, and girls were taught to expect that in their men.

5

And that society was infinitely safer and more serene than what we have now. Mugging, rape, piracy, and terrorism (in the sense of the victimization of the uninvolved) were so rare as to be sensational. In that society it would have been both futile and ridiculous for two punks to assume physical command over 159 people. They would have been quickly killed.

The idea that intended victims can overcome armed bandits is not fanciful. Some years ago two pirates attempted to take over an Air Iberia flight from Madrid to Rome. The passengers killed them, the stewardesses covered them up with blankets, and opened the bar. The flight arrived on schedule. More recently a troll seized a girl in a Philippine bank, doused her with gasoline, and threatened to burn her if he was not given all the ready money. The customers not only beat him to death, they actually dismembered him. It can be done!

Is it too late for America to find its way back to an honorable social order — one in which the goblins of the world will respect us as much as they respect Israel? Perhaps it is, but let us hope not. The current series of disasters has pressed us hard. The mood of the times is anger, fully justified. But anger is of no use to the soft, and the majority of our mentors are far too flabby to serve us well. The requisite hardness of spirit must come, unfortunately, from generations which have no evident interest in courage and no pride in victory. But the latent nobility of the human soul has not vanished. It is simply buried. Let us unearth it. Something has got to be done.

Let's do it!

"THIS MATTER OF *IMAGE*"

We American shooters are confronted at this time with a curious and unexpected difficulty. As we approach the end of the twentieth century we find that the age of electronics has converted the human race in large measure from *doers* to *watchers*. It seems incontrovertible that great numbers of Americans — especially young Americans —would rather watch than do. (As a personal view, I cannot imagine how anyone who has not played football can enjoy watching football, and yet the enormous majority of the fans have never so much as held a football in their hands.) We, as a people, have become inordinately preoccupied with the appearance of things. Possibly people have always been so preoccupied, but the situation seems to be getting worse.

Until the social watershed of World War II no one felt that his image in society was endangered by a fascination with weapons. In the elder view weapons were the tools of power, the means by which man pulled himself up out of the mud into dominion over the earth and the skies above it. Consequently skill-at-arms was not only an acceptable attribute in a cultivated man, it was, effectively, obligatory. No one asked George Washington whether he was adept with sword, pistol, and musket — this was assumed. It would have been considered astonishing if he had not been. Times change, of course, but the human spirit is more enduring and more permanent than the whims of the decade. Teddy Roosevelt was not a particularly good shot, but he certainly was an enthusiastic shooter. To say that since we no longer live in the times of George Washington or Teddy Roosevelt the place of arms in our society has reversed itself is to ignore the evidence provided by, among others, our current president.

Perhaps the most pernicious prevailing misconception about skill-at-arms is the notion that *sport* is a legitimate endeavor, but that *fighting* is not. We hear it said — often by

7

people who should know better — that weapons are the province of the police and the military, but not the private citizen. It does not take a philosopher to detect the fallacy of this. *The Second Amendment of the Constitution, to which all shooters pay allegiance, has nothing whatever to do with sport.* The sporting use of firearms is a spin-off, and a very pleasant one. A good many shooters find that sporting competition with their firearms is a source of pleasure, camaraderie, and relaxation. However, the fact that aerobatics are great fun does not lead us to believe that aerobatics are the only reason for which we need aircraft. Firearms are a deeply graven element of the American tradition, but their sporting use, while attractive, is essentially irrelevant.

Too many sportsmen ignore this. Too many sportsmen say, "Oh, well, I shoot smallbore rifle targets. I have no interest in pistols." Others say, "I shoot quail with my shotgun. I have no interest in rifles." Others say, "I shoot IPSC with a pistol. I have no interest in defending myself on the street." These attitudes are dangerous, for in the immortal words of the founding father, "We must all hang together, or assuredly we shall all hang separately." I do not shoot skeet, but I am vitally interested in the freedom of the skeet shooters to enjoy their sport. I do not hunt woodchuck, but I am vitally interested in the right of chuck hunters to take the field. I do not shoot in ISU competition, but I am vitally interested in the continuance of formal target shooting. Perhaps more pungently, I have little interest in hand-held automatic weapons, but I deeply resent the efforts on the part of some of our lawmakers to paint full-automatic fire as some sort of sin.

It is no news to anyone who has fought the battle for the Second Amendment for a lifetime that our adversaries still hold the instrument, rather than the user, to be morally culpable. The hoplophobe really seems to believe that the artifact has a will of its own. He repeats *ad nauseam* that if the instrument had not been at hand the sociopath would have been a good citizen. Shooters realize the error of this, but even we tend to categorize by image.

Consider the matter of weapon type. In the Eastern Megalopolis, most particularly in its law enforcement establishment, the revolver is "decent" — the self-loading pistol is not.
Consider that the side-by-side double shotgun is "decent" in
the highlands of Scotland, where a repeating shotgun is not.
An Austrian friend has told me that if he showed up at a
hunting lodge in his country with a rifle equipped with a
synthetic stock he would be required to use the tradesman's
entrance. Such attitudes do exist, and, foolish or not, they have
a bearing upon our future as shooters.

To the degree that we perpetuate the proposition that
"*This* is a sporting firearm, *that* is a weapon," we work to
destroy ourselves. To the degree that we perpetuate the myth
that "Sport is legitimate; fighting is not," we work against our
best interests. The man who fired "the shot heard 'round the
world" at Concord would not have understood any such foolishness, and if you believe that what happened at Concord is
irrelevant to today's problems, you simply have not kept track
of what is going on in today's world.

As our civilization urbanizes, and as more and more of
our young people never set foot off pavement, much less clean
a fish, we can no longer take for granted that our youth
naturally and automatically understands the traditions which
gave us this country, and which must be maintained if we wish
to keep it. Those traditions *must* be passed on to the young,
and they may not be divided up into so many compartments
that we shooters can no longer tell our friends from our foes.
Consider the upland bird shooter, with his tweeds, his cherished double shotgun, and his retriever. Consider the high-
power target shot, with his complex rifle, his specially-made
ammunition, and his padded jacket. Consider the sheep hunter, with his precision rifle, his climbing boots, and his binoculars. Consider the silhouette man, intent upon his "twenty
straight." Consider the householder who has just bought a
"Saturday night special" because he has reason to believe that
his home is no longer much of a castle. These may all be

different breeds, but they are united by a common interest, and only by understanding that they are of one brotherhood will it be possible for us to survive in a world in which the image of the shooter is becoming suspect.

All of us feel deeply that shooting is an essential part of the American tradition. We must not fall into the error of saying "But only my type of shooting, not his." We dare not throw even one passenger out of the sleigh for the wolves. The wolves have never been satisfied with one passenger, nor will they be now. If we are to say that automatic weapons are unnecessary and throw them to the wolves, it will be only a short time before we find that *semi*-automatic weapons are going to be banned, and then repeating weapons, and then short weapons, and then *all* weapons. The people who are against us do not want us to own weapons *of any kind*. It is difficult to formulate a composite picture of the hoplophobe, but in general he hates weapons because they represent the capacity of one man to be stronger than another by commanding skills and disciplines which he, the hoplophobe, does not wish to acquire. The man who hates weapons does not wish to acquire shooting skills because it is hard, and to him, uninteresting; and it makes him terribly uneasy to feel that there are other people who do have such skills, and that they, therefore, possess an insuperable advantage if matters should ever come to blows.

Skill-at-arms is everybody's business. It is the proper concern of all free men. It cannot be left to the public sector. It must be encouraged in all areas, and at all levels. We do not have the luxury of saying "My type of shooting is more *respectable* than his." If we take that view, our adversaries will pick us off one discipline at a time.

So let us never say that "black" guns are somewhat suspect, or that only double shotguns are sporting, or that rifles are acceptable, but pistols are not. As long as the *shooter* is respectable, his firearm is respectable. When he is not, neither is his weapon. Let us keep our focus where it belongs: on the perpetrator rather than upon his instrument. Let us firmly reject the concept that sport is legitimate, but that fighting is not. Fighting in a just cause is all that keeps man free, and it is not the sole prerogative of the state. If it were, free states would never have arrived, nor could they survive.

If we live in an age of imagery, let us concentrate upon the creation of the correct and positive image of the shooter: an image of responsibility, decency, courage, competence, and good citizenship.

NOTES FOR NON-SHOOTERS

Anyone who wishes to integrate weaponry into his life must realize that weapons do not operate themselves. One is no more armed because he owns a gun than one is a musician because he owns a piano. Firearms are easier to use effectively than musical instruments, but their use must still be learned. Naturally there is great disparity between the skill necessary to win a well-contested shooting match and that needed simply to make a firearm do what you want it to do, but a degree of skill is still essential. The piece is both useless and dangerous in unskilled hands.

Firearms are not dangerous in themselves, but a human being who does not understand them can be fearfully so if he picks one up. Safe handling may not be the absolutely first consideration in weaponcraft (if you want to avoid all danger of firearm accident just never touch one) but it is certainly a good place to begin. The N.R.A. conducts firearms safety classes throughout the U.S., and anyone who is starting his weaponry education from scratch is well advised to attend one. Actually all that is needed, however, is absolute adherence to four rules:

(1) All guns are *always* loaded. *Always. Never* assume that one is not. *Never.*

(2) Never let the muzzle point at anything you are not willing to destroy. Never assume that a piece is safe because it is "unloaded." See (1) above. And place only guarded trust in safety catches. They can fail. (This rule #2 is so dreadfully abused on target ranges that one often wonders about the viability of the human race. After decades of work with smallarms I have developed an obsession about it.)

(3) Keep your finger off the trigger until your sights are on the target. Violation of this rule seems to be the direct cause of most firearms mishaps. The shooter must train himself until the eye controls the trigger finger, and the tactile and optical reflexes are positively united.

(4) Be sure of your target, as well as what is behind it. *Never* shoot at a sound, or a shadow, or a silhouette, or anything you cannot positively identify — not even a presumably hostile gunflash.

The beginner must memorize these rules, and then implant them in his psyche to the extent that only by a painful effort of will can he force himself to violate them. Only then will he be safe with firearms.

The next step in weaponry is gun mechanics and gun-handling. Firearms are simple mechanisms, nothing like as complicated as typewriters, televisors, or gasoline engines. They are quite easy to understand and operate. A majority may be simply disassembled and assembled again without tools, and the owner should take the small trouble to learn how to operate, clean and adjust his weapons before he undertakes to shoot them. This is especially true of the non-recreational shooter, for the hobbyist needs no encouragement. *It is vital that any "non-combatants" who have access to firearms (wives, children, elderly people) be exposed to periodic re-familiarization with them.* One who does not shoot at all from one year to the next can forget how guns operate.

It is hard for those of us who were exposed to formal training in marksmanship from early childhood to realize that there are millions of citizens who know nothing at all about shooting. I have always assumed that before a boy leaves home his father makes sure that he has been taught the essential skills of life, from proper personal hygiene to driving a car. Marksmanship is certainly one of those skills, but it does not appear on everyone's list. An astonishing number of people who actually earn their daily bread photographing and writing about guns are only vaguely aware of the principles of good shooting, if one can believe what he sees in the periodicals.

The elements of marksmanship, as taught by the U.S. Director of Civilian Marksmanship in a happier time half a century ago, were these:

(1) Sighting and aiming

(2) Firing positions

(3) Trigger control

(4) Rapid fire (operation of the piece under time pressure).

All four subjects were taught, learned, re-taught, and tested before the first firing session on the range. The use of the shooting sling was emphasized, as was instantaneous, reflexive bolt operation, and speed loading. Few people now use or understand the shooting sling, which is a decided aid to deliberate marksmanship in any position in which the supporting elbow is rested.

Shooting is good fun, and those who acquire a taste for it will usually be the ones who will become expert marksmen. There are many recreational shooters who are very poor shots, but I have never known any really good shot who did not shoot for fun. However, you can certainly learn to handle a firearm well enough to defend yourself without taking up sport shooting as a hobby.

The practical person must realize that practical shooting is grounded upon the three equivalent elements of accuracy, power, and speed. Naturally we shoot to hit, and a miss is no good at all, but a hit that does not put the target down is often worse. And even a heavy, precisely placed hit is useless if it lands too late, or is not delivered at all because the target is no longer there, or has struck first. So we work first for accuracy, often with a 22. Then we select a weapon which disposes of enough power with precision, within steadily decreasing time allowances. Within certain obvious limitations, a good shot can hit anything he can see, given enough time. Using proper training techniques that time may be radically reduced. This is the big difference between a sporting target shooter and a practical marksman: The former strives for the absolute ultimate in precision, while the latter learns to hit what he has to before it is too late.

Practical marksmanship is not too difficult to learn, but it does call for positive effort. Do not buy a gun unless you really do intend to learn to use it.

THE ROOT OF THE EVIL

My dictionary describes an *obsession* as "a haunting by a fixed idea." A haunting is a nagging, continuous fear of the unreal. A fixed idea is one that cannot be altered, by truth or reason or anything else.

Phobia is listed as "fear, horror, or aversion — of a morbid character." *Morbid* is "unwholesome, sickly."

Those of us who shoot cannot help being perplexed when we encounter people who are apparently haunted by a fixed and morbid aversion to our guns. When first we meet such persons we generally respond with explanations, as is only reasonable. But with time we discover that often we are not dealing with rational minds. This is not to say that everyone who is opposed to shooting is mentally aberrant, but it *is* to say that those who latch on to an unreasonable notion and thereafter refuse to listen to any further discussion of it have problems that are more amenable to psychiatry than to argument.

I coined the term *hoplophobia* over twenty years ago, not out of pretension but in the sincere belief that we should recognize a very peculiar sociological attitude for what it is — a more or less hysterical neurosis rather than a legitimate political position. It follows convention in the use of Greek roots in describing specific mental afflictions. ὅπλον (hoplon) is the Greek word for "instrument," but refers synonymously to "weapon" since the earliest and principal instruments were weapons. φόβος (phobos) is Greek for "terror" and medically denotes unreasoning panic rather than normal fear. Thus hoplophobia is a mental disturbance characterized by irrational aversion to weapons, as opposed to justified apprehension about those who may wield them. The word has not become common, though twenty years is perhaps too short a time in which to test it, but I am nevertheless convinced that it has merit. We read of "gun grabbers" and "anti-gun nuts" but these slang terms do not face up to the reasons why such people behave the way they do. They do not adequately suggest that reason, logic, and truth can have no effect upon one who is irrational on the point under discussion. You cannot say calmly "Come, let us reason together" to a hoplophobe, because that is what he is — a *hoplophobe*. He is not just one who holds an opposing view, he is an obsessive neurotic. You can speak, write, and illustrate the merits of the case until you drop dead, and no matter how good you are his mind will not be changed. A victim of hydrophobia will die, horribly, rather than accept the water his body desperately needs. A victim of hoplophobia will die, probably, before he will accept the fallacy of his emotional fixation for what it is.

Have you noted that whenever an assassination is committed with a *rifle*, our journalistic hoplophobes clamor for further prohibitions on *pistols*? A pistol is a defensive weapon; a rifle is an offensive weapon. Yet the hoplophobes always attack pistols first because they *feel* that pistols are somehow nastier than rifles. (Though rifles are pretty nasty, too. They will get to those later.) This is the age of the "gut reaction" —that crutch of intellectual cripples — and for an interesting number of commentators it is not even embarrassing to admit that actually thinking about anything important is just too much trouble. Some of our most ubiquitous and highly paid social-problem columnists are egregious examples of this.

Not long ago a staff member of the *Chicago Tribune* held forth at some length about how the color gatefolds in outdoor magazines exemplified the same sniggering depravity that we find in the pornographic press, substituting guns for girls. What a sewer of a mind this man displays! It is undeniable that both a man-made work of art and a beautiful woman are manifestations of God's blessing, but to imply that our admiration for them is obscene is to give oneself away. For some it indeed may be, but the rest of us need no advice from such.

17

(I had thought that the fad to fantasize *everything* into a Freudian sex-symbol had gone out of vogue prior to World War II, but obviously there are a good many who never got the word.)

The essence of the affliction is the belief that instruments cause acts. It may be that certain degenerate human beings are so far gone that they will use something just because it is there — a match, for instance. (I saw a bumper sticker in the Rockies that admonished "Prevent Forest Fires. Register Matches!") One who will burn people because he has a match is the same as one who will shoot people because he has a gun, but the hoplophobe zeroes in on guns because he is — let's face it —irrational. He will answer this by saying that we *need* matches (and cars, and motorcycles, and power saws, et cetera) but we do not need guns. He will not accept the idea that you may indeed need your guns, because he *hates* guns. He is afflicted by the grotesque notion that tools have a will of their own. He may admit that safe driving is a matter of individual responsibility, but he rejects the parallel in the matter of weapons. This may not be insanity, but it is clearly related to it.

One cannot rationally hate or fear an inanimate object. Neither can he rationally hate or fear an object because of its designed purpose. Whether one approves of capital punishment or not, one cannot rationally fear a hemp rope. One who did, possibly because he once narrowly escaped hanging, would generally be referred to a shrink. When the most prominent hoplophobe in the United States Senate says that he abhors firearms because their purpose is to put bullets through things, he reinforces the impressions that many have formed about his capacity to reason.

My point — and I hope it is clear — is that hoplophobia is a mental disturbance rather than a point of view. Differences of opinion — on economic policy, or forced integration, or the morality of abortion, or the neutron bomb — these we may hope to resolve by discussion. But we cannot so resolve a phobia. The mentally ill we cannot reach. But we can identify a form of mental illness for what it is, and so separate its victims from the policy considerations of reasonable people.

The root of the evil is the unprincipled attempt to gain votes by appealing to the emotions of the emotionally disturbed. Few reasonable politicians dare to take on the Second Amendment, even in the Eastern Megalopolis. (One prominent left-liberal told a *New Yorker* interviewer that he "would rather be a deer, in season, than to take on 'the gun lobby'!") But if, as is the case with the aforementioned senator, the politician is already a hopeless hoplophobe, his advisers must turn him loose to appeal to his constituency of crazies, since their jobs depend on it. "Go to it, Senator! The nuts are all with you."

This is something we who prize our traditional liberties must face. Convincing the uninterested is the very essence of politics, in a two-party system. It is up to us to do that by demonstrating that hoplophobia is a disease, and to call upon all reasonable people to reject it as a basis for the formulation of policy.

THE COMBAT MIND-SET

Man fights with his mind. His hands and his weapons are simply extensions of his will, and one of the fallacies of our era is the notion that equipment is the equivalent of force.

For over twenty years I have been teaching weaponcraft — which may be defined as the aggregate of dexterity, marksmanship and tactical understanding — and perhaps fifty of my graduates have now had occasion to use these skills in mortal confrontations. (I say "perhaps" because I must assume that not every client sends me a report.) Of the thirty-odd who have reported, not one has said that his life was saved by his dexterity nor by his marksmanship, but rather by his "mind-set."

What, then, is the "*combat mind-set?*"

It is that state of mind which insures victory in a gunfight. It is composed of awareness, anticipation, concentration and coolness. Above all, its essence is self-control. Dexterity and marksmanship are prerequisite to confidence, and confidence is prerequisite to self-control.

Any state of mind is entirely subjective, varying infinitely among individuals. We do not feel the same about our experiences, and anyone who tells you how you *will* feel in a fight has not studied the matter thoroughly. On the other hand, we can talk to many who have "seen the elephant," and we can add to this our own experiences, and thus explore the subject — in a tentative way.

In such exploration we should bear in mind that while times change quickly, people change slowly. Abraham would be astonished at electricity, but not at Gorbachev. Lifestyles in Elizabethan England were very different from ours, but Shakespeare's characters viewed life just as we do. We may dismiss the notion that a twentieth century man reacts differently to violence from the way his grandfather did. He may be told that he will — for specious reasons —but when he looks into the lion's mouth his response will be the same. Sometimes it will be good and sometimes bad, but this will depend upon his character rather than the popularly held mood of the moment.

Combat is an unusual experience for most of us, but then emergencies of any kind always are. However, combat *does* occur, and any fully educated person knows this and prepares for it. Despite what we may hear, combat is not characteristic of any particular occupation or situation. It may come to a policeman, but it may just as probably come to a barber, a broker or a biologist. Accepting this is the first step in physical security. No one can solve any problem of which he is not aware.

In what follows we will consider the combat mind-set in three aspects — before, during and after action. I can tell you how I have felt, but that is by no means my principle research tool. On the contrary I will draw on scores of individual, informal interviews with men who were speaking with complete frankness and with no concern whatever about what their supervisors, their attorneys, their wives or the press might think. I cannot tell you how you will feel when the red flag flies, but I can indeed tell you how a great many others have felt.

The pistol is a conceptually defensive arm, intended to stop lethal aggression. Thus when used as intended it will be required with almost no warning. The man who shoots to save his life, or that of his wife or child, will rarely have any time in which to consider the situation, steel himself, say a prayer, sing a war song or go into a dance. His mental reaction will probably be astonishment rather than fear, for fear takes time to build up. Since he cannot anticipate *specifically* he must anticipate *generally*. Anyone who carries a pistol on his person is presumably aware that he may have to use it, but there is a large difference between the hypothetical possibility and the actual event.

To anticipate generally the shooter must train himself into a state of mind in which the sudden awareness of peril does not surprise him. It is essential for the man who wears a gun to react to a sudden threat with the knowledge and confidence that he can handle it. His response should be not "Oh my God, I'm in a fight!" but rather "I thought this might happen *and I know what to do about it*." Instead of feeling that the situation is unheard-of, he must feel that the situation is distinctly heard-of, and that he is in charge of it rather than his aggressor. He must regard the quick and precise use of his sidearm as "Plan B," and be fully ready to implement it when confronted with a deadly human adversary. In this situation there can be no build-up of emotion and the shooter's exercise will be entirely intellectual. He will not have time to get excited until after the fight is over.

Sometimes, however, there will be warning, and on these occasions emotion will indeed bear upon action. When another human being manifests both the intention and capacity of killing *you*, personally, and there is time enough between his declaration of intent and the actual engagement, your response will probably be one of intense alarm. (I do not like to use the word "fear" but you are at liberty to do so if you wish.) When you suddenly realize that those men, right there, are armed and prepared to kill you, there will probably be a sudden sinking sensation in the pit of the stomach. The antidote for this hollow feeling is anger. The emotions of fear and anger are very similar biologically and it is not very difficult for a subject to convert one into the other. I have experienced this personally several times and I have talked to a great many people about it. It occurs in military situations, in police situations, and in totally "civil" situations. When a man demonstrates, in effect, that he is ready and willing to kill you, your response should not be fearful but wrathful. I remember one episode involving a car pursuit in moderately heavy traffic and, after the initial understanding that this was indeed a life-and-death encounter, the principal emotional state of the subject was one of cold, concentrated rage. And it worked. The eye remained clear and the hand steady.

We may conclude that while there will usually be no time for fear to develop, on those occasions when there is time that fear should be deliberately overcome by anger in order to maintain control for the action to come.

A pistol action is usually commenced by firing on the part of the aggressor. On other occasions it can be initiated by an unmistakable movement on the part of the aggressor which indicates that he is about to fire. This triggers the combat response of the properly conditioned defender, and that response should be one of completely business-like attention to detail. Once you have decided that you must shoot, it is necessary for you to employ techniques which will enable you to shoot well. Defensive gunfights do not usually require a high degree of marksmanship, but proper technique must still be used if disaster is to be forestalled. We have known several cases in which a highly qualified marksman fired a series of atrocious short-range misses, not because he couldn't shoot but because he did not pay attention to his shooting. In these cases he seems to have been thinking about the wrong things —such as the danger in which his life was placed, the anticipation of shock, concern about official policy or other irrelevancies. *When you are being shot at there is only one proper thing for you to think about, and that is your own shooting.* All other thoughts must be blanked out. In bold red letters across your "heads-up-display" should appear *"Front sight. Press. Front sight. Press."* If you concentrate on a clear, sharp picture of your front sight, and concentrate upon a smooth, steady, surprise break, you will almost certainly survive the encounter. If you forget these things, you very probably will not.

I have heard it claimed that many police officers interviewed after shootings admitted that they did not see the front sight. Certainly we should not deny this possibility, but neither should we use it as an example of how things ought to be done. In one major police department over the past two years there have been thirty-two pistol engagements involving SWAT members. Twenty-four remembered concentrating on their front sights, and they hit. Eight remembered not seeing their front sights, and they missed. That is a 100% tally. It certainly corroborates my teachings, but I did not make it up. It was given to me by the training officer of that department.

I once asked a very prominent and experienced police marksman what he remembered about his initial lethal contact. He said, loud and clear for all to hear, "I was looking at my front sight so hard that I could see the striations across it." He got three stops for three shots on that occasion.

In my most recent field case study, just last year, the subject told me in his letter that as soon as he saw the muzzle of his adversary's gun swing toward him, he blanked out everything but concentration on his front sight and on a smooth, steady pressure on his trigger. He came out fine.

This would indeed seem to be the formula for success.

The critical point is the creation of a "mental trigger" in the mind which is decided upon in advance of the action. This mental trigger may be any one of a number of things, but it should always be sufficient in the mind of the shooter to justify his taking lethal action. Most usually it will be a shot fired at him, but it can be a weapon pointed at him or a weapon pointed with lethal intent at someone else. In any case, it must be fixed upon in advance so that there is no need to hold a conference with oneself at the moment of truth. It cannot be delayed and it cannot be equivocal. No person who has any moral reservations about the propriety of self-defense should carry a weapon in the first place.

If you accept the fact that you may have to fight to save your life, if you train yourself to use your weapons with skill and rapidity, and if you reserve your fighting stroke for conditions in which it is justified, it is not likely that you will experience any psychological difficulties in defending yourself. At least up to now I have never run across anyone who did.

Now, however, we come to a very curious and very new series of observations about how one is likely to feel *after* a successful engagement. The popular term is "post operational trauma," or P.O.T. for short. (The acronym seems appropriate.) We are told from all sides that if one wins a lethal encounter he will feel dreadful. It is odd that no one seems to have felt dreadful about this until very recently. Throughout recorded history the winning of a fight has generally been considered a subject for congratulation. It is only just now that it has become presumably tainted.

In reading our history, from the Pharaohs to the Falklands, one gets the impression that the principle feeling of the victor in mortal combat is satisfaction. Simply stated, the word we get from time immemorial down to the present is "I would not have killed him if it had not been necessary, but it *was* necessary and I am glad I did." When David slew Goliath no one records that he went into shock; nor did Theseus when he slew the Minotaur; nor did Andy Jackson when he killed Dr. Dickinson in a duel; nor did Teddy Roosevelt when he was set upon in a frontier bar; nor did Eduardo Grijalva when he shot down two assassins in front of his office in San Salvador. Nor, we may assume, did the great majority of those police officers and private citizens who have had to shoot to defend themselves on the streets of the United States in the past few months.

It may be proposed that the military situation is emotionally different from the civilian, and in a sense it may be, but upon reflection it is obvious that any resulting P.O.T. ought to be far more of a problem for the soldier. One can hardly condemn an enemy soldier for answering his country's call to arms — rather to the contrary. The enemy one kills in war may be a splendid fellow; brave, clean, reverent, truthful, and so on. But a predatory felon who victimizes innocent non-combatants on the street is a proven goblin, sentenced by his own initiative. Some men may be upset by killing him, but not anyone I have met.

But there must be something to this matter of P.O.T. It could not be so well described if there had not been a couple of police officers who experienced it. It is my belief, however, that it is primarily a public relations innovation designed to parry various sorts of preposterous litigation which have become common in our courts. Policemen are now instructed by their supervisors that, should they become involved in a fight, their attitude upon its conclusion should be one of shock, dismay, horror and hysteria. This to present a proper picture for the press. In actuality what they usually feel is pleased and proud. I repeat that I do not presume to use my own experience as a guide, but I do remember after action a definite feeling of elation. After looking right up the muzzle of one's opponent's gun there is a tendency to swagger. Jokes seem funnier, sky bluer, beer colder and bed warmer. Not for everyone, perhaps, but for those most characteristic of my investigations.

It is quite possible, of course, that certain young men have found themselves sorely afflicted with psychological woes as a result of winning a lethal conflict. It seems, however, that these are the exceptions. Throughout our history winning in a just cause has been deemed admirable and losing a disgrace. This sudden notion that there is something disreputable about winning in mortal conflict is peculiar and, I think, aberrant. This whole subject of P.O.T. may be largely an invention of the shrinks.

The combat mind-set, therefore, should be:

A. Before the fact — alert, prepared, and aware. If there is time for fear to build up it should be overcome by a conscious effort toward anger.

B. During action — total concentration upon the technical matter of placing the shot properly.

C. After the conflict — probably relief, gratification, and pride — approximately in that order. If it is advisable for the shooter to display distress, for various ulterior reasons, that is an administrative matter.

There is nothing wrong with winning. There is a great deal wrong with losing. Those who bear arms should keep that in mind.

"FOR LACK OF
THE RIGHT MIND-SET"

The assassination of Lieutenant Commander Albert Schaufelberger, III, U.S.N., was particularly distressing to us here at The American Pistol Institute. He had been accepted for instruction in May of '82, and had paid his deposit, but he cancelled when he got his orders to El Salvador. If timing had been just a little different we might well have saved his life.

How could mastery of his pistol have saved his life? Marksmanship alone might not have helped him, but, as anyone who has been here will attest, we teach a lot more than marksmanship. We also teach personal tactics, defensive principles, mental conditioning, and *mind-set*. We teach *crisis management*. And poor Mr. Schaufelberger failed to manage his terminal crisis.

Much of what I know about staying alive in WWIII I learned in Central America (WWIII, incidentally, is what we are in now, and have been in for a generation. What certain journalists refer to as WWIII is better called WWIV). I have logged a total of 16 "tours" in Guatemala, Salvador, Honduras, Costa Rica, Colombia, and Mexico. I think I know the territory pretty well. Several of my friends have been killed down there, and, while I have "seen the elephant" four times in that theater of operations, I am still alive.

We could have taught Mr. Schaufelberger many things about staying alive in El Salvador — things that the military establishment does not now teach. As a marine officer, I was taught how to conduct myself on a battlefield, but not on the streets of Central America, or Southeast Asia, or the Near East, or Ireland, or — for that matter — Houston, Texas. Neither, tragically, was Mr. Schaufelberger.

In these action areas of WWIII one does not pick up a date at the same site twice, nor at the same time. One does not sit in one's car (armored or otherwise) and wait. One does not allow a stranger to approach without making ready. One stays aware of the imminence of deadly violence, at all times and from any direction. One is not taken by surprise.

Crisis management. Yes, indeed.

The military establishment is traditionally conservative. It not only discounts this informal sort of war, it seems to pretend (or even to insist) that it does not exist. We hear that policy will now restrict jogging on the part of the advisory personnel. Jogging? On the streets of San Salvador! (Here supply your own most forceful exclamation of incredulity and dismay.)

The press, in general, throws up its hands. "We shouldn't get involved." "We shouldn't be there." *Of course we should.* And we should apply ourselves to the problems of WWIII with determination, subtlety and power. *If we win WWIII we may not have to fight WWIV.*

We needed Al Schaufelberger. His personality cannot be replaced, but others of his breed — America's gallant fighting men — will be sent to do his unfinished work. He cannot help them now, but his example can. If his sacrifice serves to delineate the nature of the conflict, others may not die unnecessarily.

May it indeed be so!

HEADS UP!

As Lee said to Jackson after Fredericksburg, "It is a good thing war is so horrible, General. Otherwise, we would enjoy it too much." This is a very penetrating remark, and it was no less in 1862 than it is today. Men like to fight, but the results of fighting are horrifying, depressing and destructive. Thus any moderately civilized man will ordinarily reject fighting if he can, but nearly always hold in the back of his mind the thought that if it is forced upon him he will carry it out — not only to the best of his ability but also with a certain enthusiasm. No sane man will invoke horror, but almost any sane man can say, "If I have no choice I may at least get what I can out of this experience, even if the zest is in no way commensurate with the disaster."

Thus we find the Walter Mitty's of this world who day-dream about the flying of shot and shell and heroic exploits carried out with calm detachment and admirable efficiency.

Almost all young, untried men who have never "seen the elephant" are torn by doubts as to their capacity to measure up to stress when it lands in their laps. In general they may expect they will do very well, because men usually do. There are exceptions, of course, but they are rarer than the left-liberal press would have us believe.

Any discussion of tactical principles begins with the assumption that there is going to be a fight, exactly as any discussion of surgery begins with the assumption that some-body is going to have to be cut on. Readers of this work must accept the premise that fighting does exist, and, moreover, that it may, under some circumstances, involve them. We can tell them that if this assumption is true, and a fight does eventually occur, (1) the results will be shocking and (2) the experience will probably be very stimulating. This is by no means an incitement to violence, but simply a flat statement of fact as observed over the decades.

To state that the object of fighting is winning would seem obtuse except for the fact that in recent times a good many people seem to have lost sight of its truth. (The classic example, of course, was Viet Nam. If you don't intend to win, don't fight. But if you choose to fight, make winning your exclusive objective until the fight is over.)

The private person who arms himself must remember that he will most likely be fighting as an individual when the flag flies. The chances of his standing shoulder to shoulder with five, or ten, or fifty close friends, strongly motivated and properly armed to confront the foe is unlikely. Therefore the individual can have only one objective in fighting and that is the destruction of his personal adversary or adversaries. He will not have the dubious luxury of giving orders, taking cover, obtaining fire superiority, moving to "close with the enemy." He will simply have to shoot to hit and to make every shot count.

I am assuming that I am speaking to decent people in these pages and therefore there will be no question of their initiating violent action against anyone else, but rather in their taking proper remedial action if someone instigates violence against them. This of course means that their strategic position will be defensive, even though they may and probably should turn defense into offense if the opportunity presents itself *after* the opening of hostilities. From this it follows that the overwhelming priority in the individual book of tactics is the first principle of personal defense — and that is *alertness.*

As Clausewitz tells us, "Everything is very simple in war but the simplest thing is difficult. Difficulties accumulate and produce a friction which no man can imagine who has not experienced it."

Just so. Good tactics are almost invariably simple tactics, but in "the bright face of danger" even the simplest thing may become extraordinarily difficult to execute. This is one of the few advantages that a defensive posture may have over the attack. The defender has — or should have — a well conceived plan for all foreseeable contingencies, and have quite a good idea of just how his responses are to be executed. The attacker, while he has initiative, still has to leap more or less into the dark and improvise his action as it develops. This is why in all violent action it is absolutely vital to discover what is going on as it happens — if possible before it happens. For example, if you are established in your "retreat" and your son suddenly tells you, "Dad, there are three jeeps coming across the north meadow. I think they've cut the fence," you have *won* that fight. If, on the other hand, you look up from your desk and see two men standing in the door of your office with shotguns, you have *lost* that fight. In neither case will your tactics matter very much.

Therefore it is obvious that awareness, the by-product of alertness, is the first principle of any sort of fighting, and especially so in the case of the man alone.

Consider the medieval stronghold, sitting there on its hilltop surrounded by its palisade and armed guards. It seems to be the very definition of security in a dark time. And so it was — but only if its master followed very important rules of alertness. He rarely slept in the same place twice in succession. He never maintained consistent hours for sleep and wakefulness. At any time of day or night, rain or shine, he could be expected suddenly to appear — fully armed and accompanied by his tall, strong sons. Only so could he be reasonably sure of opening his eyes when he lay him down to sleep. This is not a cheerful picture, but as we noted fighting is not a cheerful subject.

Eric Hartmann, the world's foremost air-to-air fighting man, has stated that in his opinion 80% of his victims never knew he was in the same sky with them. When he came in from his first contact with the allied Mustang fighter he was asked if the performance of this renowned airplane was as good as its reputation. His answer was, "I couldn't say. None of the four I got today was on full-throttle." Air-to-air combat in the days of piston engined aircraft had much in common with man-against-man combat on the ground today. The way to win is to know that there is going to be a fight before it happens. Once you know that, "your strength is as the strength of ten" because you can dictate the conditions of the conflict.

There are no set rules or drills which will enable you always to know about aggressive action directed toward you before it starts. What can help you, however, is the under-standing of the need to know it. A good fighting man has a very suspicious mind. Sometimes his actions seem furtive or even neurotic to a person who doesn't understand his problem. I recall an occasion when I had just returned from a rather difficult overseas assignment and my wife and daughter both commented about my behavior. They noted that I always knew exactly what was behind me and took nothing for granted. That was not fear but rather a prudent attitude — a course of behavior by which to eliminate fear. I'm embarrassed to say that that attitude wears off after awhile even though we realize we should not let it do so. The fact remains that good fighting men are very *careful* men. Note particularly how many of the great fighting men of World War II survived even the most fearful campaigns. Neither Lou Diamond, nor Chesty Puller, nor George Patton, nor Erwin Rommel, nor Rudel, nor Hart-mann was killed in action. The careless men died first.

So work out your G2 system. It is the most important single element of your defensive posture. Once you know what to expect, your skill-at-arms and your skilful use of ground and cover will work for you. If you don't know you're in trouble, no amount of ability on your part will save you.

BODYGUARDING?

The phenomenon of terrorism is evidence of the breakdown of social order. The Western democracies are in a state of moral uncertainty and incapable of taking concerted action against an attack of this sort. We may note that terrorism is not a problem in dictatorships, nor has it been a problem in free societies which were on the rise and successfully solving their social problems. It is clearly the decline of will which makes the acts we call terroristic possible, since terrorists by definition never have a decisive degree of physical force at their disposal. Any authority — state or private — which determines to wipe out terrorism can do so by taking draconian offensive action against the source of the problem. An example of this is that of Saladin who, when confronted with the "Old Man of the Mountain," simply mobilized his military forces and erased the terrorist base. Today we do not seem prepared to handle this problem. Terrorism will succeed and will continue to increase in our society. It is quite obvious at this time that the governments of the free world are essentially ineffective in combating this thing. It becomes therefore clear that the people who are the objects of these acts must take their own measures to save themselves.

As a professional teacher of weaponry it is my belief that the only satisfactory protector any man can have is himself. This is not, however, a majority view and many people throughout the world are seeking to employ guards of various sorts to interpose between themselves and their attackers. I teach weaponry, but weaponry alone is only a part of the capacity that a guard force must have. In a majority of terrorist confrontations the act of violence can be forestalled without gunfire, providing the people concerned are properly prepared. Careful study of such films as are available on acts of assassination and violent attack illustrate that it is the surprise with which the attacker strikes that makes his act successful. If the defender, either in person or through the agency of his guards, *expects* an attack it rarely succeeds. The problem is that it is difficult for anyone to maintain a condition of combat alert at all times — even when he is paid to do so — and even (more remarkably) when it is his life that is at stake. It is necessary for a bodyguard to be adept in the use of his weapons, but it is more important that he be properly alert whenever he is on duty. This may seem obvious but evidently it is not because the disasters we see are almost always the result of a lack of alertness.

The shooting skills necessary for efficient bodyguard work are not demanding. Any man with ordinarily good balance, eyesight, reaction time, and coordination can be taught to use a handgun quite well with about twenty-four hours of training time and 500 rounds of ammunition. Whether he will acquire the proper mental conditioning and tactical attitudes is another matter. In my opinion the greatest value that a security guard will receive from intense and highly sophisticated weaponry training will be in the building of his personal confidence in his ability to confront violent situations. This is apart from his actual shooting skills. I have studied these matters now for eighteen years and I am convinced that in most of the confrontations in which my clients and contacts report success, it was due more to self-confidence than to skill-at-arms. The difference may not be vital because one learns both at the same time.

More important than weaponry in the selection of guard personnel is personality type. The obvious difficulty is that bodyguarding is not a profession which attracts a particularly sharp person. Standing outside a door armed and ready is not a career that most men would choose as a life work. We must face the fact that when we set out to train hired bodyguards we are not going to be dealing with West Point graduates.

Much as we may regret to say it, the security business is one in which the public sector may have a built-in advantage over the private. For example, the men of the U.S. Secret

Service who guard our public dignitaries have a tradition of service and *esprit de corps* which cannot be matched by any private agency. These men are inspired by a sense of duty similar to that of a trained soldier, whereas private guards are generally in the business for the money. And here we have a problem, because anything that can be paid to a guard as wages may be multiplied tenfold by one who wishes to subvert him. No matter what salary you pay your guard, your enemy can offer him the sky to avoid his duty. The magnitude of such bribes is no problem because the briber does not intend that they be paid. A bodyguard who is bribed to betray his employer is quite sensibly killed with his employer so that he will not have any stories to tell and cannot demand his money.

A good friend and client of mine in Latin America was in the habit of maintaining a guard of four men at all times when he was abroad. I asked him what he thought bound those men to him that was more powerful than what the enemy could offer them. He felt that it was fear. He told me that these men would not betray him because they would die if they did so. He was not aware of the corollary of that observation, which is that certainly they would die, but they would not be told — and that is exactly what happened. My friend was aware of the need for irregularity in movement and he always traveled to and from his affairs by different routes. The only way he could have been set up on the day that he was killed was for one of his bodyguards to telephone the necessary information to his attackers. All four bodyguards were killed in the assault without firing a return shot. My friend was able to defend himself to the degree that he killed two of his attackers, but he was fatally wounded in the encounter and found dead later at their hide-out.

The MO of the Bolshevik bombers of the early part of the century was always to arm a fanatic with a bomb with a fuse shorter than he was told, which would result in the accomplishment of two objectives: The death of the victim and the death of the assassin at the same time.

I must confess that bodyguards make me nervous. I have been offered this type of protection several times, and after the first experience I have declined it. I don't like a man standing across the lobby of the hotel, obviously armed and watching me. I simply don't know what side he is on from day to day. When I finished a job in training the personal guard of a Central American president I told him that the degree of skill in his people was quite high, probably higher than that of the men who protect the president of the United States, but that I didn't know who they were. I told the president that I hoped that he did. He knew what I meant, since one of his predecessors in office had been murdered by one of his own guards, as was Indira Gandhi.

Probably the best service that an armed guard can provide is that of a scout. He can go through doors first. He can start cars first. He can move around buildings and relay information to his principal. In these functions he need not be armed, though he probably expects to be. One solution which is practical in some parts of the world — though not others — is to arm security personnel with a single-barrel shotgun and one cartridge. Such a man is quite efficient in a disarmed society, and he is not as much of a problem if he is subverted as if he were more dangerously equipped. It should be noted that when an armed guard is subverted he rarely is asked to kill his employer — usually just to set him up. Thus the use of his regular equipment against his principal is unlikely. Obviously the most dependable personnel that can be acquired are members of the family or extended family of the subject. This is the system used by the Mafia but is not generally available to the private citizen.

The easiest way to meet the problem of reliability in security personnel is by the unpleasant tactic of entrapment. Clandestine attempts to subvert all bodyguard personnel should be made at irregular intervals, and very convincingly. Guards should be approached by persons presumably wishing to attack the employer — but actually in the employ of the employer — in order to see just how much money or other reward is necessary to buy their treachery. If this is kept up the guard himself will never know who is trying to bribe him and thus be kept in the line of fidelity.

If all this sounds cynical it is because of the facts of life and not because anyone desires it to be so. It has been said that a cynic is one who believes that no man is worthy. A realist, on the other hand, knows that some men are worthy and some are not. Since only one defection on the part of a bodyguard is necessary to work a disaster, the realist assumes that *some* of the people he trusts are unworthy of that trust, and that he must therefore never be surprised by the defection of any one individual.

The foregoing should not be construed as the counsel of despair, but only as an indication that the problems involved in obtaining proper guard personnel are not as easy as sometimes believed. Difficult as it may be to accept, the principal himself will always remain his best and cheapest protection. His hired guards should be trained mainly in the matter of alertness and mental conditioning rather than in weaponry and marksmanship. The principal himself should be the prime marksman and his guards should act essentially as scouts, keeping him informed of the nature of hazards which he cannot always assess for himself. Primarily a bodyguard should watch and ask questions. In the notable television coverage of the attempt on the life of Imelda Marcos it was quite obvious that the aspiring assassin could have been stopped easily had anyone thought to confront him and ask his intentions. He stood out clearly in the crowd since he was of a totally foreign stamp, yet no one thought to give him pause. In this case the assassin was shot on the spot *after* he had inflicted serious damage upon his intended victim, but the entire episode could have been forestalled by proper vigilance without the necessity of violent response.

Alertness is the first principle of personal defense. No man can be fully alert at all times throughout his life, so here is the primary reason for personal guards. Bear in mind that all an armed guard need do in order to set up his employer is to relax his vigilance. He need not shoot nor take overt action of any kind; all he must do is *fail* to take action.

The terrorist will always have the initiative. He chooses the time and place for his action. His target must grant him that and still maintain a condition of readiness — around the clock throughout the year. This is clearly not easy. It is not that people cannot be hired to stand watches the year round, but that they cannot be inspired to treat every moment as if it were the initial instant of a confrontation. When we consider such "Chinese-fire-drills" as the take-over of the U.S. Embassy in Tehran it is quite clear that the force and technique employed by the attackers was not nearly appropriate to the task and could have been stopped in its tracks by people who were equipped to do so and aware of the need to do it.

In all counter-terrorist operations there must be a full measure of bitterness on the part of those carrying out operations. Terrorism is an obscene act in that it menaces the lives of the innocent in order to achieve the acquiescence of a third party. People who fear to attack their proper enemy choose to attack the defenseless and the unwary in order to work upon the humanity of the person they are seeking to influence. They foreswear any such thing as humanity on their own part and therefore place themselves outside of any considerations of humanity on the part of those who would suppress them. Once this point is fully grasped and broadcast we may have made a start toward the elimination of this nastiness. This is not to say that terrorists necessarily fear death — for some do not — but that if they are fully convinced that they not only will die *but that they also will fail*, their motivation can be severely hampered.

The essence of the counter-terror operation must be the will to carry it out. Once *that* is established speed, efficiency and ruthlessness take precedence. The sympathies and sensibilities of those related to innocent victims must not be considered, only the elimination of the criminal. For this reason, no person who is related or otherwise attached to any hostage should be involved in any counter-terror operation. If this happens coincidentally the person concerned should relieve himself from his duties. *No ransom must ever be paid.* One good start in this direction would be to make the paying of a ransom to any kidnapper or terrorist a felony in all parts of the world. This may appear to be unfeeling but it is sometimes necessary to endure one pain in order to suppress a greater one. The entire terrorist movement in Central and South America has been financed by ransoms paid by the suffering kinsmen of persons kidnapped. Much as we sympathize with the helplessness of the payers of ransom, we must impress upon all that in paying such a ransom they are feeding the very horror that has been inflicted upon them.

All persons involved in the counter-terrorist movement, especially security guards employed in these operations, should be aware of these principles and realize that when confronted with an act of insupportable barbarism a certain amount of ferocity is a proper response.

It is unfortunate that we hear primarily of those terrorist acts which succeed (from the standpoint of the terrorist). We rarely hear of those forestalled, because they are not newsworthy. One should not conclude from this that the terrorist will always win — often he fails. Everyone knows of the Schleyer murder in Germany. Hardly anyone knows of the client of mine in a somewhat similar circumstance who, when approached at the point of a submachine gun in a kidnapping attempt, tore the weapon from the assailant's hands and drove off the entire band, killing three. A terrorist does not *have* to succeed, but in order to stop him we must resolve ourselves to take such steps as are necessary and to agree upon what those steps are.

ELEMENTS OF
SURVIVAL TACTICS

(For those who have never attended Uncle Sugar's Trade School)

It is perplexing to note the curious notions about violence that have proliferated in the press in recent years. Suddenly we find previously sober people railing against even the depiction or discussion of violence as repulsive in and of itself, which is about as sensible as deploring surgery — in and of itself. Nobody wants to get cut open, but if it becomes necessary as the only alternative to something worse we want it done as efficiently and as quickly as possible. Likewise we fight only if we must, but if we must we do as well as we can, and we don't wring our hands about it.

There is, of course, an art to fighting. The operation of weapons may be a science, but the use of those weapons to win an engagement is not. "Battle drills" are good enough practice, but when the ball opens success will go to the artist more often than to the technician — other things being even roughly equal.

Let us, as Socrates was wont to say, define our terms.

Strategos is the Greek word for "general officer," thus *strategy* is the art of the general. This is the art of making use of an army to bring about victory over one's enemy. It has only indirectly to do with fighting, and a poor fighter can be a good strategist, or vice versa.

Tactics, by contrast, derives from the word for *touch* and thus implies actually touching one's foes in combat. Tactics has come to mean simply the more or less systematic conduct of a fight.

Colonel Allen, my revered Professor of Military Science and Tactics at Stanford, used to explain that arranging a date, sending flowers, buying the lady an epicurean meal, ostentatiously appreciating her catalog of charms, and finally parking comfortably overlooking the moonlit bay — these were all strategy. From that point on it was a matter of tactics.

In general, strategy applies to large units and tactics to small, though the two disciplines do overlap somewhat. Clearly a nation employs strategy while a squad employs tactics, but an army corps normally uses both. The individual, of course, is concerned with tactics, the strategic situation having been forced upon him.

While one man alone may observe certain tactical principles (e.g. keep off the skyline, slide to the flank, hit first, etc.) any study of tactics must deal with the cooperative efforts of fighting units, be they individuals, fire teams or divisions. When men fight in concert they become, whether they like it or not, soldiers. Good soldiers, in or out of uniform, stand a much better chance of winning than poor soldiers.

The essential qualities of a good soldier are five. The first two are skill-at-arms and discipline. ("Send me men who can shoot and salute.") The second three are valor, hardihood, and pride.

Whatever a man fights with — axe, machinegun, or spaceship — he must be *good* with it. He must strive to be not just good, but outstanding, in his manipulation of his weapon. ("I don't want you to die for your country. I want you to make the other guy die for his!") Napoleon to the contrary, this comes *first*.

However well a man fights, he can be taken by superior numbers, unless he cooperates skillfully, and *immediately*, with others on his side. This cooperation can be spontaneously effective only in the most simple and obvious cases. Most of the time it must be ordered, and orders *must* be obeyed.

If men who can use their weapons expertly are fully aware of discipline they can accomplish a great deal. If in addition they are brave, undaunted by hardship, and convinced that they are physically, intellectually and morally *better* than their enemies they can work wonders.

They will work such wonders — of course — tactically.

The first principle of tactics is speed.

If fighting ever becomes necessary, delays of even split seconds can be disastrous — as recent history tells us so well. The best fight is that which is over before the loser realizes that it has begun. No tactical plan is any good at all if its object is given time to understand it. Conversely even a bad plan will usually succeed if it is executed before it can be intelligently countered. Tactical principles are simple. Their instant application, however, calls for talent.

The goal of the tactician is to ensure that the fight, when and where joined, is never "fair." It is his business to bring overwhelming force to bear on a particular subdivision of his adversary's array and to dispose of it before any re-arrangement can forestall him. Immediately thereafter he can engage an enemy reduced in strength by the amount he has just destroyed. This is called "defeat in detail." Everybody, on both sides, knows about it and tries to bring it off. The skillful succeed.

It is not easy. Your foe wants to live just as much as you do, and, while he *may* be stupid, you had better not count on it. As you try to confound him he will try to confound you. The faster of the two will win. That is where discipline counts.

Consider figure 2-b. As A & B take the initiative and attempt to engage Y simultaneously, before X can engage, a skillful tactician might pull Y out of position before B could hit him, and use X and Y to pursue and wipe out A as he moved to support B.

It is all very simple in theory — simpler than checkers or even tic-tac-toe. Actually doing it, however, is hard. I know of a few fights that worked out exactly as the victor planned. They are rare, but the great commanders brought them off. Lee, Jackson, Patton, Rommel all fought actions of this type, and

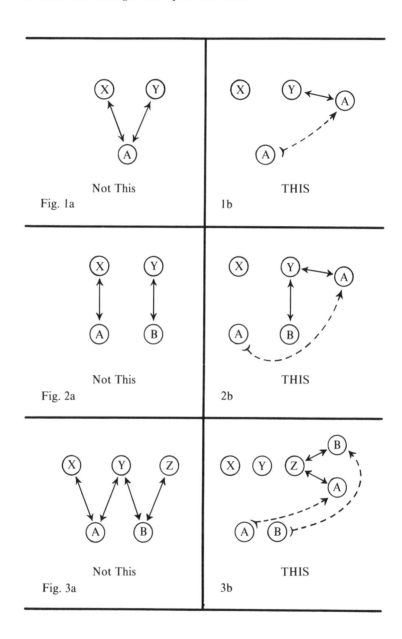

Not This
Fig. 1a

THIS
1b

Not This
Fig. 2a

THIS
2b

Not This
Fig. 3a

THIS
3b

Napoleon most of all. Superior numbers can be offset by superior talent, but such talent is never commonplace.

Still, a basic understanding of principle can be very helpful. So, whatever you decide to do, do it quickly. And no matter what *total* numbers are involved, arrange for your people to outnumber their people at the time and point of contact.

It is important to note that numbers do not necessarily mean bodies. One well situated rifleman — alert, skillful, and determined — can be the equivalent of a dozen or more untrained, sketchily armed, or badly disciplined assailants. In small unit contacts sheer surprise may totally invert numerical superiority. In planning one must think of numbers as "units of force" rather than people, and arrange his actions accordingly.

Irregular fighting will rarely involve formally constituted military units accustomed to practiced, disciplined, concerted action. Only coincidentally will good marksmanship be available, and there will be no facilities for inculcating it. It will therefore be necessary to put what can be had to the best possible use and to choose the right actor for the specified role. A quail gun, for example, will hardly suffice for a meeting engagement between two patrols, but it will do nicely for an unexpected indoor block. The ubiquitous 22 rimfire is not what you would choose for a roadblock but it will serve just as well as a more powerful piece at a short range personal threat. Nobody wants to get shot, even with a 22.

It seems hardly necessary to point out that one does not place his firearms in diametric opposition, as in the cartoon of the Polish (or Irish, or East-Frisian, or whatever sort of cultural group you fancy) firing squad. Two firearms acting against the same target normally seek a convergence angle at around 90°. We can accept 135°, but more than that may be more hazardous to us than to them.

Light forces must at all costs avoid being pinned down. Before a heavier force has spotted its gadfly the latter must have his running route selected.

Knowledge of the immediate terrain is an enormous advantage in small-unit contacts, and it is up to the irregular to know every foot of ground within walking distance of his retreat. Defense against an organized force is a losing proposition (we should never have changed the name of the War Department), but it can work against unorganized attackers —even if they come in preponderant force — if the defender knows the ground and the attackers do not. One rifleman alone, if he is good, can constitute a terrible problem for a dozen assailants, and a smoothly cooperating group of three or four such — on familiar ground — can hold off anything short of a "human wave," until fatigue overcomes it.

If you are really serious about coping with doomsday, you will select your equipment carefully, work with it until you are expert in its use, and study your local (or selected remote) geography until you know it in the dark. If you have reliable friends (*really* reliable) you will study these matters together. You will arrange a simple field code of whistles, waves and such so that you can maneuver in concert.

Then, if the evil day really does at last arrive, you will remember the watchwords — Initiative, Surprise, SPEED.

You'll have a better chance than most.

NOTES ON TACTICAL RESIDENTIAL ARCHITECTURE

It is easy to deplore the degeneration of our social order, difficult as it may be to explain it. But it is not impossible to do something about it. Before doing so, however, one must admit that it exists. The news tells us that we live in a savage society in which subhumans prey with relative impunity upon the innocent and the decent; but, as with death, these facts are hard to accept.

Since most people respond to hypothetical peril with the assumption that it will not come to *them*, the first step in adjusting to our present social situation is the hard, clear, unflinching understanding that it can indeed come to us — personally. It is amazing to read of people who did not choose to believe this until *after* they had been victimized. They all knew that burglary, robbery, assault, and murder were not only possible but frequent, but they took no precautions because they simply would not admit that they, themselves, could be the victims.

Once you accept the fact that you actually may be the next target — today — you have taken the first great step toward your own physical security. Having made this simple, if difficult, admission, you can never afterward be surprised, and surprise is the greatest single element in tactics — offensive or defensive.

Defense of your person is your first concern, and it is a very elaborate study to which we have given a great deal of professional attention over the years, but let us turn for the moment to the defense of your home. Street crime is certainly horrific, and it is our national shame that we cannot maintain safe streets in our big cities, but more shocking yet is the thought that we cannot even go home, shut out the street, and relax. The goblins follow us even there. Consider the Manson atrocities as only the most notorious on a long and horrible list.

Defense of your home may probably be stated better as defense *in* your home, for saving your life is the main concern, whether on the street or home in bed. There are things that can be done to avert burglary in your absence, but they are only effective if they are incorporated into the house as it is being built, and they are dauntingly expensive. To build a house that cannot be broken into is to build a fort, and even then it can be defeated if the intruder has the time and the wit. (The pyramids were designed to be burglar-proof, by kings who commanded unlimited wealth and labor. The tomb robbers broke into them almost as soon as the funeral flowers wilted.)

But we can make certain arrangements to insure that our homes are a good deal more secure when we are in them, and I think we should.

On a recent visit to Southern California we were depressed to note the efforts made by householders to harden their homes; first because this was necessary, and second because the systems employed did not seem very effective.

To see iron bars and barbed wire around the houses in which we grew up without even door locks is sadder than to see a city smashed by war, but still worse is to see good people relying on completely passive structures which can never succeed against an evil will. We saw great, electrically operated gates which could be climbed by any active schoolboy. We saw heavy locks on doors which could be burst open at the hinges. We saw guard dogs which could be bribed with doped hamburger. We saw nothing that was specifically designed to enable the homeowner to counterattack. Evidently the doctrine is that one covers up, keeps his head down, and calls the police.

Let us agree on one major point right here. *The police cannot protect you in your home.* If goblins break in upon you the police should be called — as soon as you get around to it —in order to write out reports and clean up the mess. *But the goblins are your problem.* Bear that always in mind.

Several features in a house can help you defend it. Some must be built in as the house goes up, but others may be added to structures already completed. In most cases they need be neither unsightly nor inconvenient.

POINT ONE:

When you are asleep you are helpless. Few things can be more nightmarish than to open a drowsy eye to see a shadowy figure standing over you in the gloom. This need never happen.

Bedroom windows must be ironed, obviously in such a way as to permit their opening from the inside in case of fire.

(A former United States senator must live out his life with the memory of his adolescent daughter who was murdered in her bedroom by a monster who simply kicked open the French windows — because he, the senator, had not protected his own child.)

But just the windows are not enough. There must be a strong barrier between the sleeping quarters and the rest of the house. A bolted door will do (dead bolt, not a pickable latch), but an iron grill is better because you can see through it — and shoot through it.

No barrier is impenetrable, but if it causes a racket if attacked it will awaken you, and that is all you need. If you are awake, armed, and *aware*, you cannot be defeated by any predator, human or otherwise. Clearly the iron grill must be fastened in such a way that it cannot be unfastened by stealth. Use your imagination here.

POINT TWO:

Sleeping quarter protection can usually be installed in a ready-made house, but door arrangement is another matter. *You must be able to see who is at the door without exposing yourself.* Peep holes are better than nothing, but essentially all doors — front, back, and side — should be recessed in such a way that anyone seeking entrance may be viewed in full, from the side or preferably from behind. When a visitor knocks on your door he should be, in effect, surrounded by your house, aware that he is in view of the people inside from several angles.

Even if he intends a *coup-de-main* he will be at such a tactical disadvantage that he may well chicken out.

Observation must include the capability to fire, so the observation ports must be unscreened, narrow, and openable with one motion. Several sorts of slit windows made for trailers serve this purpose very well if set vertically.

A proof door is an expensive luxury but it does promote sound sleep. Our lower-deck door, which is farthest from our bedroom and therefore hardest for us to hear, is a plywood sandwich with an armored filling, and fastened from the inside with cross-bars rather than a latch. It would be quieter to come through the grouted block wall.

POINT THREE:

Any house which is properly designed for the Age of Aquarius must permit its entire perimeter to be visible from inside it. This is the "Vauban Principle" and you must start from scratch to achieve it completely, but even if stuck with a blind rectangle, a single added bastion on one corner will give you coverage of two of four walls, and two diagonally placed bastions will cover all but their own backsides.

Clearly nothing is perfect. Existing structures may be all but impossible to harden, and terrain will often render specific protective features unnecessary, but this is where architectural ingenuity becomes important. (Remember Castle Dracula, protected by frowning battlements on three sides but light and airy on the fourth, which overlooked a thousand-foot precipice?)

POINT FOUR:

Roman patricians, when in town, dwelt in houses designed for an urban jungle no less savage than our own. Outside walls, right on the property line and generally rectangular in plan, were proof against anything but a ram and pierced by very narrow doors. The open living space was inside. This plan was borrowed by the Spaniards and exported to the New World as the *patio*. This design has much to offer today, where building codes permit. With one side of the quadrangle serving as a

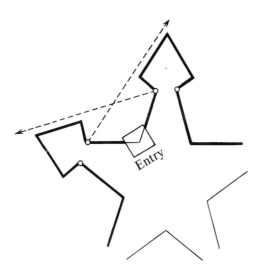

The "Vauban Star" affords observation and fire cover for every inch of perimeter, from sheltered embrasures. It is theoretically perfect and also beautiful, but prohibitively expensive. Its principles may be applied, however imperfectly, to residential construction.

garage, and bastions at the four corners, it offers a hard carapace to the outside while providing as large an interior garden as space permits.

POINT FIVE:

No inanimate structure or device can provide physical security in and of itself. Furthermore, no fortress nor sconce can withstand intelligent attack by determined besiegers. What tomorrow's house can offer, however, is comfortable living space which is hard enough to daunt the casual savage and, in addition, will permit the inhabitants to sleep secure in the knowledge that any prospective intruders must (1) make enough noise to alert the defense, and (2) be placed at a serious tactical disadvantage.

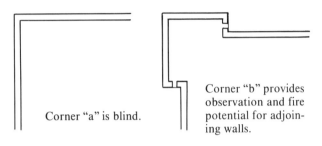

Corner "a" is blind.

Corner "b" provides observation and fire potential for adjoining walls.

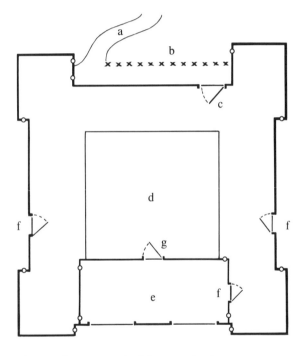

A schematic plan for a neo-colonial rectangle. A two-story tower on one corner may be added to cover roof and patio.

a. Front Walk

b. Ornamental barrier of pierced stone or framework

c. Front door

d. Patio garden

e. Garage

f. Side entry

g. Service entry to patio

-○- Embrasures

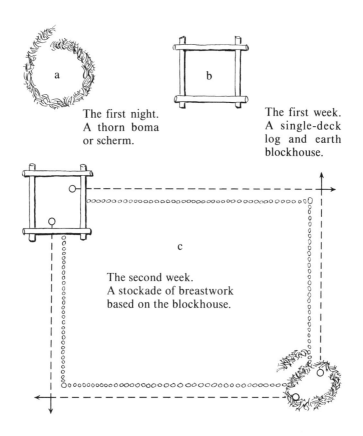

a

The first night.
A thorn boma
or scherm.

b

The first week.
A single-deck
log and earth
blockhouse.

c

The second week.
A stockade of breastwork
based on the blockhouse.

Naturally it is desirable for all walls to be relatively proof against smallarms fire — especially those which include observation ports. This is not as critical as might first appear, however, since the criminal cannot undertake a siege and must count upon surprise to gain his objectives. You can prevent this by correct observation techniques coupled with a manifest willingness to use lethal force against him. Passive defense can succeed only if the cops are within earshot — and not always then.

For those who wish to build a strongpoint in the boondocks — as opposed to a house in which to spend extended

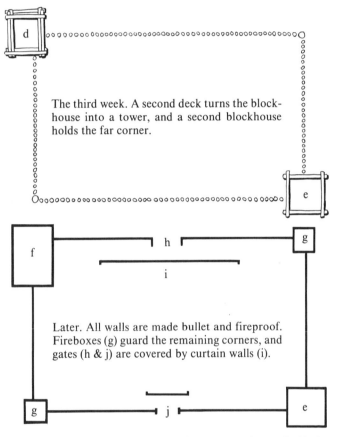

The third week. A second deck turns the block-house into a tower, and a second blockhouse holds the far corner.

Later. All walls are made bullet and fireproof. Fireboxes (g) guard the remaining corners, and gates (h & j) are covered by curtain walls (i).

Structures such as this afforded security in the expansion period before the primitives obtained cannons. The principles involved remain true today. If they turn up with bazookas you will have to go outside and scarf them up.

periods in comfort — the Army Department has a nifty field manual on the subject. This is FM 5-15, Field Fortifications. It is not classified.

It should be unnecessary to point out that the shield is useless without the sword, and that neither is of value without the brain. Lincoln and Trotsky and Castillo and Sharon Tate and the LaBiancas and General Dozier and the victims of the Boston Strangler could not have been helped by architecture. Their killers were *allowed inside.* A stranger at your door must be considered a possible target until proven otherwise. *And this is not fear,* much less the popularly misused term "paranoia." This is intelligent caution. The great leopard of Rudra-prayag had no fear of people. He was able to terrorize his district for eight years because he was very, very careful. In today's savage world we need not be afraid, but we do need to be careful.

·KIRCHNER·

THE LINE

I have seen The Line — the infernal demarcation line between freedom and slavery.

It is the worst thing I have ever seen.

I have lived two-thirds of a century, and travelled widely. I have fought in many battles, both major and minor. I have seen hospitals and prisons, inside and out. I have known much blood, suffering and terror. But I have never seen anything as horrible as The Line.

The Line slashes across the heart of Europe, from the Baltic Sea to Austria, separating the Federal Republic of Germany (BRD) from the German Democratic Republic (DDR). The BRD is "Free Germany." The DDR is "Red Germany." The Line is thus the fence of the realm of shadow —the brink of evil. It is the brand of Karl Marx across the face of humanity.

As a guest of the Third Reconaissance Squadron of the Eleventh United States Armored Cavalry, I was conducted in September of 1984 along its sector in the center of The Line, in Hesse due east of Frankfurt. The land is green and pleasant, rolling enough to be interesting and watered by the River Fulda. Patches of forest separate well-tilled fields; but, unlike most of Germany to the west, there is little or no wild game, for reasons that will be clear. In the frequent villages just west of The Line life is good enough, but it is not exactly normal. The shadow is just there to the east, and it is very palpable.

Starting at its western edge, The Line is composed of several strata. First comes the actual linear boundary, surveyed and marked to the centimeter. There is no fence here. Free people can walk right up to it — but they do not step across it. Death looms. Some ten paces beyond the marked boundary, to the eastward, is the outside fence. It is a single barrier some ten feet high, electrified and sown with directional mines set to fire along its inside surface. Beyond the outside fence is a band of dead ground some 100 meters in width, cleared of life and planted at random with pressure-release anti-personnel fragmentation mines. When the snow melts in winter thaws these go off erratically in the sunshine — "Lenin's serenade."

At the inner edge of the dead ground are the dogs — German shepherds chained to an overhead trolley that allows them to run parallel to the inner fence but not back into it (electrocution) nor forward away from it (explosion). These dogs are carefully bred and trained. In the land of evil the dogs really lead a dog's life.

At intervals watchtowers loom fifty feet into the air, manned and equipped with enhanced-vision devices, cameras, weapons, and release controls for packs of killer dogs which can be set free at command behind the inner fence.

The towers are repellently dead in aspect. There are men in them, but they shun the light. We could see their binoculars, but when we pointed ours at them they vanished. Fear. The terrible people who man The Line live in fear. Of what? Conscience, perhaps?

(I made elaborate arm movements for my hosts, in no way threatening or hostile but cryptically explicit. A lone civilian pointing things out to several military men doubtless provided much material for report and analysis. Lotsa luck, comrades.)

Behind the inner fence lies a belt of zombie-land five kilometers deep. No one moves here except those whose duties demand it. The fields produce. Roads and roofs are mended. There is an occasional dilapidated vehicle in motion. At first glance it seems a viable countryside. On closer inspection, however, it is death-in-life. There are perhaps two lighted windows where there should be scores. Such villages in which there *are* lights are inside electric fences. The sickening effect grows as the sun sets.

In the afternoon light we watched the once-living village of Ifde. It would seem to have housed a population of 10,000. Neat, red roofed, cozy — once upon a time. Now, one light— quarters for the orcs. A couple of cats hunting field mice.

Two ravens overhead. Silence, Desolation. This is Mordor, the prison of the world.

These efforts are being applied not to keep enemies *out*, but to keep an enslaved population *in.* Never before in history has any accursed tyrant, from Senacherib to Hitler, felt it necessary to do this!

With exquisite cruelty the very existence of The Line is concealed from those it contains. The east border of the 5 Km zombie zone is marked — from the East — simply as the border. Good slaves do not cross it, not because it is fearful to behold but because they are good slaves. Bad slaves sometimes do cross it, but because they do not know what they face they usually die.

My staff sergeant guide on this occasion told me of a case he witnessed. A young woman, apparently driven to desperation, dared to cross the eastern 5 Km line and lead her small child west toward liberty. As she approached the inner fence, the orcs in the watchtower loosed the dogs.

"I stood there with a rifle in my hands, but I was not allowed to shoot." He said, "I hear those screams every day. The mother's were louder than the child's. They were long and very high. They drowned out the growling of the dogs. For a while. As long as I live I will hear them."

The sergeant was black. He knows more about real oppression than Andy Young or Jesse Jackson can ever tell him.

The Line, of course, is not impenetrable. No yoke upon the human spirit ever has been. It was supposedly impossible to escape from Alcatraz or Andersonville, but men did. And people break out of the workers' paradise. Quite regularly. About one hundred a year make it. My hosts estimate that five times that number fail. They also feel that those who do cross The Line are mainly people who work The Line. No matter what sort of Orwellian indoctrination is used, man can still distinguish good from evil. Those who inhabit those troll-towers know. And they break out.

The most recent instance in the sector, for instance, involved an electrician who was checking the circuits on the outside fence. ("A dirty job, but *somebody* has to do it.") He simply disconnected some circuits and jumped from his truck to the fence. He was out of sight before the gunners in the towers could get on him. (Heads, we may assume, rolled.)

All aware people in the West know about The Line — or let us hope so. But knowing about it is not the same as *feeling* it. To look upon it is a dreadful experience, but dreadful experiences are necessary if we are to know what is dreadful.

There *is* an Evil Empire. It can be seen. It can be felt. It can be known.

Go and look — and understand!

DRAGON OF LIBERTY
The M-1 Abrams Tank

When Winston Churchill conceived the idea of an armored, tracked, fighting vehicle back in 1916, he thought of it as a means of breaking up the pattern of static warfare and thus bringing the possibility of quick decisions back to the battlefield. Everyone knows that his concept revolutionized warfare, but few of us realize how far that concept has come as we now approach the end of the 20th century. Just as the fighting airplane has progressed from the Sopwith Camel to the F-15 Eagle, the lumbering monsters of Flanders have evolved into the astounding M-1 "Abrams" Main Battle Tank of the United States Army.

In September of 1984 it was my privilege to examine and operate the Abrams now in service with the 11th Cavalry, stationed at the Fulda Gap on the eastern frontier. My host was Major C.J. Ancker, III, S-3 of the 3rd Recon Squadron. My impressions are those of a layman, since I have never been in the tank service. For this very reason I think they may be the more interesting to those who have never had a close look at a modern fighting vehicle. The M-1 has been in service for over five years, and despite a good deal of carping in the press about its putative initial glitches, it is now functioning beautifully. The bugs have been eliminated and the resulting machine is magnificent.

If the word "incredible" had not been mangled beyond recognition by pop usage, it could be correctly applied to the M-1. *Incredible* is exactly the right term for both the agility and the firing systems of this tank — that is to say incapable of belief. I cannot decide between the two. I find it hard to believe what I actually experienced.

Consider first the mobility of this mighty machine. It weighs about 60 tons, yet it can accelerate from a standing start to well over the U.S. speed limit in the space of three deep breaths. Its listed top speed is 42 miles-per-hour, but this listing draws grins from its crews. Forty-two miles-per-hour may indeed be its top speed over ground so rough as to be impassable to wheeled vehicles, but on level ground or a roadway the question amongst the crews is whether or not it will top 70. At 50 it leaps walls and ditches like a gazelle, and it stops, turns and reverses so abruptly that to ride in it without a helmet is suicidal.

It is powered by a 1500 h.p. gas turbine engine which is much quieter than the power plants of piston-driven machinery. The driving system is remarkably easy and comfortable. The driver sits in the center of the hull just forward of the turret in a sort of lounge chair which is adjustable for height, permitting the driver to operate with his head out in non-combat situations. There is only one foot pedal and that is the brake —best used gently if the driver wants to remain friends with the turret crew. A short handlebar is fitted with twin rotary throttles very similar to those on a motorcycle, but inter-connected. This handlebar is short, permitting the thumbs to touch when both hands are in driving position. The gear selector is centrally located and may be operated by either thumb. Reverse is to the extreme left, next neutral, then four forward speeds. The engine warms up very quickly and when ready for use it is switched on to "tactical idle" position, which holds it at a steady 1900 rpm. To move out, the driver simply selects first gear with his thumb and the tank starts. He rolls his hands forward to gain revolutions and, when ready, relaxes his hands, flips to second, and applies throttle again. Direction is maintained by rolling the yoke, and the whole setup can be mastered — in theory — in one short lesson. However, driving the machine operationally takes a good deal more than just moving around, and 45 days of schooling are considered necessary before a man can be placed in complete charge of the driver's compartment.

One of the minor problems of the M-1 is that it is so easy to drive fast that it is difficult to keep the young men who handle it down to economical speeds. Designed tread life, for example, is over twice what it is in field units, simply because it is all but impossible to drive the tank slowly. The problem is rather like that of giving a young man a Porsche Carrera and telling him to take it easy.

There is another small difficulty produced by this amazing speed and maneuverability. The Abrams will out-run any other fighting vehicle in the arsenal, and therefore the tanks must continually hold themselves back so that such things as scout cars and personnel carriers can stay with them.

The turret is inhabited by three men who live in a different world from the driver in the hull. Many have heard that this turret is "stabilized," but few know what that actually means. In action, this turret maintains itself where the gunner or the tank commander points it — irrespective of the motion of the hull. The tank can dash about, turn, reverse, accelerate, or stop — *and this has no effect upon the pointing of the gun.* When the gunner places his weapon on target he may feel the lurching and swerving of the entire vehicle but what he sees through his sight is stationary, because the gun stays where he points it until he points it at something else. In action, the tank commander, with his overriding control, swings the gun onto a selected target and tells the gunner to engage. The gunner then performs the fine sighting and the firing of the weapon, leaving the tank commander free to select new targets. One thing the TC may do which is startling to a novice gunner is to swing the gun out of the way of obstructions as the tank darts around amongst the trees of the forest or the buildings of a village. At an unexpected moment while the gunner is sighting, the gun may swing completely off target and then snap right back on again as soon as the tank commander relinquishes control.

The co-axial 30-caliber machine gun is aimed and fired exactly as the 105 main battery gun. A selector switch prevents the two guns from being fired with the same trigger pressure.

A second selector switch activates the night-vision heat-sensor which is another of the incredible technological aspects of the Abrams. This system enables the weapon to be aimed regardless of ambient light. It is eerie to look through the optical sighting system, then to switch to the night firing system and see practically no change in the viewer. The weapon thus is aimed exactly the same in pitch dark as in broad daylight.

Though the Abrams is some two feet lower in silhouette than the Mark IV Sherman of World War II, the interior of the turret is much more comfortable. In addition to being more commodious, it is air-conditioned. The TC sits high and right, facing 00° to the bore of the gun when in travelling mode. The gunner sits below him and forward, facing about 330°. The loader rides to the left, facing 135°. The TC instructs the driver, selects targets and points the gun, making sure that the gun barrel does not crash into things when the tank is moving quickly in obstructed areas. The gunner refines the alignment of the gun, actuates the laser rangefinder which instantly feeds the correct elevation into the tube, and squeezes the trigger. The loader selects the type of ammunition to be used, on instruction from the tank commander, loads, and keeps track of the empties, which are not discharged outside the tank. The loader also maintains surveillance to the rear of the tank when not actually loading. He must be particularly agile since he uses both hands and both feet while seated on a padded stool with the machine in violent motion. Ammunition in the magazine points straight aft, and as it is drawn out it is flipped over, pointed forward and thrust home with the gunner's right hand.

(The most modern Soviet tanks have automatic loaders, which enable them to man their tanks with one less crew member. There are certain theoretical advantages to this but they are outweighed by the additional usefulness the fourth crew member provides to the entire crew. There is also a rumor to the effect that automatic loaders tend to grab crew members upon occasion and stuff them into the gun.)

A good crew can fire very rapidly — something on the order of one shot every three or four seconds — but this is not very significant because the amazing fire control system does not normally need a second shot. *The M-1 — in violent motion, day or night, rain or shine, rough terrain or smooth —expects and achieves first-round hits, on moving tanks, to and beyond two miles, practically 100% of the time.*

With this weapon it is considered bad form to shoot while stationary. Exceptional circumstances may call for it — such as a first round from ambush — but shooting while standing still always demands an explanation.

As we drove around, changing positions frequently, it became apparent that a good tank crew must be carefully and truly mated. The four men in an Abrams must think alike, react alike and interoperate like well-tuned gears. There is subtlety about this which gives one comfort in knowing that only superior people can handle this weapon. It would appear to be beyond the capacity of potato diggers or camel drivers to master. The more I observed the operation of the machine, the more it became clear why the tank-versus-tank success in Lebanon two years ago so enormously favored the Israelis. The tanks (on both sides) in that war were comparable, but the PLO and the Syrians had almost no chance.

Of the many remarkable things about the M-1, one that struck me was the efficiency of the inter-communication system. With helmet in place the four members of the crew can speak conversationally among each other without switches, buttons or any sort of manual control. In full operation, and in the heat of action, each member of the crew is instantly aware of every word spoken. This is so far in advance of the machinery of World War II as to form a different mode of communication altogether.

The wonders of the firing and sighting system are best appreciated from the gunner's seat, the only post in the tank which is cramped for a large man. The practically automatic laying and firing system acts rather as its own simulator, and it is not necessary actually to fire the weapon to know how well one is doing. In the gunner's seat you feel the rolling, surging motion of the vehicle underneath you but nothing moves in your sight unless you move it, or unless the tank commander overrides your controls. Your body can feel movement but the view in your gunsight queerly suggests the view in a slide projector. The driver has much more of a sense of motion, since he is controlling that motion and anticipating it, but to appreciate best what is going on it is necessary to stand in the tank commander's hatch — head and shoulders out — and watch the action.

At the suggestion of the crew chief, therefore, I stood in the hatch with the tank stationary and commanded, "Full acceleration. Straight ahead. Go!"

We did not go airborne, since the terrain in which we were working did not offer us any chances to jump, but there are plenty of pictures around of the mighty M-1 with light showing underneath it.

This is the ultimate motocross vehicle. It will go anywhere, through anything, at speeds which are literally breathtaking, and it can destroy anything opposing it — day or night — with one round.

At the conclusion of my experience I told my host, "That is the nearest thing to a Roman triumph that a man can experience today."

The M-1 has certain drawbacks, which are being overcome as rapidly as possible. In 1988 it was refitted with a smooth-bore 120mm gun designed by the Germans. This weapon is more powerful than the 105, but the crews I spoke with are not as enthusiastic about it as they might be. They feel that they can destroy any enemy tank right now with the gun they have, and the larger gun will naturally reduce the amount of ammunition that can be carried. Somewhat more anticipated is the substitution of a 25mm gun in place of the current 50 cal. The 50 is the tank's primary weapon against light vehicles and APC's but new versions of Soviet equipment will resist the 50 at distance and the 25 should do a better job. It also will have a better fire control system than that currently available for the 50, which I found a little awkward since the right hand and the left are widely separated and thus somewhat difficult to coordinate.

Fuel consumption remains uncomfortably high. Time will tell whether the piston engine of the German Leopard II is a proper solution to this problem. One thing the crews especially admire about the gas turbine is that it can run on almost anything, and no special fuel is therefore required.

While there was no way for me to appreciate it, one of the points about the Abrams which impresses Major Ancker most deeply is its remarkable "survivability." Tests have been run subjecting the M-1 to abuse and damage which would seem enough to destroy a battleship, without taking the weapon out of service. Its armor construction is a military secret, which is as it should be since one of the strong points about this armor is that the Russians have nothing like it, nor do they have the technology possible to copy it. The tank is not totally invulnerable, but it is very, very tough and just hitting it once with most anti-tank weapons is not enough to take it out. Neither will tread damage from mines necessarily nor probably disable it. Its treads are so designed as to be repairable in the field, and the tank can operate quite well on a short tread.

The complete armament of the machine I rode consists of a 105 high-velocity gun firing hypervelocity (5200 f/s) dart ammunition, or squish-head, or high explosive; a remote-control 50-caliber machinegun; a co-axial 30-caliber machine-gun; and another 30 topside for bivouac protection. It mounts a set of smoke projectors but, somewhat to my surprise, no anti-personnel scrapers. Unlike any other tank, the M-1 relies on its main battery for anti-aircraft defense. Its turret is so fast, and its firing system so accurate, that its crews are confident that they can shoot out of the air any helicopter which pauses long enough to launch a missile.

With the new gun will come an over-pressure cabin system permitting the crew to operate in a poisoned environment without protective clothing.

It has become standard practice for the leftist press to rail against all American military equipment as overly expensive, badly designed, excessively vulnerable, unreliable, inefficient — or any combination of the above. The Abrams tank, however, has survived to embarrass its detractors. It is not only as good as advertised, it is better — much better. The men who use it are in love with it — and to an outsider it is awesome. My own major enthusiasms have always been shooting and driving. In the Abrams tank I discovered the ultimate shooting machine, in combination with the ultimate driving machine. Would that Churchill could have enjoyed my experience with the 11th Cavalry and have realized what has evolved from his brainchild!

"SHOOTING THE BIG ONE"

It is a great pleasure to report that practical marksmanship, an endangered art, is alive and well and living in the armored force. In an age when the common attitude seems to be "If you can't shoot well, shoot a lot!" the goal of the American tanker is to kill with the first round.

If you want to find out about this first-hand your best bet is to join the Army, but if you can live with a second-hand account, I present it herewith:

The main battle tank is king of the battlefield. Winston Churchill's brainchild has grown up, and while the big tank cannot decide the irregular actions of the freedom fighters of the world, it certainly will be the decisive influence whenever major, modern armies clash. The efficiency of the modern main battle tank is determined in large measure by its gun and its fire-control system, for the tank vs. tank fight is decided by first shot hits. What this means is that marksmanship has finally found its maximum expression in tank shooting. For anyone who loves to shoot, tank-shooting is a supreme thrill.

It has been my privilege to shoot many different kinds of guns throughout a long and active life. I cannot truthfully say which I have enjoyed the most, but as of now my vote would go to the 105mm main gun of the United States M-1 Abrams tank. The gun itself is a wonder, and though it is being replaced within the next few years with the 120mm German smoothbore, the fire-control system for both instruments is quite similar. While the new gun is more powerful than the one now in use, the shooting system is the same, and it is simply astounding. The hypothesis is that on the battlefield of the future you must shoot first, *and hit with your first shot*, if you are to survive. Whether you see your enemy before he sees you will depend upon a number of complex factors, but primarily upon your own skill and your level of training. If you do see him first, however, with the M-1 you've got him! It is that good.

In July of 1987 I was cleared to fire this mighty machine, as the guest of the 11th Armored Cavalry at the U.S. gunnery range at Grafenwoehr, in Bavaria. I had previously driven the M-1, and had simulated firing the main gun, but this time I had the chance actually to fire it. It was an offer I could not refuse, so I flew to Germany. On a damp, gray morning I presented myself as ready, and this is how it was.

The gunner's seat is to the right of the main gun, and angled to port so that the gunner faces about thirty degrees across the line of fire. His helmeted head rests against the pad protecting the viewplate. His hands grasp the firing yoke. This device consists of two slanted pistol grips joined together at the top. It is redundant in that the three switches on the right are duplicated by the three switches on the left. There is a squeeze grip for the lower three fingers, a thumb button, and a firing button for the index finger. When the gunner squeezes his lower three fingers with either or both hands the turret power is engaged. The gun is trained by rotating the yoke sideways, and elevation is achieved by tilting the yoke backward or forward. The daylight sight is an optical telescope of ten power. The reticle is an orange dot subtending about one degree. The gun-laying system is obvious and simple. The gunner places the orange dot on his target and depresses the thumb button. This activates the laser, which instantly ranges on the target, and sets the appropriate elevation into the gun for whatever ammunition is being used. If the target is in motion a computer senses the amount of traverse being applied to the turret and sets the exact lead for the exact range determined by the laser. If the tank itself is in motion the computer feeds this information into the sighting system and compensates for it. Motion in the tank itself does not affect the aiming system, since the entire turret is stabilized and stays on any target the gunner designates without affecting his aim. When the gunner is on target, and has depressed the laser button, he simply squeezes with either or both index fingers. That's all there is to it! If all systems are working properly you have a first-round hit.

I was assigned two rounds, and I resolved to give them my very best effort since they run $1200 each. When all was in readiness the tank commander sang out, "Load!" and the breech slammed shut next to my head. The range officer called for a target and up it came. It was a 60-centimeter (twenty-four inch) black-and-white disk displayed at 1200 meters. It was barely visible through the tank's periscopes, but in the gunsite it appeared to be almost the same size as the orange reticle. I actuated the power system and placed the orange dot exactly on target, obscuring it. As the tank commander said, "Fire!" I depressed the laser button and squeezed the trigger. I had been expecting an enormous blast, together with a head-cracking jolt, but I experienced nothing of the sort. Inside the tank, with the hatches buttoned and wearing the intercom helmet, I heard a report something like that of a 12-gauge shotgun fired at a distance of twenty-five yards — with earplugs. The jolt to the tank was about the same as that experienced when a heavy door on a two-door automobile is slammed — forcefully. At the report I glimpsed the brilliant crimson ball of the tracer streaking directly toward the target and obscuring both it and the orange reticle. Time of flight was so short that I could not tell what happened.

"Hit!" came over the intercom from the range tower, and the loader sang out, "Good shot, sir!"

I released the firing yoke and leaned backward, altogether bemused. "How easy! How simple! How perfect! And how *soft*!" A direct hit with the first shot, at nearly a mile, on a target no bigger than a garbage can lid. Fantastic! (I wish I could have latched on to that tin disk with a four inch hole right through the middle of it. It would make a splendid trophy for my armory.)

For the second shot we used the night-sight, which is an infra-red sensor with target definition that I simply cannot believe. The picture in the viewer is green on black, but it is so sharp that it can easily differentiate between two normal-sized G.I. cans at a range of 2000 yards — in pitch dark. It is also used in heavy rain, fog, or smoke. About the only operational difference between the two systems is that the infra-red illuminator should be left on for as short a time as possible, since it reveals the shooter's position to anyone watching with the right kind of equipment.

When a new target was displayed at the same range I used the same firing procedure, and achieved exactly the same result — a center hit with one round.

I took off my helmet and eased out of the gunner's seat as the crew unbuttoned the hatches.

"But it's so easy! Does anybody ever miss with this?"

"Oh sure, you can miss, but it's not healthy. You can depend on it that the other guy is doing his best to get on you, and if you don't kill him before he fires you probably won't get a second chance."

This fantastic shooting machine is, naturally, immensely complex. The maintenance and calibration of the entire setup is intimidating even to consider. The technicians of the armored force must be men of outstanding intellectual and mechanical ability. It is gratifying to know that we can find such people, and can sign them on at a soldier's pay. A thing that astonishes me is that the firing system must be made workable for any man at random. There was no adjustment for my eyesight or hand control, and yet the first shot was exactly on without any adjustment whatever. I saw it and I felt it, but I am still not sure I believe it.

The M-1 Abrams tank has been in full operational status for some six years. The 105 gun that I shot is now being replaced with the 120, even though the 105 is quite capable of taking out any Soviet tank that can be fielded, using the depleted uranium hypervelocity dart ammunition. The bigger gun will do the same job somewhat farther out, but its ammunition capacity will be reduced. Gun size is possibly less important than other improvements in the turret system which will accompany the 120, such as a superior tank commander's firing system by means of which the main gun and the tank commander's anti-vehicular machinegun may be used on two different targets at the same time. There will also be superior environmental sealing against the poisoned atmosphere expected to prevail upon future battlefields.

The Evil Empire fields some very good tanks, and a lot more of them than we can afford. They have always followed the policy of providing overwhelming numbers of pretty good equipment, rather than reduced numbers of perfected equipment. This hands us the necessity of producing tank crews which are not just better than those of our enemies, but a great deal better. When I talked with the crews of several Israeli tanks in Lebanon during the '82 War they were unanimous in the opinion that it is the man who wins, rather than the machine — assuming that the machinery is roughly comparable. Nevertheless I feel that the perfect shooting machine which we have in the M-1 (and which the Germans duplicate in their Leopard II) gives our soldiers a distinct advantage. We are not sure at this time just how good the Empire's firing control systems are — or at least if we do have this information it is not available to the general public — but knowing what we do about our adversary's policies and equipment it is safe to assume that they are neither capable of producing the equivalent of the M-1, nor do they wish to. Their tanks are strong, and carry very good guns, but the instantaneous one-round hit capability of the M-1 makes it the technical equal of a large number of lesser machines.

My host, the S-3 of the 11th Armored Cavalry Regiment, tells me that we are getting a higher type of soldier into our front-line units now than he has ever seen before. This is a comforting thought, considering the skill level necessary to utilize our machinery. If my experience was representative, the shooting is easy. The head-work and alertness necessary to put the machine into a shooting position at the right time are demanding. We have magnificent armor, and we hope that we have magnificent men to man it. At this time, when the powers that be deem it wise to dismantle the nuclear shield of Western Europe, it is good to know that the cutting edge of our conventional defense is such as to give second thoughts to the Warsaw Pact and their plans to engulf Europe once the Pershings have been removed.

GO AHEAD AND DROP THE *OTHER* SHOE

The *New Yorker* magazine affects a certain timid sophistication which is doubtless representative of its readership. Its editors, however, are sometimes witlessly condescending in their assumption that they, unlike us, have thought matters through.

Note this:

> "In the opinion of Hans Morgenthau, a war that was conducted with nuclear weapons would be so different from any previous conflict that the word 'war' would simply be a misnomer. As it happens, it is precisely the points of resemblance to sports — what might be called war's better side — that have been lost to war. *Physical strength and skill, strategic brilliance, and personal courage have all been rendered superfluous,* [italics mine] together with the combatants themselves, who would hardly have time to report for duty or put on their uniforms in the half hour or less that it would take for intercontinental ballistic missiles, travelling at some fifteen thousand miles an hour, to reach their targets."

But what then? Shortly after the buttons are pushed most of us will be dead. The dead will have no problems. *But the living will.* The survivors will structure the new world, and in that endeavor "physical strength and skill, strategic brilliance, and personal courage" will *not* be superfluous. On the contrary, they will be overwhelmingly, decisively important. The nuclear threat has far from invalidated the individual warrior. He will survive, in very small numbers, and his victories will determine the future of the race.

PROBLEM TWO

The charge was murder. The plea was self-defense. As was eventually decided, the deceased attacked the defendant with deadly intent, because of which the defendant shot the deceased eight times with a 380, causing him (the deceased) uneasiness, cramps, loss of morale, desuetude and — eventually — death. All seems in order, except that the gendarmes flang the defendant immediately into durance vile, and the county prosecutor (here read *persecutor*) took it upon himself to hang a conspicuously bum rap on an innocent man. Not just once (hung jury), but twice! The defendant is a free man today, but he spent most of a year in the *carcel* — without bond —while the matter was being kicked around. This seems to me a pretty poor show.

Problem One is defending yourself. Problem Two is explaining it to the boys with the bracelets. One is more important than Two, but only until it is solved, at which point Two can become a bloody bore. It is all very well to declaim "He tried to kill me. A bad mistake. He won't try it again. OK with you guys?" But sometimes it isn't OK. Sometimes people don't believe you.

I was called in on this case as an expert witness. It is my firm belief, which I always try to make clear to my clients, that you only want an expert if you are innocent. An expert — if he really is one — may uncover some truths. The truth shall only make you free if you are not guilty.

The sticky point in question was the large number of shots. You are not supposed to keep on shooting a creep after he is no longer a threat to you. Eight shots! Doesn't it take time to fire eight shots? He must have been *hors de combat* after the first couple of hits, but you kept right on socking it to him. Such socking is shocking! *You murdered the bum!*

Now this is not necessarily so, but nobody connected with the case knew much about the effects of pistol fire. That is why I was called.

First item: How long does it take to fire eight shots (with sufficient control to stay on a man at ten feet or less) out of a 380 pocket auto? On the first try it took me 2.8 seconds. With an unfamiliar hand, perhaps four seconds. With practice, two seconds. That is not very long. That is well within the span of "hot blood." It by no means automatically establishes deliberation.

Second item: Can a man keep coming after being hit repeatedly with a 380? Absolutely! Among many examples is a particularly choice one in which the deceased shot *himself* amidships four times with a 380 Webley. Presumably the first three hits did not convince him.

It was pretty obvious that, whatever other considerations bore upon the case, deliberate, cold-blooded homicide was not evident from a technical standpoint.

The villain here (if we excuse the peculiar vindictiveness of the county attorney, who may well have had something else against the defendant) seems to be that crummy pistol. It was purchased for its handiness, light weight, large magazine capacity (it was a 13-round Beretta) and its large(?!) 38 caliber. Bruce Nelson has stated that a large magazine is most useful "if you plan to miss a lot." Quite so. But if you don't miss, and just keep hitting your man with no effect, you are likely to chew him up so much that he will almost certainly die. And then you may have to explain why you did all that shooting when all you claim to have been doing was saving your life.

On being released, the first thing our man did was to turn in his 380 on a serious pistol. We hope he never has to shoot for blood again, but if he does he will be much better off.

I have long ago lost count of cases in which a minor caliber pistol failed to solve Problem One. This is the first in which it very nearly lost on Problem Two.

II. THE PISTOLERO

MILITARY PISTOLS

The handgun began as a military arm — a means of extending the reach of the cavalryman beyond that of the infantry pike while allowing him to manage his horse with his free hand. The original horse pistols, especially the wheel-locks, were both too expensive and too bulky for use by any but special troops (rather as anti-tank rockets are today) and the pistol's general value to armies did not become apparent until the mid-nineteenth century — a matter of three-hundred years or so.

Sam Colt was to handguns as Henry Ford was to personal ground transportation, and his development of a powerful, accurate, *repeating* sidearm was one of a half-dozen achievements that civilized the world in the age of colonization.

For a time during the mid-eighteen hundreds the Colt revolver, and its imitations, became the ruler of close combat all over the world. Though less powerful than the musket, it was still powerful enough to stop an adversary reliably with one good hit, and it was much handier. A soldier could carry two major-caliber revolvers more easily than one Minié-rifle. If he knew how, he could hit reliably from farther out. *And he could keep on shooting.*

In our American Civil War this flowering of the handgun was especially obvious, and if pistols had not been so much more costly to construct we might well have wound up that epic with regiments of pistoleros in conflict. Amongst the cavalry raiders such as Mosby and Cantrell this almost came to pass, as their success-enriched troopers went into action without carbine or saber but with four revolvers — two on the belt and two on the saddle. Experience indicated that a man who could not handle a fight with twenty-four well-placed shots could not handle it with anything.

But the repeating rifle put an end to that. The Mauser tribe replaced the Colt tribe with the coming of smokeless powder, and the pistol slipped into a different role. It ceased to be a decisive weapon and became instead a confidence-builder, and it has stayed there since.

We hear great tales of the pistol in war. We see Custer in the Anheuser-Busch lithograph facing death with a Smith & Wesson Schofield in each hand. We see Teddy Roosevelt bounding up that hill in Cuba and rolling over a Spaniard, "like a rabbit," with his pistol. We see Winston Churchill riding through the Fuzzy-wuzzies at Omdurman, shooting his "Broomhandle" dry (an unforgiveable *gaucherie*) and decking six for ten. We see young Douglas MacArthur dropping the guerrilla chief off his fine horse on the railroad track near Vera Cruz. And we see Lieutenant George Patton reporting to General Pershing with the body of General Armendariz "as ordered" — secured by one shot from his 45 Peacemaker.

And we know about Herman Hanneken and Alvin York and Sam Woodfill and Audie Murphy. If our records were good enough we would know about hundreds more — splendid men in splendid conflict — pistol soldiers whose exploits should be rendered into song beside those of Leonidas and Horatius and Roland and The Cid.

It is currently fashionable to declaim that there is no glamor in war. The truth is that while there is *little* glamor in war, what glamor there is can be very glamorous indeed. And it is by no means a thing of the past. Despite the best efforts of the "rabbit press," accounts dribble back to us steadily from all those places where armies are clashing while you read this. It is happening now!

The de-glamorizer of war is distance. There is nothing heroic about being blown up by something fired from out of sight, but excitement builds as the range closes. When you finally confront your enemy face-to-face you truly "see the elephant," and that is when the pistol comes into its own.

Personal face-offs affect the lives of individual men, but they only affect the outcome of wars in that the men who survive them may go on to become important commanders. Such commanders are a minority among their peers, and even they tend to forget their juvenile adventures. Since commanders do not fight, they often do not know how. Consider that a conspiracy of very senior German officers — men who knew how to mobilize industry, organize armies, command battle fronts, and direct grand strategy — proved *technically* unable to kill Hitler. The generals were not up to a private's job! Consider that James Dozier, a brigadier general, states that he had never any training or preparation in how to deck a handful of two-bit punks at indoor ranges. I recall with deep sorrow the death in Lebanon of a personal friend — also a one-star general — who was killed at little over arm's length in a situation that might have been well met by a good pistolero.

This problem is one of attitude, or "mental set." If generals do not think of themselves as fighting men, how can they be expected to take the sort of personal, intimate, even sensual interest in arms that is essential to proper evaluation? The answer is that they can't. The old Marine Corps attitude that every Marine was a *rifleman* first, and anything else from truck driver to division commander only second, produced generals who could appreciate personal weapons. We do not see that attitude in today's military establishment.

What effect this has upon the design and procurement of military pistols is depressing. Its effect upon the design and procurement of rifles has given us the M-16. Have you ever met an honest-to-God, people-shooting infantryman who had anything but contempt for that one? Neither have I. We may be sure that the people who gave us the M-16 would be glad to hand us a pistol of equal merit if they could. (And now, it seems, they have.) For the time being, however, any new U.S. military pistol is on the financial back-burner, and we are luxuriously stuck with the Hanneken/York/Woodfill/Murphy pistol. Isn't that nice?

If we could get our military chiefs to think seriously about personal combat for a bit, not perhaps as a factor in winning wars but just as an element of warfare which suggests that we field better soldiers than our enemies, we might get them to come up with something productive. (Something better, for example, than replacing all the old 223 barrels with new ones with a tighter twist intended to keep a "fine new" 65-grain bullet, as opposed to the "terrible old" 55-grain bullet, point on. I have no idea of how much of your money and mine is being spent on this rancid sow's ear.)

This is not to say that we can make better soldiers just by giving them better personal arms, but it certainly should help. And we have *got* to have better soldiers, since our enemies will always have *more* soldiers. Superior troops can normally handle superior numbers (see Afghanistan, the Falklands, and Lebanon) but they must be truly superior. My own view is that we will not reach that needed individual superiority without Universal Military Training, but that is a political matter.

Too many of our people have been demoralized by the disaster in Viet Nam, and they assume that our morale problem is insoluble. It is more likely that the trouble with Viet Nam was the lack of an objective, and that if American troops are given a properly military mission they will fight just as well after Viet Nam as before. Be that as it may, the Viet Nam generation has just given up on individual weaponry, and tells us, in a roundabout way, that today's soldiers simply cannot be trained to shoot the way their grandfathers could. If that is true, no improvement in smallarms is reasonable. Let us hope that it is not true.

To shoot a rifle well takes skill. To shoot a pistol well takes more skill. To the military bureaucrat (as opposed to the fighting man) it seems pointless to try to train a soldier to use a less efficient weapon when the same effort can make him more skillful with a more efficient weapon. That is a reasonable attitude. It overlooks, however, the intensely human view that the individual soldier takes of his own life. No matter how deadly his anti-tank gun, or his mortar, or even his rifle, he still likes to feel that he can survive a totally unexpected short-range brawl. That is why men always acquire pistols, one way or another, in campaigns of any duration. In *Blitzkriegs* they haven't time to assess the situation nor loot much.

Three questions arise.

First: Do modern soldiers need a handgun?

Second: Can modern soldiers be trained to shoot a handgun well enough to give them confidence in it?

Third: If the answers to both of the foregoing are affirmative, what *kind* of pistol is indicated?

DO MODERN ARMIES NEED A PISTOL?

If we disregard the administrative structure of large modern armies, which include everything from prison chasers to orderlies and plain-clothes detectives, and consider only combat troops, the question as to the necessity of a sidearm is indeed moot. It is generally conceded that the Israeli Defense Force (*Zahal*) fights very well indeed, and on the occasion of a personal visit to the Beirut area in the middle of the invasion of '82, three things were conspicuous in their absence: hand grenades, girl soldiers — and pistols. The Israeli troops displayed very good weapons discipline, and I never saw a soldier separated from his personal arm. This personal arm was, however, an M-16, a Galil 223, or an Uzi. No motor drivers, nor artillery crews, nor tankers, nor communicators wore any sidearms that I could see. This might suggest that a modern army does not indeed need a handgun, since *Zahal* is as good as any around.

But the Israeli thrust through Lebanon up to Beirut was indeed a *Blitzkrieg,* and one may still wonder if the Israeli troops would choose to be pistolless if they had that choice.

It may be supposed that one of the reasons for the popularity of the pistol in WW1 was that the principle infantry arm of that conflict was a bolt action repeater, and in the event of close, rapid action the virtues of semi-automatic fire were obvious. In World War II, however, the American troops did have a semi-automatic battle rifle — the illustrious Garand — and still our forward-area people were very partial to the acquisition of sidearms of all sorts. This was also true in Korea and Viet Nam. Allowing for the measure of swank which many soldiers feel in wearing a pistol in a battle zone, there are the matters of readiness and handiness.

The following episode derives from World War I, but it will be seen that the circumstances could be paralleled exactly today.

"I had the prisoners climbing out, and we all picked up our loads and started on, when one slid back into the trench and reached for a grenade. Very fortunately, the last man in our party was one who was wearing a pistol. He dropped his load, made one of the quickest draws I've ever seen, fired twice, and shot the man twice through the knee joint, almost smashing his leg apart. All this was done and over within much less time than it has taken me to tell you about it — and none of our party could possibly have unslung a rifle and fired in time to stop that action."

From *A Rifleman Went to War*
by Herbert W. McBride

To bring the matter up to World War II, an incident of immediate interest to me involved an officer on forward-artillery duty and temporarily "bewildered" in Kunai grass (a Marine officer is never *lost*). This man attempted to climb a broken tree to locate himself. He could not have done this with either rifle or machine pistol. As his head cleared the vegetation he was face-to-face with one member of a Japanese patrol at a distance of about twelve paces. The Nip attempted to pivot to bring his rifle to bear, but the Marine officer was able to produce his pistol in time to shoot one-handed and stop the action.

To bring matters up to Viet Nam, we hear of the case in which a hospital corpsman — unarmed by regulation but too far forward to worry about such things — was attempting to load wounded into the side door of the helicopter when he was hit by a squad of Viet Cong, which he stopped by using his service pistol efficiently to kill five of the attacking wave.

A matter remains debatable. For every soldier you know of who esteems a pistol in action, you will find two or three who never heard of one's being used successfully, and who doubt if the weapon has any purpose at all. It is probable that the cases in which the pistol has been used to save a soldier's life have not been statistically impressive. The fact is, however, that on those occasions where it was so used it seemed extremely important to the user. A statistician could simply write off all those soldiers who saved their lives with pistols and insist that the provision of pistols to a modern army is not cost effective, since it would cost more to provide handguns than the losses that their absence might entail. Statisticians can look at it like that, but a soldier still wants to live, if possible. He carries a pistol because he feels good doing so. A three-tour veteran of Viet Nam once told me that his knowledge of how to use his sidearm, acquired in California competition, made his third tour entirely different from his first two. He felt a peace of mind the third time out, which, justifiable or not, was entirely due to that weapon on his belt, and his knowledge that he could use it well.

It is not up to one observer to decide whether or not the armies of the world need pistols. My personal view is that armies probably don't need them, but if *I* go to war, *I* want one.

Since a pistol is primarily a confidence-builder, and since confidence is a personal matter, the policy of having officers select, purchase, maintain, and train with pistols of their own choice has much to recommend it. It was general during the

Victorian period, and it worked well. It also saves a little money, as budgeters will be quick to note.

CAN MODERN SOLDIERS BE TRAINED TO SHOOT A HANDGUN WELL ENOUGH TO GIVE THEM CONFIDENCE IN IT?

Shooting a pistol well enough to save one's life with it is about as hard as learning to ride a motorbike well enough to be safe in traffic. It is certainly not impossible, but it does take concentration and time and effort. A pistol to a duffer is a dangerous nuisance. In highly-skilled hands it is not only a confidence-builder, but it can be extremely efficient. An alert man who knows what he is doing can place controlled shots with great speed, at short distances, and keep his weapon continuously in action as long as he has spare magazines available. Witness the fact that a par score on El Presidente is achieved by placing twelve center-hits on three different targets at 10 meters in 10 seconds, including reloading the pistol.

The question is how much training and how much motivation is necessary to achieve this sort of skill? The armies of the world dismiss modern pistol training, as developed in practical competition, as fanciful. They appear convinced that it is impossible or impracticably expensive to teach a man to shoot a pistol well. This is entirely a matter of *which men make up the army*. It is self-evident that the armed forces of any free nation must represent an accurate cross-section of that nation's population. Universal Military Training — not the draft — is the obvious way to obtain this. When the people *are* the army, and the army *is* the people, there is no risk of a military assumption of political power. A professional army is safe only so long as it is kept small — probably too small to meet the needs of any major power at this time.

If our soldiers represent a true cross-section of the populace, coming from all walks of life and all degrees of education, then clearly they can be trained to use weapons well. If they are drawn into the army only because it offers wages and shelter, then it is possible that our troops are indeed untrainable, at least to any serious level. To say, however, that men cannot be trained to shoot a pistol well within the budgetary and time considerations of a military training program is to betray ignorance of the facts. In a top-grade, private-training center, students of middle to high quality are brought to a fair degree of pistol competence at the end of twelve hours of supervised instruction and a four-hour period of unsupervised practice, involving a total expenditure of little more than seventy-five rounds. Twenty-eight hours of instruction, plus the expenditure of about 500 rounds of ammunition, brings the same type of student body to complete command of its immediate environment — in more than 50% of the cases. Admitting that the students in a private school are more powerfully motivated than troops in the service, we can still maintain with complete confidence that the amount of time and ammunition necessary to develop a satisfactory degree of skill with the pistol is not out of the question in a representative training budget.

The question of motivation is, of course, important. Monetary reward for excellence in the performance of weaponry tasks was a feature of the military in days gone by. It is probable that this policy should be revived.

WHAT KIND OF PISTOL IS INDICATED?

Any satisfactory service pistol must possess the following three essentials, in equal measure: A. Dependability; B. Power; C. Controllability. (From a procurement standpoint, it is also very desirable that it be cheap to produce. Several excellent pistols from the past are no longer worth consideration by the military, simply because they were too costly to make.)

A pistol is a life-saving instrument. *It must work.* Perfection may exist only in the mind of God, as Plato insists, but in the matter of life-saving devices we still seek the closest thing to perfection that we can. When a pistol is drawn and employed to save a man's life, it absolutely must function. A reliability factor of 999 in 1000 is not unreasonable. This is to be expected of a fairly well-maintained piece. It is unreasonable to expect a weapon to be treated badly and give good service, though it is surprising how well some do in this regard. It is not unreasonable to require troops to take care of their weapons. It has been done, and it can be done. To those officers who claim that this is not realistic, we can only say, "Step down!"

A satisfactory service pistol must be sufficiently powerful to stop a determined adversary with one solid hit in the torso, more than nine times out of ten. The capacity of pistol cartridges to do this is a complex study, but fortunately we have a century of experience upon which to draw. It is indeed interesting that the armies of the world in the 1980's are still using cartridges developed near the beginning of the century. Nearly world standard is the 9mm Parabellum, developed by the Germans and adopted in 1908. It was not a particularly satisfactory round then and it is no better now. Attempts to improve it by changing its bullet shape and configuration are a waste of time. It disposes of enough power to put a man down if he is hit many times in succession in the chest, as is often the case when it is used in machine pistols. It will not do so reliably when shot successively as in a pistol. The chances of its turning off an adversary with one well-placed hit (which does not damage a major nerve center) remain at about 50%.

The United States developed the 45 ACP cartridge and adopted it in 1911. It is the cartridge of the Hanneken/York/-Woodfill/Murphy pistol. It is quite good. It is almost twice as good as the Parabellum. Over the generations, the 45 auto-pistol cartridge has been achieving one-stop shots in about 19 cases out of 20. Listen again to McBride:

"There never was a Luger or a Mauser made to even come within hailing distance of our Service Colt.

"Say — wait a minute though. I do happen to remember one instance in which the German Luger had wallop enough to do the job right, and maybe I had better tell about it right here. The incident occurred down on the Somme, where I was working along with the advance, commanding a scratch crew of machine gunners. There was a lull in the fighting and we were waiting on something or other at the time, the Germans having all pulled out of their trenches and moved back a bit to the rear. So I decided to look about the German trenches and dugouts and see if we could locate some loaded belts of their machine gun ammunition, as we had just found two perfectly good Maxim heavies that might as well have been put back to work.

"Calling upon a couple of the gun crew to come along with me, the three of us crawled over into the main German trenches and commenced searching around for some loaded belts. One of the chaps who accompanied me was evidently a new replacement, at any rate he still had the souvenir bug in his head, and tried to pick up everything lying in that trench. I soon put a stop to this, and made him throw away most of the junk he was carrying, but he held on to a Luger pistol which was in a holster slung onto a black leather waist belt — this find I decided to overlook. Those trenches were the usual deep and well made German affair, showing the result of months of hard pick and shovel work, but they had been pretty badly battered by our guns and the bottom was mostly covered with a layer of loose dirt, upon which we made no noise as we crawled around the traverses and bays.

"The souvenir hound kept sticking a bit in front of us, I suppose he wanted another pistol or two, but at any rate he kept ahead, swinging that Luger from the buckled belt held in his right hand. In this manner we stepped around the end of a deep traverse and our 'point' almost fell over a big Heinie who was down on his knees going through the pockets of a dead British officer — the Dutchman was so busy he never even knew we were around. It was all over in a second — the kid just swung the belt and that holstered Luger made a circle and came down on top of the German's head with a 'womp' —and we went on, leaving both dead men lying there. And that is about the only time I can remember a 'slug' from a Luger having sufficient wallop to do a 'bang up' job of things."

The issue is closed. There is little point in beating a dead horse. Those who wish to do so are invited to consult the reams of copy prepared on the subject, both by those who know and those who don't.

A satisfactory service pistol must be controllable. That means that it must be relatively easy to hit with. A difficulty here is that it is not always agreed *what* the pistol is expected to hit. I will postulate that what the pistol is expected to hit is the vital zone of a human enemy, at distances of up to hand-grenade range. Note that nothing is said of "accuracy," since almost any pistol, in good condition, is more accurate than the shooter. Some, however, are easier to control than others. Trigger-cocking, for example, always interferes with ease of control. There are those who maintain that any powerful pistol is difficult to control, and such people simply indicate that they do not understand the modern technique. It does not take weight or muscle — it takes knowledge. That knowledge can be imparted fairly easily by those who know how.

With the foregoing considerations in mind, let us look at some of the classics, together with some of their successors, and consider what ought to be done about this item of equipment.

The Classics

The Broomhandle Mauser.
This marvelous old gun, the world's first successful auto pistol, has a special place in the history of smallarms. It was never officially adopted as a G.I. sidearm by any power, but it was extremely popular at the turn of the century and continues to fascinate us to this day. With its elaborate wooden carrying case doubling as a shoulder stock, its ten-shot stripper-fed magazine, and its fanciful rear sight (graduated clear out to Fort Mudge) it was every bit as much a carbine as a pistol. Its extraordinary interlocking mechanism, devoid of pins or screws, is unique in weaponry. To see it is to covet it. To know it, however, is not necessarily to love it.

The Broomhandle was dependable. That was possibly its strongest single point. It was powerful — in an odd way. The thirteen-hundred foot seconds of its little 87-grain bullet gave it plenty of energy, a flat trajectory, and good initial penetration, but such stopping power as it had was dependent entirely upon what was struck. Fairbairn saw it used extensively in China and his conclusion was that its projectile produced quite good stopping power if bone was struck, but not otherwise. In controllability and handiness it was a failure. The curious round handle, from which it gets its nickname, is comfortable to no hand I have ever discovered. It is about as handy to use as a bicycle chain, and its ignition system clanks like a barn door. These things should not be held against it since it was, after all, the pioneer of the type; but despite Winston Churchill's affection for it, the Broomhandle was never a really satisfactory military pistol.

The Webley Mark VI.

This fine old revolver was the mainstay of the British forces in the First World War. It was a first-rate weapon, combining reliability with good power and controllability. Its slow, fat, soft bullet delivered very reliable stopping power for modest recoil, and its single-stroke loading system provided better continuity of fire than obtainable with any other revolver. It was somewhat fragile, and very big and clumsy, but it gave good service while it lasted.

The Luger.

Here was another marvelous mechanism, with a very special esthetic appeal. It was adopted by the Germans in 1908, together with its cartridge which has since become standard in European armies. Somewhat like the Chinese alphabet, this cartridge was a great step forward at the time, but it has held its users back ever since. The pistol for it was a wonder, being compact, handy, strong, accurate, and controllable. It featured an interesting butt shape, which is very comfortable to the hand, but only if the hand is improperly placed upon it. To those who do not understand shooting, this is no drawback, and consequently the Luger has a great following among people who do not shoot very much.

The drawbacks of the Luger were an open mechanism which is quite prone to malfunction when exposed to foreign matter, and the sensitivity that its design requires for reliable functioning. It depends for proper operation on ammunition perfectly suited to its system of cams and springs. Other ammunition will not work it reliably. The Luger also suffers from an ignition system which works through so many corners that a conventional trigger pull is all but unreachable. Instead of a break, Luger ignition offers a continuous, smooth, spring tension which lets go somewhere along the line. This can be mastered, I am told, but since it is only found on this one weapon, few wish to take the trouble.

Except as to its stopping power, the Luger was a successful battle pistol, and was the tactical equivalent of any of today's offerings which take the same cartridge.

The Colt 45.

This weapon is so well known and so widely used in the United States that it requires no history nor description. Since it combines dependability, power, and controllability in a way that no other sidearm ever has up to now, it holds the title as the world's best service sidearm. It is used by all serious contenders in international practical pistol competition throughout the world — in which no restrictions are placed upon the type of weapon used.

Its drawbacks include a certain complexity which has been found unnecessary in subsequent designs, unsuitability for small hands, unsuitability for left-handed shooters without modification, and inferior sights. Also it is occasionally found with an atrocious trigger pull, though this is not due to its design and can be easily corrected.

The Browning P-35.

This weapon was Browning's idea of an improvement over his 45 auto (which was called "Colt" after Colt bought the design from Browning). He cleaned up the mechanism of the earlier weapon, making it simpler and more easily maintained. He improved the butt shape, and installed a double-column magazine for the 9mm cartridge. He also removed the grip safety, which had been required by U.S. contract stipulation in 1911.

The P-35 is a first-rate military sidearm and became world standard during World War II and the actions following it. Its drawback, as with the Luger, is its cartridge.

New Ideas

The new generation of military automatic pistols features double-column magazines and double-action. The large capacity magazine seems hooked to the concept that "more is better." I have studied the matter long, and I have yet to find a situation in which a man was able to save his life because his pistol carried an unusually large number of rounds in its butt. I do know of one case in which a police officer discovered, in time, that simply shooting at a van that was trying to run over him was not the answer. Having fired fourteen rounds out of his pistol, he then reloaded, found the way of truth, and shot at the driver. This is an equivocal example, since the number of rounds in the weapon was not the issue, but simply the need to think. There is certainly nothing against a large-capacity magazine, but one should not make magazine capacity a primary attribute in selecting a battle pistol. Far more important than magazine capacity is stopping power, and one is wise to trade the former for the latter.

The double-action, or "trigger-cocking," feature in auto pistols is deemed essential by a great many of today's procurement officers, presumably on grounds of safety. A cocked pistol on the belt fills a good many of the world's desk warriors with horror. They seem to think that a cocked hammer is a disaster looking for a place to happen. One sometimes gets a feeling that our military and police bureaucrats are more concerned about accidents than about fighting. Perhaps this is because accidents affect their careers, whereas fighting probably does not. We see a continuous stream of inventions, devices and designs which are intended to make a pistol so free from accidental discharge that it cannot be used for its real purpose. This is a good example of redoubling one's efforts after having lost sight of one's goals.

The essential weakness of nearly all new military pistols is that they continue to be made for what has been long proven to be an unsatisfactory cartridge, the 9mm Parabellum. The best of the new official designs is the Czech 75, and if that weapon were available in a serious cartridge it would be the brightest thing on the horizon.

TRIGGERS,
TRIGGER CONTROL,
AND OTHER ESOTERICA

It has been baldly stated that there is nothing to marksmanship but pressing the trigger when the sights are aligned. This is true. It is also true that there is nothing to playing the piano but hitting the right keys at the right time.

The issue is simply the coordination of hand and eye. A man blessed with perfect coordination could shoot perfectly, with anything, any time. But we are not so blessed, and even the very best of us need all the help we can get. Thus it is that a good trigger is a very important feature on any hand-held firearm from which reasonably precise bullet placement is to be expected. I will go further and say that, in my opinion, a good trigger is the single most important element of a good gun.

What, then, do we mean by "a good trigger?" We do not mean its configuration, but rather its action. Trigger configuration can be a matter of esthetics or of comfort, but trigger action is what matters for precise control. What is wanted is *imperceptible movement*. The trigger must move, in order to release the spring-loaded igniting mechanism, but we don't want to know about it. As finger pressure reaches the designed level, the "break" should occur without any movement that the finger can feel. The trigger should break, as the old timers say, "Like a thin glass rod." To achieve this paradox of movement without motion takes some doing. It is a vital element of the gunsmith's art.

It should be noted that preliminary motion of the trigger, before it arrives at its disengagement resistance, is no impediment to good action. This is correctly called "slack" or "take up," and it is a feature of many excellent modern triggers, including all semi-automatic actions and a good many bolts.

When a marksman "takes up the slack," he moves the trigger from its rest position into its firing mode. A good take-up is light — say one-half to one-and-one-half pounds — its travel is one tenth to one quarter of an inch, and it terminates cleanly at its release point. From here on no movement should be apparent. This sort of trigger is often called "military" or "two-stage," as opposed to "shotgun" or "single-stage" triggers, which include no slack. (The Swiss are fond of a *three-stage* trigger, which is pretty peculiar but seems to suffice.)

A really good single-stage trigger, such as may be found on certain high grade revolvers and many target rifles, is a baffling delight. When you press it (on an empty chamber) you *feel* nothing, you just hear it click. This sort of thing is a great aid to good marksmanship — probably the greatest single aid we know.

I do not feel that the single-stage trigger is superior to the two-stage except in that it is easier to learn. Proper management of the military trigger calls for taking up the slack as the piece is presented, and duffers have been known to "go through" the second stage inadvertently to a premature discharge.

Either system will do very well, and one should not feel that it is either necessary or desirable to take the slack out of a two-stage trigger. Especially beware of the gun butcher, amateur or professional, who suggests blocking take-up with a mechanical stop. This was done widely to military bolt actions right after WWII, and it is an open invitation to disaster since it removes all barrier to accidental discharge as the bolt is closed.

Trigger weight — the pressure on the trigger needed for ignition — may vary from a few ounces to as much as ten pounds, but two pounds can be dangerous and five pounds can be awkward. Two-and-a-half to three-and-a-half — clean — is a good spread, but I would prefer five pounds clean to two pounds creepy.

"Creep" is the standard term for apparent motion in the trigger, after take-up, on the break. It is an obstacle to precision, in any degree, and in bad cases can render the piece nearly unmanageable.

"Backlash" — in marksmanship — is the common term for trigger movement which takes place after the ignition break. It bothers some people more than others, but it is hardly serious. The platonic ideal of trigger, existing only in the mind of God, has no slack, no creep, and no backlash. We cannot achieve it, but we can approach it. (As with other desirables, such as liberty and justice for all.)

Europeans are fond of the "set trigger," in which the releasing mechanism is spring-loaded and deliberately cocked — or "set" — just before firing. This can provide trigger action so light as to be imperceptible — the merest touch will fire the piece. It works, not only for deliberate fire but for speed shooting, as Gerry Gore showed me on running rabbits in Natal. It is, however, somewhat weird if you are not raised on it. I am not convinced that it makes for better shooting; besides which it is necessarily delicate and complex, and if "un-setting" it after a false alarm is neglected, it is unsafe. Set triggers normally offer the option of a "regular" action if the trigger is not set. On those I have tried, this un-set action has never been good.

About half the firearms you may encounter will have good triggers as issued. The odds on quality bolt action and lever action sporting rifles are good. High grade revolvers usually have fine single-action triggers, and late model Colt autos are often as excellent as earlier versions were egregious. The semi-automatic rifles are difficult, since the weight and violence of their actions tend to jolt off a nicely tuned trigger on closure. The Garand family (M-1, M-14, M1A, BM-59, U.S. Carbine, Mini-14) are better than most in this respect and can often be found with very nice triggers — possibly not Grade One but good Grade Two. The true "assault rifles" (*Sturmgewehre*) have uniformly poor triggers, and fixing them is so difficult as to be beyond the skill of most gunsmiths, even those with much experience.

Accessory triggers — Canjar, Jaeger, Timney, etc. — are available for most bolt actions, and can be "plugged in" to a military bolt gun to replace its two-stage mechanism. Canjar, in particular, enjoys a fine reputation, and I have used one on a custom Enfield for years with complete satisfaction. However, nearly all late-model sporting bolt guns come with good single-stage triggers and it is best to make sure that you really need an accessory trigger before buying one, which will cost about as much as 100 rounds of factory 308.

The trigger can be managed in three ways, the easiest and most useful of which may be called the "open-end surprise-break." "Surprise break" is the marksman's term for a break which occurs at an instant not specifically chosen by the shooter. "Open-end" signifies that the finger pressure is steadily increased until, at some indefinite point in time, it suffices —and the shot is fired. This is the standard system used for deliberate fire from stabilized positions — bench, bipod, prone and sitting with rifles; and prone and braced-sitting with pistols.

The combat pistol shot must quickly learn the "compressed surprise break," in which the surprise is compressed into a selected time interval, which may be very short but still encompasses a true surprise. The rifleman engaging running targets uses this technique.

For unstabilized firing positions — principally offhand with either rifle or pistol — it is not possible to use the compressed surprise break since the sights may well waver during the chosen time span. The open-end version is possible but nerve-wracking, as waiting for a perfect sight picture may take forever. The great offhand shots, I am told, use the "nudge." They nudge off the shot just as the sights are right. For a duffer to try this is disastrous. That is why we see so many really bad offhand shots.

With any of the three trigger presses, however, a good trigger is essential. Finger placement varies — among good shots — but I favor the pad of the first phalange with the pistol, and the crease between first and second phalanges with the rifle. Pressure should be straight to the rear. With a trigger much below two pounds it becomes tricky to present the piece when using any finger pressure at all, and this is why most do not favor very light ("hair?") triggers for general use. The renowned Julian Hatcher tells of using such a hair trigger in the Olympics by actually reversing the direction of his finger. He would carefully place his finger on the side of the feathery trigger and push gently *forward*. Then when sight alignment was perfect, he just released his trigger finger and the piece fired. Interesting, certainly, but hardly practical. Special "release triggers" were at one time in vogue with clay-bird shotgunners, but they are rarely seen now.

I have shot steadily now, season after season, since before ordinary American families had cars, radios, or refrigerators. That is a lot of shooting. I can manage a bad trigger — barely — but I do not enjoy it, and I do not think it is necessary. If your weapon comes out of the box with a good trigger that is just fine — you are ahead of the game. But if it does not, get it fixed. That is what gunsmiths are for. Do not be content with a gritty, spongy, or stubborn trigger. "Three pounds, crisp" is the word. Four may be better with auto pistols, but not five. But whether it is three, three-and-a-half, or four — *crisp* is what you want.

PRINCIPLES OF
PISTOL SIGHTING

While a lot of defensive action takes place at just outside arm's length, the majority of defensive shots are sighted, or would be more effective if they were. All pot shooting is sighted. So we have sights on our pistols. You may have seen pistols without sights. You may have seen a car without a reverse gear, too. Even if you don't think you'll need them, you'd better have them.

The sights on a pistol function on a different principle from those on a rifle. Non-telescopic rifle sights may be set far enough apart so that front and rear lie at significantly different distances from the eye. The farther they lie apart — the greater the "sight radius" — the more precise may be the alignment they afford. However, the greater the sight radius the less it becomes possible to focus on both sights at once. Therefore the aperture rifle sight is better than the open rifle sight since the latter requires a short radius, with the notch set well forward on the barrel, while the former allows the ring to be set close to the eye, to be looked *through* rather than *at*. With a well-designed aperture rifle sight — large diameter, thin rim — you may disregard the rear sight as long as you are looking *through* it.

With pistol sights all is different. The sights are necessarily close together and held farther from the eye than the distance between them. Their geometric efficiency is low but they lie in nearly a single focal plane. They do not afford great optical precision but practical pistol shooting rarely demands it, while they do provide satisfactory and almost instantaneous *verification* of alignment. This point is most important. A correct firing stroke — from leather to line-up — aligns the pistol reflexively, once it is neurologically programmed. The sights are not used to align the weapon, rather they are used to verify an alignment already achieved by means of a trained presentation. Your mind does not command "Up. Right. Down a hair. A hair left. Now that's about right. Squeeze!" It simply says "OK, go!" This is called Flash Alignment, and it works beautifully once it is understood.

I was amused a few years back to hear of an F.B.I. instructor who dismissed the modern technique because it is entirely sighted. "What do you do in the dark, where most fights occur?" Not having been to school, he didn't know that a good stroke works just as well in the dark as in daylight, since, as it is perfected, verification becomes so automatic as to be almost unconscious. You always seek it, but if the lights go out you go ahead anyway, and if you have done your exercises you hit.

These instructions apply to defensive shooting. Hitting a squirrel in a tree in the head is another matter. If you have developed a sound stroke, however, you will have little trouble with the slow, target alignment used for the pot shot.

Modern pistol sights are nearly all of the "Patridge" pattern, a combination of a square rear notch and a square front post. This provides a precise index of elevation, which is not true of any bead or "V" arrangement. The front sight must be prominent enough to be seen sharply and quickly. The G.I. front sight on the 45 auto is especially bad in this respect. It is good enough for slow fire but extremely hard to pick up in a hurry. Thus proper sights are almost the first accessory needed for the big auto.

Pistol sights must be zeroed, just as rifle sights, to bring the mean point of impact into coincidence with the sight line. In general, subsonics should be zeroed for dead center at 50 meters, printing about 1½″ high at 25; and supersonics at 100, printing about 2½″ high at 50. Naturally this is facilitated by adjustable sights, and most quality handguns are so equipped, but fixed sights are always more durable, as well as being less expensive. It is a nuisance to zero fixed sights, but once they are set they stay there.

Both front and rear sights on any practical weapon should be de-horned. Sharp corners tear hands, clothes, and holsters, and should not be found on the exterior surface of any hand tool. Unfortunately neither gunmakers nor gunsmiths agree with me in this, and bloody hands are commonplace on the practice range, as are perforated sport coats on peace officers. The front sight must be ramped — neither undercut nor vertical — and the wings of the rear sight face must be smoothly rounded, both laterally and longitudinally. A proper rear sight presents a plain flat surface to the eye, without shelves, recesses or steps.

I prefer black-on-black, but many people do very well with colors. If a shooter thinks contrasting colors help his shooting, they just may. One thing does seem certain — white-on-white or grey-on-grey sights are not good. If you have such, best touch them up with enamel or nail polish.

Much work has been done on so-called "night sights" for pistols, following the sound notion that most pistol confrontation occurs in dim light. Those systems I have evaluated do not impress me, so far. It is easy to demonstrate that, using the right technique, you can hit reliably in very dim light with the sights that you use in broad daylight. When light becomes so poor that you can no longer identify your target you obviously should not shoot. At the very narrow lower limit of shootable light certain kinds of illuminated or light-gathering sights can actually help, but this is not a fair trade for the efficiency they lose in broad daylight.

If there is one thing that is most vital about pistolcraft it is concentration on the front sight. When the bugle sounds the charge in your mind, you think FRONT SIGHT as your piece lines up. Don't think about your target, think about your front sight. Concentrate on it, *and focus on it.* In any action, live or simulated, there is an overwhelming tendency to focus on your target. Surmount it! This is quite literally a matter of life or death.

A pistol is primarily a defensive instrument, for use in unexpected encounters with armed men at short range. It can, however, be used quite efficiently to put meat on the table. The same handiness that makes the handgun the ideal device for instantaneous defensive reaction suits it well to the sort of fleeting target of opportunity that may be encountered by anyone doing ordinary chores around a farm. The pistol rides on your belt as you cut wood or till the soil. The rifle at the house, or even in the truck, may be out of reach when you spook a rabbit in your cabbages or a feral hog in your corn.

This opens the subject of glass sights for hunting handguns, since we mainly agree that a scope is usually the best sight for a hunting rifle. My view is that a telescope is definitely useful on a 22 pistol (rimfire, that is) but much less so on a centerfire. On any sizeable target your problem is not seeing it but holding and squeezing properly. At ranges at which you need optical help you can't hold well enough to hit reliably with a handgun — or at least *I* can't. (I confess that reading some of my gunwriting friends humbles me very much. "A" is dead certain on jackrabbits at 350. "B" can hit 20 aspirin tablets with twenty shots at 100 — every time. "C"s wife can hit a golf ball ten straight at 200. Marvelous! My competition record is pretty fair, but I guess I must have been competing against cripples.)

THE FIRING STROKE

The handgun is a means of stopping violence initiated by another. It will rarely be out and ready, still less "aimed in," when the need to fire it becomes apparent. Most often the decision to shoot will be taken when the pistol is holstered, with the hands unready and well clear. (The cocked, or "cowboy," ready position is used only in the cinema and in carelessly run contests.) Thus the movements of the shooter's body between the internal "Go!" signal and discharge of the piece constitute what we have come to call the "firing stroke." It may also be called "the draw," or "the quick draw," but whatever it is called it is made up of a sequence of movements which must be carefully learned and just as carefully practiced by the aspiring handgun marksman.

For decades "quick draw" has been eyed askance by conventional shooters — military, police, and civilian — not because it is not essential to sound pistolcraft, but because it has been regarded as dangerous. As a matter of fact it *is* dangerous, to the shooter himself, if he does not know what he is about. For a novice to buy a gun and holster, withdraw to the city dump, and start trying to see how fast he is, is indeed to invite a mishap. So we don't go about it like that. We learn the moves in correct sequence, and then we have no trouble.

Until recently I could say that no properly trained pistolero had ever had a premature discharge on the draw; and that, conversely, every drawing accident to come to my attention happened with an untrained hand. This year I saw my first (*and*, I trust, my last) exception to this rule. The shooter had been carefully schooled, but he was under intense competitive pressure in a man-against-man contest and he simply drove himself a notch beyond the limits of his own coordination. Damage was minor, and nobody's day was spoiled, but my absolute statement was invalidated. I don't know how many thousands of draws I have seen, but the one exception in that total is about as significant as one reluctant lemming in a migration.

The firing stroke is one fluid movement, devoid of any unnecessary motion, but it should be considered by the novice as a series of distinct steps. These steps are first learned staccato — by the numbers — and then blended together smoothly. There is no need to try to be fast at first. If you are smooth you *will* be fast. The incentive to be quick will supply itself if you ever have to draw for blood. The problem in a live encounter is more often to slow yourself down than to speed yourself up, once your gunhandling has been successfully programmed.

Step One

Facing your target, place your right hand on your pistol butt in a solid firing grip, except for the thumb and the trigger finger. The thumb rides high, above the safety on an auto pistol, and the index finger points straight forward along the frame. If you cannot comfortably place your second finger snugly up against the bottom of the trigger-guard, change your holster.

Simultaneously place your left hand "in grab" — about a foot in front of your belt buckle, palm vertical, fingers extended, thumb pointing straight up.

Keep your left elbow against your body.

Step Two

Break the piece clear of the leather, upward if you use a pouch holster, forward if you use a break-front. *Do not move it further than just clear. Do not depress the safety. Do not insert the trigger finger in the guard.* This is most important. Failure to heed can hurt.

(Note: At least one master marksman pops the safety in the holster. That is his method and he is welcome to it, since he will make no mistakes. He does not gain speed that way, however, as others just as fast as he do not do it. Leave the safety on until the third step.)

With trigger-cocking ("double-action") weapons the trigger finger *may* enter the guard at Step Two. Three is safer, however. (Note: With a cross-draw keep the muzzle below the supporting arm as the piece is advanced.)

Step Three

Advance the piece halfway from the holster to the waiting left hand. Depress the safety. *Keep the index finger straight.* (Except with double-action, where there is no safety latch and the finger enters the trigger guard.)

Step Four

Join hands and initiate counter-pressure, right hand against left. Now, place the finger on the trigger. (D.A.'s commence squeeze.) Keep the muzzle depressed about 15 degrees below line of sight and maintain focus on the target.

Step Five

Line up. Force the left elbow away from the side. Increase counter-pressure. Shift focus from target to front sight. Take up trigger slack, if cocked. If double-action, press trigger about halfway back. (You can still check your complete stroke at this point, with practice.)

Step Six

Press smoothly, thumb against forefinger. Do not pull. Do not jerk. Do not milk. *Press smoothly.* Quickly, but *smoothly.* If the piece is unloaded the muzzle will not dip and the sights will not twitch. If it is loaded you will have a center hit. After the shot, stay right on target, locked-in for a second, to verify your hold and be ready for a second shot.

That's it. Practice it very carefully — by the numbers —until all motions are sure. This will take about 100 strokes, unless you are especially well coordinated. Then put them together slowly, eliminating all traces of lost motion, such as crouching, twisting, "slapping," or "bowling." Only the arms may move, though a slight dip of the head is permissible.

Try another 100 of these, preferably under observation by a coach. When arms and hands begin to ache, stop and continue tomorrow.

Eventually you will develop a very smooth and very strong stroke, well within a second and powerful enough to smash a champagne bottle with your gun barrel. Then you can try some live shooting.

Remember — DRAW QUICKLY — SHOOT CAREFULLY!

THE FLASH SIGHT-PICTURE

Of the five elements of the modern pistol technique, the second usually presented is the "flash sight-picture," or *Blitzblick*. The "sight-picture" is what one sees when he looks at his sights as they are aligned on target, and it is a *flash* sight-picture when he picks it up instantly.

There is an opinion commonly encountered among the unenlightened to the effect that pistol sights are not useful in social work because (a) there is no time to align them, and (b) they cannot be seen in dim light. On the contrary, sight alignment achieved by means of a properly conditioned series of reflexes can be verified in a couple of thousandths of a second. Furthermore, in light so dim that one cannot verify alignment (with adequate sights) shooting is unjustifiable because the target cannot be identified.

We use the sights, even at maximum speed. If we dismiss the speed-rock draw as impractical — since it cannot be executed except from a "ceremonial" holster — we do not lose any time in coming to eye level. If we come to eye level, that split-second view of the front sight, in sharp focus, acts as the "GO" signal to the nerves completing the trigger press, and produces a nice center hit just as quickly as one can move his piece from leather to line-up.

On the training range, we can read the student's target as he works on his firing stroke. A widely dispersed pattern, generally distributed, indicates inconsistency in grip, stance, or position. It also, though less frequently, may mean a focus on the target rather than the front sight. (This possibility is second only because of our intense emphasis on front sight focus during introductory instruction.) It is oversize groups, distributed *high*, that point to visual loss of the front sight. Other placement patterns tell us other things, but if we find a suggestion of front sight loss we work hard to correct it before getting on with the program.

When a student moves from the base range into tactical exercises there is always a strong tendency to lose his concentration on his flash sight-picture. This is natural because his attention is strongly preempted by the need for target location and identification. When forced to make a quick tactical decision in a simulated life-or-death situation it is indeed difficult to freeze one's concentration, at the last instant, onto that little metal extrusion. That is why the training range saves lives. It is certainly better to make mistakes in practice, and to learn thereby, than to make them in a fight — and lose.

As a student enters the Fun House we tell him, "You will now lose your ability to concentrate on your front sight." He usually resents this. How *can* he lose his front sight? He has been locked onto it for three days! Then he runs through the first "scenario." More often than not he comes out, thinks hard, looks at the instructor, and says, "You know what? *I lost my front sight!*"

That's OK. After a little work he will not — ever again —we hope.

It is important to distinguish between stereoscopic convergence and monocular focus. The first is a matter of the relationship of the axes of the two eyes, while the second has to do with the flexion of the lens in one eye. Stereoscopic vision provides our ability to judge distance — at least up close. Focus provides accurate optical definition of the object viewed. Both are important but, in shooting, the latter is more so.

It is better to shoot with both eyes open, if possible. The more one eye dominates the other the easier this will be. You can quickly determine which of your eyes is "master" by looking fixedly at a definite point at middle distance and quickly raising a ring of some kind (thumb and forefinger will do) at arm's length, placing it so as to encircle the selected point visually. Do this quickly, and do not move ring nor eye to adjust. Now close one eye. If the point jumps out of alignment the eye you closed is master. If it always works the same way it is strongly master, and you can probably shoot easily with both eyes open. If it goes sometimes one way and sometimes the other your eyes are roughly equal and you may find it better to squint slightly with one in order to make sure that the other always controls.

With the pistol it does not matter which eye is master. It may be very slightly more comfortable to shoot right-handed with a right master eye, and left-handed with a left, but the difference is too slight to matter. Some very fine shots shoot "cross-eyed."

None of the foregoing has to do with focus, which is a matter of one eye only. You check focus with one eye at a time, obscuring or closing the other. To do this select an inscription which you can read at some distance, such as a road sign at 50 meters or a diploma on the opposite wall. Close one eye, raise your index finger, and point at the writing. By conscious effort you can shift focus in and out, alternately reading the inscription and examining your fingernail. Practice this until you know exactly what you are doing and how to do it at will. On the range you will extend this exercise to the shift between target and front sight — in, out — in, out — and repeat. The vital reflex that you must groove into your brain is that nearly instantaneous focus shift from target to front sight, just as you press. Al Nichols, one of the Senior Masters, once told me that he had succeeded in burning a "fail-safe" circuit breaker into his nerves, so that he simply could not apply final trigger pressure unless the front sight was in focus.

Our preoccupation with the front sight leads to some reasonable curiosity about the rear sight. What is *it* for? With the open sighted pistol (as opposed to the aperture-sighted rifle) the two sights are very close together and both are rather far from the eye. Holding the pistol in a proper firing stance, both sights can be held nearly in one focus, making alignment all the easier. Actually, while we do strive for precise sight alignment we attempt to achieve it — in combat shooting —

with the hands rather than with the eye. If we practice our presentation until it becomes automatic, we find that alignment of front and rear sights also becomes automatic, and that the arm and hand harden into a gun mount which will not let the front sight stray. When this happens, front sight focus includes rear-sight alignment, and the result is speed.

As a degree of proficiency is achieved in drawing and presentation, the next step is a "blind draw." After a number of warm-ups, and without moving his feet or body, the student starts a stroke and closes his eyes just as his hand touches his piece. He completes the stroke to hammer fall with eyes shut, holds steady, and opens his eyes. If his stroke has been good he will be exactly on target, as his sights will verify.

All this takes practice, but it is well worth it, for the trained shot will eventually reach a sort of "look-down, shoot-down" capacity quite similar to that of the fantastic gunsight helmet now in use with our ground-attack airmen — what you look at, you hit! This absolutely does not mean that you rise above the need for sights. It does mean that you use your eye to verify an alignment already achieved with the hands, rather than using it to align the piece after presentation.

Thus it is that the seasoned pistolero almost never fires a continuous string in practice, the way a target shot may, but works always at his quick presentation, usually firing once, and never more than twice, without re-presentation.

Yes, we use the sights. It is possible, with experience, to do very good close-range work without them. It is also possible to ride well without a saddle and to swim well with one arm. It may be very good fun, too. But if your life depends upon your very best performance, as it may in defensive pistolcraft, you will use your strongest technique.

THE MANAGEMENT OF THE DOUBLE-ACTION AUTO

There have been surprisingly few technical innovations in handguns since World War I, and such as there have been are not especially impressive. In the "Century of The Common Man" (!) scant emphasis has been placed upon the expert use of sidearms, but much upon making such pieces so "safe" that not even an idiot can hurt himself with them. This is foolishness, of course. A weapon is a weapon, and if it is absolutely safe it is absolutely useless. (Would that our courts could be made aware of that!)

In this futile search for a "foolproof" sidearm, however, one modern development stands out. This is "double-action" in the auto pistol. While not esteemed by the expert, it is vastly admired by the duffer, and in a popular vote between experts and duffers guess who wins. Whether we like it or not, the d.a. auto is here to stay.

Double action indicates an ignition system that can be operated in two ways: from either a cocked or an uncocked condition. Thus the expression "double-action only" is contradictory, even though we know what it means. Most d.a. autos are in truth double-action, while those that are called "double-action only" are actually single-action.

When the Walther company, then of Zella Mehlis, Germany, announced its PP and PPK double-action pocket autos in the early thirties the excitement was intense. The notion of carrying an auto pistol in Condition Two — hammer down on a loaded chamber — and firing it from that condition by merely pulling the trigger, seemed to be a decisive forward step. Of course that was before we knew much about pistol technique, but so it seemed at the time. Then when the famous P-38 appeared in A.F. Stoeger's catalog, for sale in the U.S., my frustration knew no bounds. I just had to have one, but the price was out of my reach. Less than $100 seems a negligible figure for a sound pistol today, but for one who just does not have it, $100 might as well be $100,000. Stoeger advertised the P-38 as available in 45 ACP and Super 38, as well as in 9mm Parabellum. A factory P-38 in 45 ACP might not bring $100,000 today, but you could certainly get an ample fistful of 100's for it.

The war came, and the P-38 was G.I. in the up-to-date German army, but pistols are not important weapons of war and we did not think much more about them until peace broke out. At that time I was at Quantico and discovered that the Marine Corps Equipment Board was commencing a pistol evaluation that included a whole trunkful of liberated P-38's. I was not attached to the Board but a close friend was, and together we got a good long look at this first d.a. service auto. We were somewhat underwhelmed.

Double-action in revolvers is generally held to be a good thing, though it does call for extra skill and a bit of hand-tuning to make it really efficient. If it is good in a wheel-gun, why isn't it in an auto?

Well, in the first place, it is not all that great in a revolver. We have seen Jack Weaver break that 140-yard balloon — first try, under pressure, double-action. We have also seen him print paired V's (10″) at 100 yards — double-action. But Jack is a remarkable marksman — an all-time great. Even such masters as Elden Carl and Al Nichols cock a revolver when they need maximum precision. Trigger-cocking can indeed be mastered, but it is *not* an *aid* to control; it is rather an obstacle to be overcome by intense concentration.

Secondly, the flywheel action of a revolver can be made to be very smooth, light, and consistent. Quick, controlled pairs in coarse shooting can be developed with no prohibitive expenditure of effort. On the other hand, the trigger-cocking action of d.a. autos is uniformly poor, by comparison, and it does not lend itself to much improvement.

Third, with a couple of exceptions, double-action autos really have a *double* action, shifting from the trigger-cocking mode into self-cocking automatically with the first shot. This means that the instantaneous two-shot response that correct tactics demand is very difficult to control, because both the placement of the trigger finger and the muscular action of the hand in firing are different between first and second shots.

There may be those who hold that these points are quibbles, but I am not speaking theoretically. I have now had the opportunity to see hundreds of d.a. autos used in training —one entire class used nothing else — and I can state positively that extensive field work has proved that the d.a. auto is distinctly more difficult to shoot well than either the d.a. revolver or the normal self-loader. This is providing the d.a. auto is used in its designed mode, trigger cocking for the first shot. There are other possibilities, as we shall see.

The premise behind the double-action auto is safety. Most people have a sort of morbid prejudice against a cocked firearm, and really do think that it is likely to "go off" all by itself. A policeman who carries the 1911 in Condition One (cocked-and-locked) is frequently told by well meaning observers, in frightened whispers, that *his gun is cocked.* (!!!) With the thumb safety on, the grip safety operative, and a retaining strap locked in place between hammer and firing-pin, that 1911 may be as "safe" as any loaded firearm can be, but the fact that it is *cocked* just seems to shake people up. In any case, with a d.a. auto you can carry your piece *un*-cocked but still ready, at least for a coarse shot. Since most defensive shooting is coarse shooting, this is the theoretical answer, albeit to an uneducated question. In actuality the d.a. system is somewhat more prone to inadvertent discharge than other types. Both in courts of law and on the range, I have had occasion to observe this at some length. It is not that the weapon itself is necessarily at fault (though in some versions the hammer-dropping action of the thumb lever is subject to disruptive wear), but the various manipulations it requires can be confusing, and applied out of correct sequence. For whatever reason, I count on a couple of accidental shots out of the 500 rounds that are fired in the basic course when a student uses a d.a. auto. That is why we keep that muzzle down range.

So I am not sure the d.a. principle is a safety feature in the auto pistol, but whether it is or not, it does pose control problems. Their solution is the object of the exercise.

There are people who can print quick, accurate pairs with the first shot trigger-cocked and the second cocked by the slide. Not many. It is well to start the student using this "crunch-tick" system, to see if he can handle it, because that is how the piece was designed to be used. However, as frustration sets in, as it usually does, we may talk of other methods.

The first and most shocking technique we can suggest is simply to carry the pistol cocked and *un*locked. This, of course, wipes out the whole theoretical purpose of the d.a. system, but if the holster covers the trigger guard it is not so wicked a solution as one might think. I do not actually recommend it, but if a student simply cannot cut it any other way, I will not forbid it.

In most d.a. autos, and all those based on the original Walther system, depressing the thumb safety drops the hammer, without firing the piece (usually), so one cannot put the safety "on" without placing the action back in the trigger-cocking mode. Incidentally, once that safety is depressed, it should always be flipped back up to horizontal. On the new model Walthers it is spring-loaded and returns to position automatically — a good feature.

If we cannot quite face up to carrying the pistol in "Condition Zero," we can try some other systems. One is to thumb-cock the hammer on the draw, preferably with the thumb of the supporting hand — the left thumb if the shooter is right-handed. Several people I know do this very smoothly and well, but if you try it remember to flip the thumb instantly back to the support side, to avoid being cut by the recoiling slide. Correct technique is to train the trigger finger to stay straight

— outside the trigger guard — until the thumb has completed the cocking action and is back in position.

Most d.a. autos have exposed hammers, but the Heckler and Koch P-9 does not. On this one there is a cocking lever located forward of the stock on the port side, by means of which the shrouded hammer may be operated. While the lever may be depressed with the right thumb of a right-handed shooter, this action cannot be done with the hand in a firing grip — at least not by any hand I have seen. You have to shift your grip, unless you operate the cocking lever with the left hand, which seems to me the better method. Unfortunately it is difficult or impossible for a left-handed shooter.

The P-9, unlike the Walther-type pistols, does not drop the hammer when the thumb safety is depressed. It thus offers a type of "selective double-action," in that the wearer can select Condition One or Condition Two at will. The drawback to this is that thrusting the safety forward and up is awkward and unnatural, compared with depressing the thumb piece on a Browning-type pistol simply and easily as the hand assumes the firing grip. It can be learned, of course, but it is not handy.

Various new d.a. autos do not come over the counter with selective double-action, but they can be easily altered to that condition by removing the sear-release lever. Without this part in place, the thumb safety can be depressed without dropping the hammer. This does not prevent dropping the hammer by pressing the trigger, but it does keep the piece from firing if this is done. (Or it should. Things can go agley in this arrangement, and the Walther instruction sheet recommends that you lower the hammer gently with the thumb whenever possible.) With the sear-release lever removed, these pistols can be placed on safe, locking the firing-pin but not the trigger nor hammer. You can then stab the safety forward on the draw as with a P-9. This is unhandy but probably better than "crunch-tick." Of course if you get butter-fingered and touch the trigger before you stab the safety, you will wind up pulling like mad with no results, until you release the trigger all the way and start over. This may not be the complete answer.

And then, of course, there is that preferred form of d.a. auto that offers trigger-cocking in conjunction with a convenient Condition One override. This truly selective double-action is a feature of the Czech 75 and the Seecamp Conversion of the 1911. This system offers the best of both worlds.

One might well ask why, if you prefer a Condition One carry (as you do if you know about pistols), do you bother with double-action at all? Two answers: Live storage and left-handedness. Many people, myself included, prefer a pistol in a desk drawer or glove compartment to rest in Condition Two. (I should note here that Bruce Nelson, who knows as much about serious pistolcraft as anyone, *never* uses Condition Two. I do not fault him, but I like the hammer on an untended pistol to be all the way down — possibly because I am used to houses full of children.) It is easy enough to cock a single-action pistol as you pick it up — you do not "quick-draw" from off the mantelpiece — but trigger-cocking might just be a help under these peculiar conditions. You can always cock it if you have time, and if you have not your range is likely to be arm's length.

The other point is the problem of the southpaw — that one man in six who has simply been ignored throughout most of the machine age. (In sword-wielding armies you used your right hand, even if you were left-handed. Besides being regarded askance in the days of superstition, left-handers fouled up the battle drill.) New pistol designs will feature ambidextrous safeties, such as are now available at considerable expense for the 1911 series. Until they become standard, however, double-action will offer specific advantages to the "sinistrous sixth" of the population.

There are those who insist that, when all is said, "double-action-only" is the only way to fly. Pioneered by the venerable *Manufrance Type Armée*, an auto pistol action that remains uncocked and must always be fired by a trigger that both compresses and releases the mainspring on the same stroke does have a certain appeal. Instead of "crunch-tick" it goes "crunch-crunch," and the action of the firing hand and finger are constant. The Czech 38 pistol had such an action, and today it may be found on the Marshall and Semmerling pocket pistols, as well as the weird H&K VP-70. A very smooth, light trigger action can be well controlled, no matter how long it may be. Weaver stoutly maintains that with a trigger that travels an inch or more you cannot possibly flinch since you have no idea where the end of that travel may be. That is certainly an interesting point, but I have not yet found a trigger-cocking auto with a really good trigger stroke, and I do not believe that the effort necessary to design one would be well spent even if successful.

Single-action autos work just fine (except for lefthanders) and it is hard to see how a man can protect himself better, or print better targets, or pot squirrels better, or untangle a leopard better, with a trigger-cocker. However, double-action is demanded by "the market," so from now on auto pistols will be double-action. Aside from introducing a degree of unnecessary complexity into the mechanism this is OK, as long as such pieces are truly and conveniently *selective*. With a non-selective example we can still manage, if we will take time to learn how, but it does seem bothersome in the face of all the other things we have to learn. Designers, one might think, should make mechanisms easier, not harder, to use well.

But we might take another view. In the eyes of some people firearms are *dangerous*. If we made them so hard to use that they could not be fired at all, under any circumstances, we would dispose of the danger. I will bet I could sell that notion to certain people in Washington — but let's not.

For the present, we need not make too much of the double-action feature in auto pistols. If it is there, we can handle it, one way or another. If it is not, so much the better.

THE ULTIMATE IRON PISTOL

Pistol Silueta shooters will be interested to hear of a new and conceptually improved handgun for the Unlimited Class. If successful it should provide the perfect technical solutions to the problems posed in this branch of the shooting sports. It is tentatively called the Peabody Spoonbill, after its inventor, James O. Peabody, of Belleview, Arkansas.

The Spoonbill disposes its four, 14" barrels vertically, adjusted so that each barrel places its bullet exactly on the second intersection of the line of sight with the trajectory at each of the four fixed ranges. Thus no sight change nor over-hold need be used. Each barrel is stamped with the appropriate silhouette, to obviate misunderstandings.

A side-break is utilized in order to reduce rotary movement between frame and barrel assembly. The butt frame is plastic for increased thermal and hydroscopic stability.

The prototype is being produced in 44 magnum caliber for testing, but production models will be chambered for the 45-75 Winchester cartridge (350 grains at 1380 f/s) which approximates the performance of the 45-70 Govt. cartridge in a shorter, fatter, bottlenecked case, more convenient for handgun use. The heavy bullet assures knockdowns on every hit. Recoil, in this 5¾-pound piece, should be quite acceptable, in view of the radical sighting and ignition system under development, to which flinching is not relevant.

The essence of the Spoonbill's superiority lies in its unique target-acquisition capability. Since iron silhouettes may be detected quite precisely by modern technology, a single 3.7mm laser beam is projected coaxially with the optical sight. Interruption of this beam actuates a solenoid which, in turn, actuates the electric ignition system. Thus the piece will not fire unless the laser is on target. Obviously this arrangement works just as well from offhand as from a bench rest. The only care

PEABODY SPOONBILL PAT. PEND.
(ARTIST'S CONCEPTION)

the shooter need take is not to let his wobble stray onto the adjoining target while the trigger is depressed. The acquisition cone encompasses 6.7 degrees as now set up. It may be desirable to reduce this to about 5 degrees on production models.

Shooting the Spoonbill is simplicity itself. The shooter slings his power pack over one shoulder and plugs it into the butt socket. If all systems are in order a small blue light on the receiver tells him so. When any barrel is loaded (after power is on) a tiny illuminated green silhouette of the appropriate animal — chicken, pig, turkey, or ram — is displayed under the blue light. As the shooter aligns his optical sight on the target, he squeezes the trigger which actuates the laser, turning the blue light to red. When the laser acquires the target it fires the piece, and all lights go out. The shooter need not observe his strike — if the piece fires at all a miss is not possible, assuming everything is properly tuned and wind velocity is less than four knots.

Tuning the Spoonbill is fairly simple for a trained engineer who has access to the appropriate laboratory equipment. Full instruction will be packed with each piece. Naturally any variation in loading the ammunition will call for re-tuning. It is also desirable to tune the piece under climatic conditions exactly the same as those where the match will be shot.

Mr. Peabody, who realizes as well as anyone that in future competition you will be either a Spoonbill shooter or a dead duck, is naturally very secretive about his invention and would allow no photographs to be taken. The barrel adjustment mechanism is a marvel of ingenuity, employing Swedish differential screws, and he feels that its principles must not be revealed until the piece is ready for the market.

With any luck at all, the Peabody Spoonbill should be available soon. At a price of less than $9,500 per unit, it will be a bargain for anyone who is serious about his hobby.

REFLECTIONS ON THE NEW ORDER

There is probably no one who can read who does not now know that the people who took away our 30-caliber rifles and gave us a 22 have now decided to take away our 45-caliber pistols and give us a 36 (9mm Parabellum). The wails which have greeted this quaint decision come from people who know about shooting, but who are still innocent enough to believe that shooting — specifically the shooting of smallarms — is an item of importance to those who are responsible for modern war planning. The obvious fact is that the war planners, the procurement officers, and the weapons designers *are not fighters*. The whole concept of fighting has become so foreign to the thinking of the defense departments of the world that it is unfashionable even to bring it up in conference. The warriors in our military establishment have for the most part been "invited out," and they have been replaced by management engineers.

We should perhaps not list the embarrassing examples of personal combat failure which we see regularly in the public press, but the fact remains that fighting is today almost the last thing a soldier is expected to do. That being the case, it is clearly unsound to worry about the quality of the instruments he is supposed to fight with. Much as this pains the "old guard," it is a fact of life and should be recognized as such.

So here we have the Beretta 92S service pistol, selected by the Pentagon as the American soldier's friend for the new era. We have been shooting it here at the school for some time and can present a fairly generalized view of its characteristics.

First the good news: Our test piece (serial number C 27870 Z) was very nicely fitted and finished. Its function was completely reliable and it came in a nifty little carrying case. Naturally reliability cannot be tested with one gun and a few thousand rounds, but as far as we are concerned the 92 is completely reliable. (Curiously enough the case has its label affixed upside down. There may be something significant here but I am not sure what it is.)

That is the end of the good news.

Our overall impression of the weapon is that it is excessively large, blocky and "busy" for best use. A pistol taking this small cartridge could be made about two-thirds as big as the 92 without loss of efficiency. There are far too many switches, buttons, levers, pins and exposed moving parts on the outside of the weapon. Every one of these can break or hang up under hard use and — in accordance with Murphy's Law — probably will.

The common opinion is that the 92 is "uncomfortable." Lest it be advanced that our hands are accustomed to the 1911, few of us feel that the 1911 is the most comfortable pistol we know — that vote going to the P-35 Browning, the Czech 75, or the Bren X.

The sights are not bad but could be a good deal better. A two-vertical-dot system is used for alignment accentuation, but this is not as good as three horizontal dots. The outside surfaces of the rear sight are properly rounded to avoid tearing clothing and hands.

The "double-action" feature *is not selective.* The pistol may be carried only with the hammer back and the safety off, or with the hammer all the way down. In the latter case it will be fired by a long pull on the trigger or by thumb-cocking on the way up. The double-action pull is far too heavy for serious use. Presumably, in accordance with the current Austrian philosophy, the first shot will not be fired to hit anyway. If this weapon is to be carried in a serious defensive mode it will have to be holstered in "Condition Zero" — cocked and unlocked —which is doubtless contrary to various regulations. As we know, the closer one gets to the front line the less attention one pays to regulations of this sort.

The pistol mounts a curious two-sided hammer-dropper on the top rear of the slide. When this switch is depressed it drops the cocked hammer safely on a live round. Why it is desirable to be able to do this on both sides of the weapon is not clear. Dropping of the hammer on a live round is not the sort of act one needs to perform in a hurry, and might just as well be handled by a skate key.

Oddly enough the magazine release, of the type we are accustomed to in the Browning family, is reversible so that it may be placed on either the left or right side of the weapon at choice. This is an interesting feature since the original Browning buttons were all placed on the *wrong* side of the weapon —for a right-handed shooter. We can now change this on the 92 by replacing the button on the right side, where it is more easily operated with the index finger than with the thumb. Since either system can be learned easily with a little practice, this would seem to be an unnecessary complexity.

The trigger-pull, in the cocked mode, is unsatisfactory. People who are concerned with practical accuracy (as opposed to intrinsic accuracy) should take note of this. We are often amused at the notion that the old 1911 is somehow "inaccurate," despite the fact that, except in worn-out examples, it will always shoot better than the shooter. The trigger on the 92 is far more of an obstacle to practical accuracy than recoil.

A curious feature is the placement of the slide-stop so far to the rear that it is normally depressed by the firing thumb when shooting. This, of course, prevents the slide from locking open on the last shot. The slide-stop should properly be placed on the right side of the weapon, since here again is a device which is never needed in a hurry.

Another curious feature is the exposure of the trigger-bar, so that the weapon can be fired by pushing forward on it without touching the trigger. This is not easy to do, however, and should not be equated with the execrable firing mechanism of the Japanese Type 94, which permitted that pistol to be fired when squeezed. You can fire the 92 without touching the trigger, but you do have to work at it.

The weapon cannot properly be "press-checked," as with the Browning family, but it does incorporate a chamber indicator which is designed to serve the same purpose. Personally I would rather look and see than put my trust in a gadget.

It is interesting to note, in the era of girl soldiers, that this new 92 will prove very difficult for our girls to use. The trigger is too far forward for a small hand, and the pull is too heavy for any but a muscular shooter — and not easy even for him. The operation of the slide is much stiffer than on most current auto pistols, and we may even find women who cannot work it at all. One might think, in view of the peculiar comments we have seen in the press about the "bone-wrenching recoil" of the 45, that any new sidearm should be easier rather than harder to manage than an older weapon.

The unanimous and independently reached impression of those who shot the piece here at the ranch is that it was not designed by, or for, shooters. This is not remarkable since very few weapons *are* designed by shooters, and even fewer gun manufacturers think it necessary to submit their designs to a knowledgeable test group before freezing them into a production model. It is certainly clear that no one seriously interested in riflecraft could have passed the M-16 rifle for service use, and it is equally apparent that the committee which ran the tests on the 92 was not composed of experienced pistoleros. It is possible that this policy is intentional rather than accidental. Perhaps we should *not* utilize experts to check our equipment before we issue it. Perhaps experts would seek the wrong things, but eventually the decision must be made as to the *purpose* of the instrument to be produced. The critical question about any weapon must be *What is it for?**

---

*In this age of innovative technology, one can make himself very unpopular by asking what a particular innovation is *for*, since the innovator often does not know, and this embarrasses him.

Now I and those in attendance here at the school — both faculty and students — have a pretty clear notion of what a pistol is for. *A pistol is to stop fights.* A pistol must provide its wearer with the ability to turn off the threat of deadly force at close range, with as much certainty as is possible in an uncertain world. The 92 does not seem to be the best solution to this challenge — since it is essentially complex, difficult to use, and under-powered.

It would appear that those who ran the tests on the various test pistols were tremendously concerned about mechanical safety. They went to great lengths to build a foolproof weapon — flying in the face of the ancient Egyptian truth that *nothing is proof against fools.* The safe operation of a weapon is a matter of the brain of the user — not of switches, gadgets and arrangements. It does not seem to us that the Beretta 92 is any safer than any other handgun, despite all its buttons, signals, blocks and levers. If a man wants to do something stupid with a pistol, he can do it with a 92 just as easily as he can with a double-action revolver, or any other sidearm.

What is most important, above every other consideration, is the power of the pistol to turn off an enemy with one well-placed hit. Anyone who has gone deeply into the matter understands that the 9mm Parabellum cartridge is not a reliable man-stopper. Just this week we had a report from a major department in California which last year had 26 shooting incidents, using the 9mm cartridge, and achieved *two* one-shot stops — both of which were head-shots. This is only one of an endless series of examples, but the people who have decided to saddle us with an under-powered sidearm are obviously not interested, primarily because they do not see a sidearm as an important instrument. Perhaps it is not, but I can give you one recent example of evidence to the contrary. In the Lebanese War of 1982 a one-star general, whom I knew slightly, decided to move his command post from the roof of a high-rise building to a deck below. Being a proper forward sort of leader, he burst into the room he had chosen and ran squarely into three enemy soldiers armed with assault carbines. Neither he nor they had any anticipation of this confrontation, and it is my considered belief that if he had been a qualified pistolero he could have terminated all three of those people before they could have got their AKs into action. As it happened there were no survivors, but there were observers from outside the room whose testimony suggests to me that there was plenty of time for an expert pistol response. *But not with any 9.* The chances of putting three enemy soldiers out of action with three shots from a 9mm are almost nil. On the contrary, the chances of doing that with a major caliber weapon are pretty good.

Seen in this light, the question is not whether the United States should surrender its major-caliber 45 for the minor-caliber 9, for the answer to *that* is clear. We have, however, ignored that answer, so the question is: since we are going to a 9, which 9 should we adopt? It seems to us that there are several 9's on the market which are conspicuously better than the 92. My own first choice would be the Czech 75, but there is a strong minority view that if one is going to carry an underpowered pistol he should carry the neatest and handiest one available, and that is the Heckler & Koch P7. (And if you insist upon the smaller caliber there is nothing much wrong with the old P-35 Browning that a little tinkering will not fix.)

One does wonder how the decision of the Pentagon to buy the 92 was reached. The fighting capacity of the weapon itself cannot have been weighed significantly — at least not by people deeply instructed in handguns. Evidently the view must have been that pistols do not matter anyway, so all that is important is who gets the contract — and in return for what?

The fact remains, as we attempted unsuccessfully to get across to Mr. Weinberger, that a modern army probably does not need a pistol — but that if it does, the old 1911 Colt is the best thing in common use at this time. It does seem curious that at a time when budgets need to be cut the Pentagon has seen fit to spend perhaps $600 million of your money to make our armed services a little bit less efficient.

In 1860 the Union Army was sent into combat with a 44-caliber cap-and-ball single-action revolver, a defensive sidearm far superior to that which we have adopted in 1985.

When we went to war in 1941 the United States handed its young men the best personal fighting tools the world has ever seen. Times, however, have changed.

III. THE RIFLEMAN

·KIRCHNER·

THE GENERAL-PURPOSE RIFLE

The progress of modern technology has been curiously uneven. We have conquered polio and smallpox, but not the common cold. We have landed on the moon, but we cannot move conveniently around our cities. We build word processors, but not a satisfactory writing stylus. And while certain varieties of missilery have taken great strides, little of importance has been done to improve the rifles with which we greeted the turn of the century.

Well hold on now! We have semi-automatic actions and telescope sights, haven't we?

Of course we have, and these improvements do deserve consideration, but the first matters only in the military mode and the second is still only partly understood. Rapid repeat shots do little for the individual rifleman, whose primary object is to hit with his first shot, and glass sights have, in a sense, retrogressed since the pioneering efforts of Rudolph Noske and some others in the 1920's.

When I first went after big game in 1937 I used a rifle very similar in style, weight, size, practical accuracy and ballistic potential to one that might be bought over the counter today. It worked very well (and it still does) so we might well ask why anyone should wish to improve upon it. This is like asking why we should improve on *anything* that works. (If an outhouse works, why install indoor plumbing?) The fact is that we improve things for three reasons: to make our lives more convenient, to gratify our curiosity, and to make money. These motives have not conspicuously affected riflery until quite recently. We have dwelt too heavily on cartridge variation, forgetting that all modern cartridges will do very well if they are shot well. In a sense we have concentrated so hard on the aircraft that we have ignored the carrier. It is only in the last ten years or so that rifle design has come alive, but now it has (though only a few realize it) and we stand on the brink of a new era.

Any instrument is built for a purpose — presumably. What is it for? Certainly we see endless gadgetry being promoted for which the purpose is pretty obscure — answers in search of questions — but that does not invalidate the premise. We cannot sensibly improve on rifle design unless we decide what a rifle is to be required to do. If we specialize overmuch in this thinking, we come up with instruments well-suited to a specific task but not to any others. Possibly the ultimate special-purpose rifle is the new Walther 2000, which does not perform its special task conspicuously better than a more generalized piece, but which is almost totally useless for anything else.

It is much easier to specialize than to generalize, and the definition of a general-purpose rifle is a complex task. Let us attempt it by declaring that *a general-purpose rifle is a conveniently portable, individually operated firearm, capable of striking a single decisive blow, on a live target of up to 200 kilos in weight, at any distance at which the operator can shoot with the precision necessary to place a shot in a vital area of the target.* This involved statement will not meet with everyone's approval but certain elements of it must be accepted before we proceed. Convenience is important. Power is important. Practical accuracy, as opposed to intrinsic accuracy, is important. If we add the desirability of ruggedness, versatility and speed of operation, and finally throw in a touch of aesthetics, we complete a workable set of parameters. Such a piece is eminently suited for taking the vast predominance of four-footed game, and equally so for men.

In 1983 a conference was convened at the Gunsite Training Center in Arizona to examine the subject of the modernization of rifle design. The members of the conference included gunsmiths, stocksmiths, journalists, marksmanship instructors, inventors and hunters. It was called the First Scout Rifle Conference ("scout" being the term settled upon for the definition of the new concept) and it adjourned with the objective of exploring all elements of design during 1984 and meeting again in October. When the second meeting was held much progress had been made. The project is not complete, however, and at this point certain technical innovations remain to be perfected. At this time we are held up by the unavailability of certain important components, but when the completed instrument is ready for demonstration and examination it ought not be too difficult to persuade certain manufacturers to accommodate us. Riflemen tend to be a conservative lot, and anything which departs from past procedures is viewed with skepticism. There is also the problem of cost, for innovations are always expensive. However, the scout project has proceeded on the assumption that a better mousetrap will sell itself — eventually.

The Concept

The idea behind the scout rifle is not new. The famous old Mannlicher 6.5 carbine was a step in this direction, as was the equally famous Winchester Model 94 30-30 carbine. The British "Jungle Carbine" of World War II was another example of the breed, and finally there came the ill-fated Remington 600 carbines of a decade ago — excellent guns in most ways but ahead of their time. I acquired a 600 in 308 and fitted it with a Leupold 2X intermediate-eye-relief telescope. This laid the groundwork for the scout concept now being studied by the conference. This little gun was an absolute delight, and it sits in my rack today. Its decisive drawback, of course, is that neither the rifle nor the telescope is any longer manufactured. Also it is imperfect in some other ways, and the builders of new versions of the scout rifle will seek to overcome all such weaknesses.

The consensus of the conference was that modern technology enables us to produce a rifle which need not sacrifice either power or accuracy to convenience. The new-wave rifle is neither more powerful nor intrinsically more accurate than the rifles of the past, but it is much, much handier — shorter, lighter and quicker to operate. The current guideline is a length limit of one meter and a weight limit of three kilos. (This weight is measured with all accessories in place but with the weapon unloaded.) Immediately these limitations point us toward short actions, short barrels, compact sights, and synthetic stocks. A further feature which distinguishes the modern scout rifle from its predecessors is the telescope sight, but that in a certain particular mode. The modern scout uses a low-power telescope mounted just forward of the magazine well. In recent decades, progress in the development of telescope sights has been to a certain extent negative in that telescopes, instead of becoming stronger, smaller and faster to use have become larger, more cumbersome, more fragile and almost necessarily mounted too high above the bore. Current Zeiss glasses, for example, are marvelous optical instruments but clumsy sighting devices. Since most modern shooters are used to these things they do not understand the advantages of a radically different system, but there is little doubt in the minds of those who have used the scout telescope that it is the only proper general-purpose sighting system for a rifle.

The Forward Telescope

For those who have not tried it, an explanation of the advantages of the forward telescope is in order. First, and most important, the forward glass does not obscure the landscape. With both eyes open the shooter sees the entire countryside as well as the crosswire printed on his target. For this reason it is important that the magnification of the telescope be no greater than 3X (some hold that 2X is maximum) in order to avoid excessive disparity between the vision of the two eyes. This forward mount, properly used and understood, is the fastest sighting arrangement available to the rifleman. (Many students at Gunsite are capable of taking straight-away clay birds at the end of one full training session.) There are those who think that a glass of low power is necessarily less precise for long-range precision work, but we have not found this to be the case in any sort of realistic test.

There are many additional advantages to the forward telescope mount. It is out of the way when the rifle is carried at the balance. It may be mounted as low over the bore as the diameter of the bell permits. It avoids pinching between thumb and bolt handle when the bolt is operated. It permits stripper loading if desired. It greatly facilitates single-loading with eyes on target. It completely eliminates "telescope eye." Without exception, those who have tried the forward mounted glass in a full course of rifle training are unanimous in their conviction of its superiority.

Unfortunately telescopes of proper eye-relief (minimum 6″, maximum 12″, optimum 9″) are not readily available. The old issue of the Leupold M-8 2X is the glass most used on the prototypes, but it is out of production and no longer obtainable. The new versions of this glass have an optimum eye relief of 14 inches. The new Burris "Scoutscope" is now a production item, and works fine.

Mounting

The problem of mounting a telescope properly in its forward position is severe, since no current manufacturer is ready to produce the necessary components. On Scout I the old Buehler mount locked the Leupold glass to the plastic rib on top of the barrel in a most satisfactory way, but such equipment is no longer manufactured. The mounting system used on Scout II is extremely efficient, being strong, low and simple, and utilizing the barrel lug to resist recoil in compression. It is a custom proposition at this time, and thus expensive, but when the entire project is completed standardization will reduce this difficulty. Since scout barrels are as thin as compatible with safety there is no way to screw anything onto the barrel at the forward telescope mount ring. Therefore some sort of extrusion must be applied to the barrel in order to provide a proper base for the front mount. On Scout I this was the plastic rib that came on the Remington 600. On Scout II a machined steel ring was slid over the barrel and sweated into place to offer foothold. On Scout III the standard Ruger quarter rib of the single-shot rifle was affixed to the Ruger Ultralight to provide a forward footing. On all subsequent scouts the barrel is machined with intrinsic rings in place.

Metallic Sights

Reserve iron sights are held to be desirable for a proper scout rifle. The forward mounted telescope allows the positioning of an aperture sight on the receiver bridge, and the barrel extrusion which constitutes the forward telescope mount offers a proper base for a front sight. An aperture sight on the receiver bridge, in combination with a front sight at the forward telescope mount, offers a sight radius of about 11 inches — quite sufficient for reserve use. This system avoids the necessity of hanging the front sight out on the end of the barrel, where it catches on things, breaks, snags and muddies up. The ZKK 601 action incorporates a retractable aperture sight in the bridge and therefore is used in conjunction with the new type front sight on Scout IV, V, VI, VII, and VIII.

Stocks

Light weight is important in a scout, and therefore the conference has settled upon synthetic rather than wood stocks. I think we must admit that wood stocks on rifles are in their closing period. Wood is warm to the touch, traditional, and in its luxury aspect very beautiful. However a good piece of wood is frighteningly expensive and old-fashioned hand-checkering is pretty much a thing of the past. Wood is also somewhat fragile, subject to thermal deformation, ambient moisture and staining. Synthetics — when properly constructed — are better in every way except one. They look cheap. Fortunately this can be corrected. It is not possible to make a synthetic stock look convincingly like wood, but no one should try. It is possible, on the other hand, to make a modern synthetic stock look very handsome to the eye. A synthetic stock need not be checkered, since its whole finish may be made "crinkly" and thus non-skid. Attractive forest-leaf patterns have been worked up which may offend the traditionalists but have a definite beauty of their own. And a high grade fiberglass, Kevlar, or graphite stock is stronger, lighter and much cheaper than good grade wood, in addition to being inert and unaffected by moisture or heat.

Barrels

The barrels of the scouts are short and light. A short barrel does sacrifice something in velocity but not enough to balance considerations of handiness. All scouts up to now have been in caliber 308, and the chronograph insists that proper loading can start the 150-grain bullet from a 19-inch barrel at a couple of clicks over 2700 f/s. These ballistics served Theodore Roosevelt and Stewart Edward White very well in Africa, and they still can. The 7-08 affords slightly better ballistics, if that matters, and one can go to the now defunct 6.5 and 350 Remington Magnums while still using a short action. For targets of greater weight than 700 pounds a standard-length action will be necessary, adding about an inch and perhaps ¾ pound to the whole assembly. (Medium caliber scouts have been built up now on the 350 Remington cartridge.)

The consensus at the first conference was that stainless was the proper material for barrels, not so much because it is resistant to corrosion but because it offers a better coefficient of friction. It is "slipperier" than normal steel and therefore should provide slightly greater velocity for the same charge. In practice it has been found that stainless steel is very difficult to control as to quality, and that it differs from batch to batch. There are barrel makers now who will not attempt a light-weight stainless steel barrel, not because it could not be made but because they do not know that *they* could make it — since they do not make their own steel.

Whether a barrel is cut, buttoned, or hammer-forged does not seem to be as important as some maintain. Hammer-forging has many advantages, but it is necessarily expensive and can only be applied to production runs in large numbers. The handsome Mannlicher barrels are uniformly brilliant in accuracy, and offer the curious advantage of being slightly tighter at the muzzle than at the breech, but they cannot be had as components at this time.

The heavy barrels so popular on target guns have no place on the general-purpose rifle. Barrel diameter adds weight without any appreciable increase in accuracy, and serves mainly to delay heating. This is desirable on the range but not in the field, and the natural habitat of the scout is the field rather than the bench.

Self-Loading

Much thought has been given by the conference over the years to the subject of semi-automatic actions for scout rifles. If a semi-automatic action were made which was sufficiently compact and otherwise acceptable, it should certainly be considered, but at this time there is no such action available. The whole concept of great rapidity of fire in a rifle has been weighed and found, not exactly wanting, but somewhat inconsequential. About the only circumstance in which a rifleman might need a volley of quickly repeated shots would be in the unfortunate and unexpected event of a "house clearing." Such a problem *might* arise for a lone rifleman but the chances are very low. The primary purpose of a rifle is a first shot hit, whether the target is game or a human antagonist. Semi-automatic fire does not assure this. As a matter of fact it sometimes detracts from it by letting the shooter believe that if he misses with his first shot he can always make up with a second. This is a bad attitude for a rifleman. As a result of these deliberations all prototype scouts will be bolt action unless and until something new in the way of the semi-automatic action appears.

Actions

The conference was unable to reach a consensus as to action desirability. Actions considered have been the domestic Remington, Winchester and Ruger, plus the '03 Springfield, and the foreign ZKK, Sako and Mannlicher. All have drawbacks, though the ZKK 601 is the closest to the guidelines.

While the conference was not fully content with any one action now available, it did conclude that certain things are desirable in a proper bolt action. Two-lug, ninety-degree rotation was favored, as was the traditional Mauser claw extractor and positive ejector. Smoothness and reliability were found wanting in most modern commercial actions, and these things should be given attention. The bolt knob should be smooth and round — not checkered — and positioned far enough forward of the trigger to avoid pounding of the index finger during firing. The safety should disconnect the trigger mechanism rather than blocking it. It should be strong and positive and work from front to rear. The magazine should be so constructed as to protect the points of soft-point spitzer bullets as they ride in the magazine. The action should offer a built-in aperture sight on the receiver bridge, and some sort of magazine cutoff permitting the weapon to be used in the single-shot mode with the magazine in reserve. The trigger system should be smooth and clean, and provide a three-pound "glass rod" release. No rifle action now in production offers all these features, though some come reasonably close.

Only the Mannlicher now affords a shoulder-holder to protect points in the magazine, and also a detachable rotary box magazine. No current action offers a magazine disconnector, such as that found on the '03 Springfield. (The magazine disconnector was not put on the '03 rifle by accident. It is an extremely useful accessory, allowing the rifle to be single-loaded while retaining the magazine in reserve for emergencies. In the game fields it permits the rifle to be topped off continually without the danger of a double feed.)

As an alternative to the magazine cutoff, thought has been given to the fitting of a detachable box magazine with a double detent. Such a magazine could be inserted to its first stop, which would not allow the bolt to feed it. When desired, the magazine could be pressed into its second stop, permitting the bolt to pick up the top cartridge.

Accessories

Three additional improvements were displayed at the 1984 conference. The CW sling, discovered in Guatemala and described in the *American Rifleman* for June '84, is now standard. It is most efficiently installed with Pachmayr flush sockets — three on each stock, permitting two modes of attachment.

On all forthcoming prototypes the heel of the butt will be rounded to avoid snagging on the shirt in quick mounting.

In 1983 the leather butt-cuff was used to provide ready ammunition for shoot-one-load-one situations. The butt magazine neatly carries ready ammunition out of the way and instantly available at the fingertips as needed. This not only facilitates instantaneous one-round loading in the single-shot mode with eyes on the target, but it offers a most convenient way of carrying ready ammunition when the rifle is unloaded in camp.

At the 1983 conference it was decided that a form of retractable bipod should be perfected which would not be offensive to the eye nor extrude from the stock. The Clifton system holds the most promise. There are those who claim that any sort of bipod is somewhat "cheating," but the purpose of shooting is hitting, and if a bipod increases the certainty of hitting it should not be scorned.

The Next Steps

Scout I was improvised from available equipment and it worked very well, but its components have become obsolete. Scout II has been assembled from components and is an extremely successful rifle — light, quick to operate, handy, convenient, and extremely accurate. Unfortunately it is very expensive. Scout III was made up nearly stock from the Ruger Ultralight and the Ruger Mark I rib. Unfortunately it is fitted with a telescope which is no longer available. Scout IV is made up on a ZKK 601 action and uses a Burris Scoutscope built to the demands of the Scout Conference. It is also the first proto-type to feature the new iron-sight system and a disappearing bipod.

For the time being the scouts stand as described, and Scout VII, even though it does not include everything we desire, is so far ahead of anything which can currently be purchased as to make enthusiasts very discontented.

Accuracy in Scouts I and III is quite satisfactory — fully up to any reasonable field requirements — while Scout II is a tack-driver. If it were half as accurate as it is, it would still be twice as accurate as it need be. And it is hardly more cumbersome than a swagger stick. Of course it features a hand-cut premium barrel. One usually gets what he pays for.

The Scout Conference is in no position to produce weapons — only to assemble them. At such time as all the proper instruments have been assembled completely there will be an opportunity for a forward-looking manufacturer to take advantage of modern technology and make a great leap forward for the rifleman. Meanwhile we must build to order.

SOME MISCONCEPTIONS
ABOUT UTILITY RIFLES

We have been more than a bit perplexed in the conduct of our rifle instruction by the widespread notion that only a twenty-shot semi-automatic rifle has any general utility in today's scene. People have suggested that they would be interested in learning to shoot but they cannot afford a semi-automatic battle rifle in order to have something with which to work. There are indeed some good points about the semi-autos, but they are by no means the only answer to the rifle problem.

It seems that there is a basic misconception about purpose here. Before leaping to conclusions it might be well to examine just what a rifle is supposed to do — in whose hands and under what conditions.

The basic attribute of the rifle is *reach*. A powerful rifle enables a man to reach "way out past Fort Mudge" and strike a blow that will stop not only a man but a truck or a horse dead in its tracks. Whether or not an individual rifleman might ever be called upon to do that again and again and again — ad infinitum — is at least moot.

In battles between opposing forces of infantry the need for continuity of fire in order to suppress the enemy and gain what is known as "fire superiority" over him is quite evident. Whether a man alone may ever have any such need is not so evident. In the marvelous tale *Brown on Resolution*, by C.S. Forester, the story is told of how a British seaman — a prisoner of war aboard a German raider — was able to block the escape of that raider by jumping ship, swimming ashore, and stopping all repair work with a rifle. The rifle in this case was a Mauser G-98 (in caliber 7.92) and, despite the fact that the Walter Mitty's of our age extol the AK-47, the job was better done with the G-98 than with anything issued to troops today. The point is that the work on the cruiser was stopped by an intermittent series of lethal blows delivered from different points on the beach, the source of which was impossible to discover in time to counter it. If Able Seaman Brown had had — say — a G-3 and had attempted to fire all twenty rounds from any one point, he could not have done the damage he did because he would have given his position away and been disposed of in short order.

In studying the circumstances under which an individual owner might be called upon to use a rifle in defense of his life and property, one is drawn to the conclusion that a battle scene is almost certainly not going to be involved. A solitary rifleman, or a small group operating individually from cover, can do enormously effective work — but rarely with more than two shots from the same firing position. It thus becomes a question as to whether rapid repeat shots delivered from a large capacity magazine are of any real value. More important might be a beautifully crisp trigger and very accurate shooting.

Anyone familiar with irregular combat can tell you that when one is fired upon from long distance, without warning, it is extremely difficult to tell whence the shot came. The "bolt from the blue" is followed by a moment of bewildered silence, during which time the recipients adjust themselves to the fact that someone has just decked one of them. This will nearly always give the rifleman a chance for a second shot, even if his rifle is a single-loader, but the third shot is definitely going to pin him down. At that point his adversaries (who can be expected to outnumber him) will either flee or get after him. If they flee he has won his point. If they get after him he will be faced with the problem of changing his position so that they will be attacking into thin air.

What I am driving at is that in nearly all individual situations the rifleman is going to need range, power, control, and ease of movement more than volume of fire. There are exceptions of course, but before we dismiss the precision rifle in favor of the *Sturmgewehr* we should know why we are doing so. I certainly will not fault a man who has considered every angle and decided that he can only be happy with a SIG 510, but I am suspicious of those who reach this conclusion without having examined the matter in depth.

Those who are deeply instructed in riflecraft agree that the most important single factor in precision riflery is trigger action. A clean, motionless, "glass rod" break, of some two and one-quarter pounds, is almost the first thing to look for in a rifle which is to be used at any distance. It is certainly true that good men, by dint of hard work, can do very fine shooting with bad triggers. It is also true that a track star can run a mile carrying a 50-pound pack. However, it is not what he would choose to do, and it will not win races. The semi-autos are rarely equipped with good triggers. The conspicuous exception is the Garand family (M-1, M-1A, BM-59) which usually have triggers that are quite serviceable even for precision work. They won't be target triggers but they will do. But I have never seen a satisfactory trigger on any of the Phase III battle rifles, with the exception of my own personal HK 91, which is the exception to the rule. Its trigger was put in by a highly skilled gunsmith and it is on the order of a good M-1 trigger, but even this gunsmith has been unable to duplicate that job on other people's rifles. Heckler & Koch advertise a so-called "sniper trigger," which is indeed a great deal lighter than that of the issue weapon, but if anything even more spongy. The fact is that the battle rifles of the world are simply not intended for precision work any more. The mission of the rifle has changed since the early part of the century when battles were actually won with the individual weapons of infantrymen. Consequently we cannot do with today's military weapons what we did with those of our fathers. The Krag, the SMLE, the '03 Springfield and the G-98 Mauser are fine material for "customizing." The same, unfortunately, cannot be said of the FN FAL, the G 3, the SIG 510 or the SIG 542. (Note that I am not including the Kalashnikov family or any of the 223's. These weapons are by our classification battle carbines rather than rifles and serve a different purpose.)

The more I ponder this matter the more I am led to believe that a man alone, fighting for his survival, is probably better armed with a good, strong, modern sporter than he is with any form of battle rifle. If it comes to equipping "private armies" we deal with a totally different subject. If I were called upon to equip a private army I would probably go to the H & K line, though there is a good deal to be said for the SIG 542. I would do so because of interchangeability of parts, durability under rough use, modern manufacturing methods, great strength, and a number of other things. I would — if I were in this position — make certain stipulations to the factory which I have brought up in the past, only to be told that the German army did not specify those things. I would call for a device to hold the bolt open after the last shot was fired, an easier magazine insertion system, a totally different rear sight, and a reworked trigger mechanism (which did not have to stand up to being dropped out of airplanes without a parachute). These rifles would be made up in quantity for a large number of men who could not be expected to learn to be expert shots. For my expert shots — call them snipers if you will — I would design a short, light, handy, bolt action rifle with a detachable box magazine and a strong, low-mounted, low-powered, fixed-power telescope sight.

The main problem I have encountered with the rifles currently called sporters is fragility. In modern design their extraction and ejection systems have been rendered less reliable in the interest of greater strength to support the high pressures of what may be called freakish cartridges. Such high pressures are by no means necessary in a weapon to be used in a combat role. (For that matter I have serious doubts about their utility in the hunting field as well — but I am in the minority on this point.) I am somewhat concerned about the sixty-degree rotation on the new bolt actions and about their general daintiness in operation, though they are obviously strong enough to withstand the high pressures of their cartridges. The new sporters are seldom easy to reload and we increasingly see heavily shrouded ejection ports which make the action hard to get at. This does not mean that none of these new bolts is satisfactory. Many of them work very well despite what seem to be design flaws. I am very nervous about the extractor on the Remington bolt action but I must admit that it has not failed me on either of the two examples I own. Of course, a failure to extract is a type of malfunction that may get you killed — and you don't want to have it happen even the first time.

The point is this: Do not feel that you are not with it because you do not own a *Sturmgewehr*. As in all forms of conflict success is much more a matter of the man than of his gear. Success in riflecraft is a matter of good shooting, and —generally speaking — good shooting is more easily conducted with a good grade sporter than it is with a military rifle. It is important to note also that good quality sporters can be bought today — complete — for something like one-third the cost of even an inferior battle rifle. Just think of all the ammunition you can buy with the money you did not spend on the semi-auto! And practice, they say, makes perfect.

ELEMENTS OF RIFLE SIGHTING

The sights on a rifle enable the shooter to bring his optical line of sight into fairly close coincidence with the gentle curve of his bullet's trajectory. For practical purposes a line-of-sight is straight. A ballistic missile (such as a bullet) travels in a curve as gravity pulls it toward the earth's center. This curve is not constant, being quite flat at inception and decreasing in radius as missile speed is reduced by the resistance of the air through which it passes.

Thus, to be useful, a rifle must be "zeroed" by adjusting its sights so that the sight line intersects the curve of its trajectory at a predetermined distance from the muzzle. Since the sights are normally situated above the barrel, the bullet starts its free flight below the sight line, rises to its initial intersection a short distance out, travels above the sight line for a longer distance, curves back to its second intersection ("zero"), and then falls away rather quickly below the sight line as it loses velocity. The distance at which a rifle is zeroed will depend upon the type of shooting it is intended for and the ballistic efficiency of its bullet, but mainly upon its initial velocity. Ideally what is sought is a trajectory that does not depart enough from line of sight to require the shooter to hold either low or high, on the size of target he intends to engage, out to a distance beyond which his holding ability is not good enough to stay on that target. This ideal can be achieved in some cases. For example, a rifle intended for deer hunting may be adjusted with the assumption that the target zone necessary for a clean kill on a small deer is represented by a circle about eight inches across. What is wanted is a sight setting that will place a bullet some- where within an 8-inch circle, if the shooter's hold is exactly centered, out to where he cannot hit an 8-inch circle — from a field position, under time pressure.

With a 170-grain flat-nosed 30-30 starting at 2200 f/s we might choose to zero at 150 yards. With this setting the bullet will be travelling about 1½″ above the sight line 50 yards out, 2″ above it at 100 yards, intersect at 150 yards, and drop 5″ below it at 200. This will be quite suitable for shots up to 175 yards, but at 200 the center of impact will have dropped below the bottom of the 8-inch circle. If, on the other hand, we zero this piece for 200 yards, we find that the bullet is travelling 4½″ high at 100 — calling for a deliberately low hold at typical deer ranges. This would seem to label the 30-30 as a 175-yard deer-gun, which is just about right. And it is indeed a fine deer gun. People who can hit an 8-inch circle 80% of the time at 175 yards — in a hurry — are extremely uncommon.

But we can reach farther if we choose. The very popular 270/130, starting at some 3100 f/s, can be zeroed at 250 yards without having its bullet 4″ above or below the sight line out to about 325 yards.

If we go to extremes and start a 190-grain 30-caliber match bullet at 3200 f/s (!!) we may theoretically zero the piece at 300 yards and stay in our 8″ circle from muzzle to 350.

In practice, we generally zero 22 rimfire rifles at 60 yards, centerfires of the 2100-2300 f/s class at 150, 2400 to 2800 at 200, and the 3000-footers at 250.

Manufacturers make an effort to set up some sort of zero at the factory, but this is never a precise operation, nor should it be. In the first place, the very coarse open sights generally furnished as factory equipment do not permit exact optical alignment, and, second, only coincidentally will the same zero serve two different shooters. If good aperture sights, or telescope sights, are used, *each shooter must zero his own rifle*, and do so with the same load he intends to use for record.

Rifle sights may be metallic or of glass. Metallic sights are of two types — open and aperture ("peep sights"). Glass sights are usually telescopic, affording some measure of magnification.

In untrained hands, the open sight is fastest and least precise, the aperture is more exact but slower, and the scope is most exact and slowest. For the skilled marksman, however, while the open sight remains the least exact, it also loses its speed advantage. I believe that a low-powered telescopic sight, properly mounted and used correctly, is slightly faster than any metallic sight. And I have found that, for me at least, a large-ring aperture, placed close to the eye, is slightly faster than an open sight and permits more precise placement at equal speed. As to practical accuracy, target aperture sights and target telescope sights produce about the same results in competition.

The primary advantage of the telescope sight is its single focal plane. With open sights the shooter must try to focus on three points — rear sight, front sight, and target — each of which lies at a different distance from his eye. With the aperture sight he must try for two — front sight and target. But with the scope the sighting index ("reticle") is projected right on the target, requiring only one focal distance.

While a telescope sight is little, if any, more precise than a good aperture sight on sharply defined, highly visible targets such as bullseyes, it permits surer bullet placement on targets which are hard to see, such as a rabbit in a brush pile or a lion in dry grass. Magnification is naturally a factor in this, but magnification ought not be thought of as an end in itself. FourX is not necessarily "better" than 2X, nor 10X than 4X. As magnification goes up so does apparent tremor; and field of view decreases, as does sharpness of definition. A "variable" glass gives the shooter his choice of magnification, within limits, but a variable sight is bulkier, more expensive and usually has too much gadgetry immediately forward of the rearward cone for it to be mounted properly forward. (As a rule-of-thumb, the rearward lens of a telescope sight should ride no further aft than the rearward curve of the trigger-guard.)

Open, metallic sights have served riflemen for centuries, and are still popular with thousands of outdoorsmen. Obviously they will do, but they are the least satisfactory of the three systems. To be visible at all the rear notch must be set well forward on the barrel, necessarily reducing sight radius and corresponding geometric precision. The customary round front bead provides a poor index of elevation and the shooter is never really sure how far down into the rear notch it should go — especially when in a hurry. Additionally, that rear notch is very rarely capable of other than haphazard adjustment.

A properly designed metallic aperture sight is far better, but it must indeed be properly designed. It cannot be in unit with an open sight (Springfield '03 and German G-3 to the contrary) because apertures are looked *through*, not *at*, and must be placed close to the eye — the closer the better. One does not consciously center the front sight in the rear aperture — he lets his eye do it naturally. Thus he uses the front sight only. With a fairly large ring this process can be very quick, and no precision is lost.

A good front sight should be a rectangular post, not a bead, for only a flat top provides a sharp index of elevation. This may not be necessary on a charging elephant at 15 steps, but a red insert on a post is just as quick as a bead, and has an extra margin of precision to boot.

On modern sporting and combat rifles there is seldom any need to set sights when afield. Modern rifles shoot flat enough so that one setting will suffice out to distances where effective work is limited to specially trained and equipped snipers. The peculiar sights found on turn-of-the-century military rifles — adjustable (after a fashion) to 2000 yards and more — were designed for area fire by massed riflemen. Such tactics are no longer with us, and never did apply to the individual shooter.

The novice rifleman must understand the theory of his sights, and then work with them until their use in practice is quite clear to him. Good equipment is nice to have and can be a joy to operate, but it is no good in the hands of one who will not trouble to learn it. A fine marksman with a second rate rifle is far more effective than the reverse.

RIFLE POSITIONS

It is a continuing source of irritation to any trained rifle-man to see the way general rifle marksmanship (as opposed to formal team shooting) has degenerated since the Korean War. This will have to be the assumption if we accept the illustrations in the "trade papers" as indicative. Centuries of experiences have established that there are right and wrong ways to shoot a rifle, yet some editors appear to believe that as long as the negative is nice and sharp, what the picture illustrates does not matter. Not long ago the back cover of an important national magazine showed a young lady (let us assume that she was indeed a lady) holding a sporting rifle in a way that could serve as an almost perfect study of how *not* to do it. I feel sure that she was simply posing, and did not actually shoot from that position, for if the piece had had any considerable recoil it would have rolled her over backwards.

While it is obviously true that all one needs to do to hit his target is to align the sights and press the trigger at the right instant, it is equally true that ways have been developed which make this operation easier, more precise, more consistent, and more comfortable. They have been taught, and generally well taught, for over a hundred years in Uncle Sam's trade schools. It seems foolish to disregard them.

In high school R.O.T.C. I was shown the offhand, kneeling, sitting, and prone positions. I learned these positions well enough to make the rifle team. When, upon graduation, I went after my first big game in Alberta, I took four prime trophies with four shots. This is not meant as a boast, but only as evidence that Uncle S. really did have the answer.

Today we can add three more positions, at some risk of complicating the study but possibly worth it. These are standing, Indian, and bipod. There is also the possibility of shooting from a rest, which should be understood and accepted.

A knowledge of correct firing position is essential to good riflecraft. Without it good shooting is possible but much more difficult. Life is hard enough without gratuitously adding to one's problems. As the man said, "Why be difficult, when, with a little more effort, you could be impossible?" Why make good shooting harder than it already is? Learn the right firing positions.

Offhand

The offhand position is the quickest to assume, and it is high enough to let the shooter see over cover. It is also the least steady of all rifle positions, affording the lowest hit probability. Deliberate fire from offhand is widely practiced and good fun, but it has almost no utility. The quickness of offhand is its virtue. If you have time you will use a steadier position. Offhand practice should always be conducted starting with the piece off the shoulder and locked safe. Four seconds from whistle to shot is appropriate for novices, and two seconds for experts.

To assume the offhand position, stand fully erect and facing between 70 and 90 degrees to the right of your direction of fire, depending upon your individual build. Feet should be one short pace apart. Hold the rifle with the hands in place on the checkered areas of the stock — or where the checkering will be when you can afford it. The left hand may be placed a bit forward if desired, but not rearward. Turn your head to the left and look directly at the target. Now, without moving your head, neck, or shoulders, raise the piece into line, so that the sights are aligned exactly between your right eye and the target. Bring the rifle up to your eye, do not lower your eye to the rifle. At this point the butt plate (on modern stocks) will be higher than your shoulder. Holding the rifle with the left hand only, point your right arm straight up, and then lower your hand and upper arm so that you can take a firing grip. Your right elbow will now be level with or somewhat above your right shoulder, which will solidly back the butt. The forestock rests flat in the palm of the left hand, fingers limp, and the left elbow is directly under the rifle. On most rifles, the right thumb stays where it came to rest as it unlocked the safety. I prefer the right hand to ride forward and to press the trigger right at the first joint of the index finger, but there are good shots who both cross with the thumb and fire with the fingertip. The cheekbone rides right on the forward tip of the comb.

Once this position is understood, make it quick. If you fancy a bolt gun, learn to operate the bolt as the piece recoils, without removing the butt from the shoulder. Your first shot *should* do the trick, but be ready if it doesn't.

The Standing Position

This is not quite as quick as offhand but somewhat steadier. It is used when a bit of time is available but intervening cover makes it impossible to lower the sight-line and still see the target — or when standing up to your waist in a mangrove swamp. It is also used in some popular forms of competition, albeit difficult for the rule-makers to justify.

The body is placed much as in offhand but the left upper arm is brought back against the torso and the piece is supported by the fingers and thumb of the left hand — first three fingers on the floor plate and thumb under the trigger guard. On "free-rifles" a palm rest extends beneath the piece and rides in the palm of the left hand. The spine slants somewhat rearward, and is not vertical as in offhand.

The standing position does not afford a quick swing and it is not suitable for conditions of exertion where heaving lungs jostle the supporting arm, but for that rare "high deliberate" shot it is useful.

The Kneeling Position

This is slower than offhand but quicker and higher than sitting. It is steadier than either offhand or standing. It can be assumed in a flash and quitted just as quickly. You can leap out of kneeling but you must squirm out of sitting. This is naturally more important to a soldier than a hunter, and kneeling has more military than sporting utility. My personal hunting experience is not notably extensive, but I have hunted broadly and only once have I taken a beast from kneeling.

In this position the left elbow is supported but not the right. The shooting sling can thus be used to advantage here, as is not the case where the left arm is free. (The loop sling ties the rifle to the left shoulder as long as the left elbow rests on a firm support, relieving all muscle tension in the left arm. Widely unappreciated today, it can increase your hitting probability up to 35% whenever there is time to rig it.)

In the kneeling position the body is profiled to the right and lowered so that the right knee is on the ground and the right buttock rests on the right heel. The toe of the right foot is flexed some 90%, a cause of much distress and objurgation in some people. The left elbow is placed just forward of the left knee, so that its apex does not roll around. *It is most important that the left foot, left knee, left forearm, left wrist, left palm, and the forestock of the rifle all be held in the same vertical plane, so that the rifle is supported entirely by bone, with no muscle under tension.* The right elbow is carried high, as in offhand and for the same reason.

If you have time to get into kneeling, you usually have time to get into sitting, which is a lot more solid, if somewhat lower. The thing is that it is easier to get *out* of kneeling than sitting when in a hurry.

The Indian Position,
or "Military Squat"

This one has been adopted since my time in basic training, but I have tried it and it works. It is especially adapted to rifles with military style stocks, such as the G-3, the AK 47, and the M-16. It is as fast as kneeling, in and out, and a bit steadier because both elbows are supported. It is not as solid as sitting, because it constitutes a two-point rather than a three-point gun mount, but it is excellent for quick, precise single shots from successive firing points at mid-range.

To take it you just face 45 degrees to the right of your direction of fire and squat, like an Indian at a campfire. Both feet are flat on the ground, but your posterior remains airborne. Both elbows are supported by the knees. As always, the forestock rests squarely in the palm of the left hand, fingers limp. Finger tension in the supporting hand is the mark of a duffer.

The Sitting Position

This is the classic position of the open-country hunter. It is slower than the previous positions, but not so slow as to risk the loss of the shot once you learn how to get into it. It is very nearly as steady as prone, and enough higher to let you see over grass, rocks, and low brush. Unlike all other positions except offhand, it affords wide variation in elevation. You can shoot anywhere from 20% down to 30% up — most convenient in broken country or mountains. Ideally, it permits time to loop up and lock in while the quarry is still in first flight, then, when he pauses for that last quick look back, the shot is delivered as from a bench rest. (Obviously we do not recommend sitting for stopping charges.)

To assume the sitting position, face 45 degrees to the right of the line of sight and sit down. Spread the legs some 45 dcgrccs and dig in thc heels. Lean well forward so that the torso is nearly parallel with the thighs. (It helps to have done this since high school. If you are not limber enough, take a short course from Jack Lalanne and report back.) Your upper arms slide well down inside your shins — do *not* sit erect and balance elbows on knees, point to point. Shoot right over your left elbow, forearm in the same vertical plane as the rifle. To get full value you really should use the loop sling — you can loop up as you plank down — and keep it well up on your left arm, loop in the armpit. It may take you around ten seconds to deliver a perfect shot from sitting — starting standing in safe carry —but if you have the ten seconds you are well advised to try, because from a really good sitting position you can shoot almost up to your rifle.

The Prone Position

Theoretically, a proper prone position eliminates human error. Actually it does not, but with a good man it comes close. Tiny groups off a bench are technically interesting, but what delights the heart is a one-incher shot from prone. And this can be done. Not always but often.

The trouble with prone is not so much that it is slow — it can be taken just about as quickly as sitting — but that it is restricted. It calls for a piece of fairly clear and level ground large enough to spread out on, and this is not often available under field conditions. The target and the shooter must be on approximately the same plane as the shooting platform, and even a low obstruction can block your view. You always use prone if you can, but very often you cannot.

To take the prone position face about 45 degrees to the right of the direction of fire and lie down. Raise your chest off the ground with your elbows and place them so that when the rifle is mounted against your shoulder your left elbow is directly under the piece as you point at the target. Adjust deflection by rotating your whole body right or left, and adjust elevation by positioning your right elbow — out for up, in for down. Needless to say you should use the loop sling. If you do you can go dead, with every muscle in your body relaxed, and your sights will stay right on target.

A variation, called "low prone," may be taken by lying flat, chest on the deck, letting the toe of the butt rest on the ground and resting the forestock on the clenched left fist. This works only if the slope of the ground is exactly right, and is thus probably too limited for general use.

The Bipod

The integral bipod is an innovation scorned by the traditionalist but probably here to stay. Being a conservative, my first reaction to the bipod was negative, but when I first saw it used in open country hunting I changed my mind. It works so well that it can even compensate for a crummy trigger. A proper bipod should lock in the open position, and should permit some degree of rotation between it and the rifle, without which uneven ground will cause unacceptable canting.

An interesting advantage of the bipod is that the shooter need not spread himself out behind the piece if terrain does not permit. I found this out when I had to shoot from a patch of cholla (the man-eating cactus) and had to curl up around the rifle. (When doing this be careful to keep your feet to the front out of line with the muzzle. Loss of a toe can spoil your whole day.)

Oddly enough, quite good shooting can be done with a military rifle equipped with collapsible stock and bipod — with the stock folded. You just support that "firing handle" by placing it on your clenched left fist. Works fine!

Rest Position

We have not spoken of rest shooting so far because there is little to say about it. A careful man always shoots from a rest if one is available, but it is unwise to come to count on one. Just keep in mind that you should never let the rifle itself rest on anything hard, such as a rock or a log. Barrels twang like a tuning fork on discharge and a hard bearing point usually causes a wild shot. Interpose your left hand between the rest and the rifle, so the weapon will not know that you are cheating and jeer at you.

CW —
THE *ONLY* WAY TO SLING

When the renowned John Paul*, his ship afire and sink-ing, was called upon to surrender, he is said to have shouted back, "I have not begun to fight!" Whereupon a marine was heard to mutter, "There's always some clothpate as never gets the word."

Well, so it seems. Since "nineteen-ought-thirty-four" I have been shooting rifles for fun and profit, but not until nineteen-*eighty*-four did I get the word about sling systems. There was the military loop sling, there was the "hasty" sling, and there was the carrying-strap. The loop gave support, but it was slow to get into. The hasty did nothing for shooting except get the leather out of the way. The carrying-strap was just that — not an aid to marksmanship. We all worked hard on a quick loop-up, but a lock-time of five seconds seemed about all we could count on. There had to be a better way.

Most postwar riflemen just gave up. "Nobody shoots with a sling anymore." Cobra straps and bipods appeared, trending in opposite directions. The target shooters had plenty of time so they saw nothing wrong with the conventional military loop, and the hunters — no longer trained on the '03 and the M-1 —just ignored the whole subject. The advantages of the shoot-ing sling began to fade into the realm of the arcane.

Let us consider the function of the shooting sling, and see whether or not we really do need it. Properly used, the shooting sling binds the rifle to the upper body in such a way that, if the supporting elbow is rested on something solid (like the ground

---

*Aha! You thought I was going to say "Jones," didn't you? The fact is that John Paul had no father and no last name until he picked "Jones" out of the air when on the lam for a murder-two charge. As John Paul Jones he is logged in the U.S. history, but actually that is an alias.

or the knee), the piece is held firmly in the vertical plane by bone and leather rather than by muscle. In any firing position in which the elbow is supported, the shooter can "go dead" —relaxing all muscles — and the sights will not sag off target. This is accomplished by tying the rifle to the supporting hand and to the upper arm simultaneously, so that the angle of the elbow is positively locked by the strap between the two. The higher the loop is on the arm, the more positive is the lock.

Using the systems taught in the marksmanship schools (at least those marksmanship schools we know about), and using slings as conventionally attached, the loop must *encircle* the upper arm, and be firmly tightened in place, if it is to render proper support. The loop must pull *forward* to the front attachment, and any connection with the "butt swivel" is irrelevant. Target slings, or "shooting cuffs," have no such connection, but they do not serve to carry the rifle.

A proper sling, however, must be both a shooting aid *and* a means of carrying the weapon. A carrying strap does one job and a shooting cuff does another. What we need is a device that does both, and which can be used instantly.

Or do we? Many do not think we do, maintaining that field shooting needs no artificial gadgetry. The point may be moot, but I do not think so. The shooter of running rabbits, the brush-country deer hunter, or the African pro who only shoots to stop charges may not need a sling. Anyone who shoots only from standing positions does not. But the *generalized* rifleman does. No one man's experience may be taken as definitive, but I have shot for a long time, and under various conditions, and my guess is that the loop sling is needed six times in ten. It has always been used when there was time, but it takes five seconds to put on and that is not always available. It increases "hitability" — the probability of a first-shot hit, under stress, from an elbow-supported position — by about 30%. That is important.

The Olympians play the Biathlon game, which had a certain practicality before it slid down to the rimfire level (sling-shots next?). In the Biathlon one skis from firing point to firing point. He needs a sling both for carrying and for shooting. I checked this out and was informed that a "biathlete"(!) can loop up in one to one-and-a-half seconds. Good show! The catch is that the biathlete wears his cuff on his arm, as part of his shooting jacket, and simply snaps a hook on his sling into a waiting D-ring on the cuff. A rifleman cannot go through life with a D-ring laced to his biceps. No solution here.

At the First Scout Conference, in 1983, this matter was considered in depth. The Burroughs loop was demonstrated with good response, but lock time was still about three seconds. John Pepper came up with a well-designed metal hook for a web strap that was also quicker than the military loop, but still not in the one-second bracket.

Frustration!

Then, at the home of Carlos Widmann in Guatemala, the lights came on. He showed me his Mannlicher SSG, on which a conventional QD stud had been fitted as an extension of the forward floor plate screw. What for?

"An old British system," he explained, detaching the sling from the butt swivel and re-fastening it to the floor plate stud. "You use it thus." Arm through, around, and in — just as in "hasty." But, unlike in hasty, there is now positive load on the upper arm, pulling forward on both studs.

! ! ! ! !

Why didn't I know that? Why wasn't I told? Why aren't all rifles fitted this way? Where have we all been!?

Immediately some thoughts occurred. The system does not need loops and keepers. A single strap will do. A cobra strap, *reversed*, is ideal, if given a half-twist forward to keep the leather smooth against wrist and forearm.

And Pachmayr *flush* sockets complete the improved assembly. These do not project and can be hooked up instantaneously. (Don't leave home without them!) Three sockets should be installed; forward, aft, and intermediate.

Since the sling is first a shooting aid, and only secondarily a means of carrying the piece, the *normal* attachment is to the two forward sockets. The weapon may be carried quite comfortably this way, either right-side, muzzle-up ("American") or left-side, muzzle-down ("African"), as long as one hand is free to steady it. If violent exercise is expected, or if both hands must be free to climb or manage a bike, the front hook is snapped into the butt socket and the intermediate into the forward. Three seconds. Now the piece may be slung cavalry style, diagonally across the back.

As soon as I got back to Gunsite an intermediate Pachmayr socket was plugged into Fireplug II — a Remington 660 in 350RM, with Leupold IER 2X in Bechtel's forward mount. We rushed off to the *vlei*, our largest rifle reaction range, and checked the combination out. As expected, it worked like a charm. We particularly noted how much better than a loop it is in the "spider walk" when topping a low ridge.

This system is truly a "great leap forward." I have been in need of it for a lifetime. It has been there all along but I, like John Paul, didn't get the word. But neither did anybody else I knew, so at least there was plenty of company in ignorance.

I showed the photos to Creighton Audette, a fellow director of N.R.A. and an old-time big-bore rifleman. He said, "Yes. That's the old British 'two-point' system. They used it back before the turn of the century."

O.K. So nothing is new under the sun. But excellent wisdom is often lost with time; witness the techniques of Lizst and Paganini. The fact remains, however, that this sling system, which I have named the "CW" after its re-discoverer, is *the* answer to a long sought goal — positive sling support in one second. All serious riflemen will fit it to all serious rifles from this day forward.

THE CALIBER GAME

It is obvious to any competent observer that our cartridge catalog is grotesquely over-complicated. Just try to prepare a one-hour lecture on cartridge designation and selection and you will see what I mean. From a utilitarian standpoint this seems silly, but we know that elemental utility is not generally characteristic of the shooting sports. This is no bad thing in itself, for without a certain amount of playful pedantry shooting might be no more than a dull mechanical exercise.

We could probably get along just fine with about ten different calibers — rifle, pistol, and shotgun — but we would not have as much fun. And the manufacturers of sporting arms and ammunition would suffer grievously.

Thus the "telephone directory" from which we now pick our calibers may be foolishly over-stuffed but it is nonetheless interesting to read. And even with its redundant profusion there are still gaps to fill. For example, the 10mm auto pistol cartridge has yet to be marketed, though it promises to do a job no other round can do as well. The 25/223, brain child of John Wooters, could be the finest light-game caliber yet. And I think the 460 G&A Special should replace the 458.

On the other hand, we frequently come up with something we think is new out of mere ignorance, not knowing that what we seek to invent has already been invented — sometimes many decades before our time. This is often observed as we cross continental frontiers.

Take the case of the "big bottle" 25's. There are a whole platoon of these, viz:

(.257″)	(.263″)
25 - 35	6.5 Jap
25 - 36	6.5 Swede

25 Remington	6.5 Mauser
250 - 3000	6.5 Portugese
25 Krag	6.5 Carcano
25 Neidner	6.5 Mannlicher
257 Roberts	
256 Newton	

This is the old list, and not complete at that. (I know that 257 does not equal 263, but the difference is so slight as to be tactically if not technically insignificant.)

In this bore the best ballistic coefficient works out at about 120 grains of bullet. To get a bullet of that weight up to an i.v. of 3000 f/s (the magic number!) is not feasible with any of these cases except the Neidner and the Newton.

So — onward and upward — we put our feverish little post-war minds to it and came up with:

25 - 06 Remington	120 at 3120 (list) and 3090 (test)
6.5 Remington Mag	120 at 3220 (list) and 3100 (test)
*257 Weatherby	120 at —NFL— 3100 (test)
*264 Winchester	120 at —NFL— 3300 (test)

(*Not factory loaded at 120 grains.)

Not bad at all, but was all this really necessary? Along about 1930 Schuler designed the 6.5x68, and DWM put it into production for sale in 1938. *The factory 6.5x68 starts a 123-grain bullet at a clocked 3450.* You can probably match this in a 264 Winchester, if you use a 26″ barrel, but you'll be right on the peg. The point is that the two cartridges do exactly the same job (I'm not sure what that job is but they do it exactly the same.), so why did anyone bother to design the 264 Winchester when the 6.5x68 was already there, and had been for more than a generation? Can it be that the Winchester designers just did not know about the 6.5x68? Or maybe they *did* know but thought *we* did not. One may well ask what one needs a 25-caliber, 120-grain bullet at 3450 f/s *for*, but, if it is needed, the 6.5x68 will provide it. Both Mauser and Mannlicher rifles are chambered for it.

Let us take another case — that of the "big sevens." The modest 7x57 is a great cartridge — compact, well-balanced, highly accurate, gentle to shoot, and suitable for anything up to 400 pounds in weight — much more if well handled. (Consider Bell's countless elephants.) But we cannot make that magic 3000 with the 7x57, and everybody knows that a rifle that will not top 3000 is suitable only for a museum, so we must have a *big* seven — a sort of king-size 270 — if we are going to be taken seriously down at the hardware store.

So OK. Here come the Big Sevens! In 7mm (±.284") we achieve our best ballistic form with a bullet of around 160 grains. What cartridge case will boot it out at 3000? Neither 280 Remington nor the 284 Winchester, both relatively new ('57 & '63), will make it. Neither would the old 280 Ross, the 275 Rigby's (rimmed and rimless), nor the 275 H&H. So suddenly we marketed the 7x61 S&H, the 7 Weatherby, and, in 1962, the 7 Remington Magnum, today's popularity leader in the U.S. The thing is, Jeffery produced *his* 280 (140 at 3000) in 1915, and Brennecke introduced the 7x65R (also 140 at 3000) only a couple of years after that. Somewhat later the imposing 280's of Halger and Vom Hoff appeared, to dazzle my innocent eyes from the pages of Stoeger's *Shooter's Bible.*

I will be the last to derogate the great 7 mags, though I have no personal use for one. They are indeed a bit more potent than the venerable 7x65R, but neither the shooter nor the target can tell the difference. Just about halfway between the illustrious 270 and the box-office 7 RM, the 7x65 has been around *since before WWI.* Being rimmed, it is almost the standard cartridge now in European combination guns. For long-range use on middle-sized game it just cannot be topped.

Now, then, how about a big *eight*? We have all heard about the wondrous "new" 8mm Remington Magnum. We also know about the less recent but still young (1958) 338 Winchester. There is also the 340 Weatherby (1962). Well, the 8x68 is not senior to WWI but it does anticipate WWII, and it slightly out-performs all three newcomers, thus:

8mm Remington Mag	185 at 3080 (list) — N.A.
338 Winchester Mag	200 at 3000 (list) and 2960 (test)
340 Weatherby Mag (26″)	200 at 3210 (list) and 3200 (test)
8x68 (25″)	198 at 3200 (test)

What is more, it does this without a belted case, which can be something of a nuisance.

The 8x68 is available in Mannlicher and Mauser rifles, plus custom guns.

Here again I must confess that I do not know what a big eight is *for*. Doubtless it is a fine elk cartridge. So is a 30-06. If you cannot fetch your elk with a 30-06, a magnum-eight is not likely to do the job for you either. Possibly spring hunting for brown bears in the alpine tundra may now and then offer a very heavy, resistant target at a range so great that only a master marksman should risk the shot. In such cases a big eight might be about right. On the other hand a 375 might be better. Well, to each his own.

As to the mighty and distinguished 375, we may here note that the continental 9.3x74 is both contemporaneous and ballistically quite similar. Both cartridges are elderly, Holland's appearing in 1912 and the 9.3 a few years earlier. The 375 is a bit stronger — 270 at 2700 against 258 at 2620 — but just a bit. The 9.3x74R is rimmed, suiting it for double rifles and combination guns, while the rimless 375 is more comfortable in box magazines.

In truth there is not much new under the sun, and in sporting arms most of what purports to be is sales gimmickry.

There is nothing wrong with gimmickry as long as we recognize it for what it is, but we should not be deceived into thinking that more is necessarily better, nor that newer is necessarily nicer. The simple principles of smokeless powder cartridges for sporting arms were well understood by Teddy Roosevelt and (some of) his contemporaries. We are a nation of gadgeteers and it is quite understandable that we should believe that science must bring us newer and more marvelous gadgets with every passing year. It is well to remember, however, if we consider our guns judiciously, that "It ain't necessarily so."

THE ROLE OF THE FIVE

"Smallarms" are those weapons which are intended to be managed by a single man, without help or support from another. Those in present use are the rifle, the carbine, the pistol, the shotgun, and the machine pistol. (The "machine-gun," taking a full-sized rifle cartridge, is a crew-served weapon.) While the purposes to which smallarms may be put overlap somewhat, the five types listed have different characteristics, and each is better for some uses than for others. There is some confusion about this, and it is the purpose of this disquisition to sort the matter out. Categorization is always open to dispute, and exceptions occur to any system of classification, but what follows is generally supportable in informed debate.

The Rifle

The rifle is the queen of weapons — "the brother of Allah" — and it does more things well than any other smallarm. The skilled rifleman can strike a decisive blow, in a very short time, at any distance at which he can clearly make out his adversary. There are all sorts of rifle types, but the one we speak of here takes a full-sized military cartridge such as the 30-06 US, the 7.92 German, the 303 British, or the 7.5 Swiss. In the hands of a skilled operator the battle rifle is a formidable instrument —far more so than is generally realized in an age where most casualties are inflicted by high explosive. It can kill a man, or a horse, or wreck an automobile, with one round, at distances of half a mile or more, and when used in massed area fire it can be effective at two miles. At the other end of the scale, it can be used with split-second precision in close combat.

The rifle is a very personal arm, or it should be. It is not at its best when kept in racks and handed out indiscriminately to troops as they may need it, but rather issued to one man and made his personal responsibility for the duration of his assignment. It is thus something of an elite weapon, since only troops who can be trusted may be issued rifles and allowed to maintain them personally. If you are not sure of the reliability, loyalty or trustworthiness of your troops you had better not give them rifles.

Rifle marksmanship is demanding. It calls for a very high degree of concentration and self-control. Only certain kinds of people make good riflemen, and mostly they are derived from cultures in which there is a tradition of rifle marksmanship. The Central European *Jäger*, the American frontiersman, the Afghan tribesman, and the South African *Boer* are examples of the sort of people who can, and have, produced supremely efficient riflemen.

For reasons which would appear obvious, hunting cultures tend to produce the best riflemen. While severe and demanding training, conducted by skilled instructors, can do a good deal with a city boy, it is not possible to introduce him to the varied and unexpected circumstances which he may encounter in the practical employment of his rifle. Generally speaking, the townsman tends to be excitable, and to forget the things he learned on the range — when the chips begin to fly. On the other hand, the experienced hunter, while he may be no braver, is used to concentrating upon his marksmanship under conditions of stress, and tends to be less easily distracted from the essentials of holding, aiming, and squeezing.

Therefore the close of the 20th century may see the end of the era of the rifleman. It is not that the rifle has been rendered obsolete, but the rifleman may have been. A prominent military historian concluded after the Korean War that men could not be trained to shoot the rifle well in battle. My own limited experience leads me to doubt this, but even if it is true it raises the question as to why men could be so trained in the first half of the 20th century but not in the second. If it was possible for a young man to keep his head and pay attention under the terrible lash of artillery fire in 1918, it would seem possible for him to do it again 70 years later, but the people who determine such things in today's armed forces seem to have given up on the entire matter. Still today the rifle remains the queen of weapons — in the proper hands. The fact that there are few such hands is a sociological rather than a technical matter.

A really good rifleman, with a really good rifle in his hands, is a man of stout heart. He knows what he can do and he looks down upon those who cannot do the same. I was once told by a very experienced and battlewise officer, who later became Commandant of the Marine Corps, that he would rather attack ten machineguns working together than one platoon of riflemen who could shoot. He was fortunate to serve in the Pacific, for it was never possible for the Japanese to field a platoon of men who could shoot, because shooting is not part of their tradition.

Tradition has it that the Boers could shoot, and that tradition is probably true, if somewhat exaggerated. The South African farmboys shot the British to pieces, with rifles, on many occasions, and inflicted about double the number of their combatant casualties upon much larger forces of trained soldiers.

When the Germans were scraping the bottom of the barrel at the conclusion of World War II they put together several units composed of over-age Bavarian and Austrian professional hunters. These men were not up to long marches or parachute jumping, but when the crack British "Blue Devil" division was inadvertently dropped right on them, beyond the Rhine, the Blue Devils were wrecked by precise, deliberate rifle fire in open forest.

Today the Afghans fight on against communist imperialism — very largely with rifles. They may be going over in large measure to carbines, since that is what they can steal from the

Russians, but there are still a lot of good rifles in those mountains, and the invader doubtless knows about them.

It is important to remember that the rifle is an *offensive*
weapon. It is an instrument with which to take the fight to the
enemy. With a rifle one can attack with terrible effectiveness, if
he is good enough; but he must be good enough, and that is
why the rifle is the patrician smallarm — marvelous in the
hands of the few, but uselessly powerful and unnecessarily
accurate for use by the masses. There will probably be no true
rifle in the hands of the world's conscripts in the 21st century.

The Carbine

This term is very old, dating back to the origins of firearms, and it has been used in various ways through the centuries, but today we may classify a carbine as a "reduced rifle." It
cannot be grouped with the true rifle, in that it takes a small
cartridge, disposing of less power and less range. To the extent
that it succeeds in its mission it does so because of the reluc-
tance on the part of the military establishments of the world to
bother with careful and extended rifle marksmanship training.
No man can do with a carbine what he could do with a rifle, but
if what he can do with a rifle is not much, a carbine may serve
him just as well. The carbine is the weapon for mass armies,
whose motto is "If you cannot shoot well, shoot a lot." Modern
battle carbines are almost all capable of fully automatic fire,
and are thus mistakenly called "machineguns" by the unenlightened. These battle carbines — termed "assault carbines" in
Europe — are a development of World War II, in which it was
discovered that troops exploiting the armored breakthrough
were usually fighting under confused conditions at very short
range, and had more need for a lot of shots than for precisely
placed shots. Whether this theory is sound remains to be seen,
but it was adopted by the Germans and later by the Russians.

Today all the major powers of the world issue some sort of carbine to their troops. The most common now in use are the AK47 of the Russians and the M16 of the Americans, together with various modifications and adaptations of both. They are essentially the weapon of the masses, to be issued to great numbers of people who cannot be given adequate training. When one tries to train a good soldier to shoot well with one of these battle carbines the frustrations involved become almost intolerable. If, on the other hand, the order is to take a large number of green troops whose "dedication" may be quite low, who cannot be trusted to take their weapons with them off the range, and to whom only a few hours of instruction are going to be available anyway, a carbine has much to recommend it.

There is a current opinion that the battlefield of the future will be so poisoned that a pedestrian will only be able to survive if he is wearing a sort of space suit, and that no one in such a rig will be able to shoot with any skill. I think this view oversimplifies, because brush-fire wars seem more likely than total wars, and chemo-nuclear pollution may possibly never be encountered at all.

It is possible that in the future military forces may be separated into categories, just as are most law enforcement agencies in the United States. Today if a police officer in a big city gets into trouble he runs for cover and calls for tactical backup — SWAT. Likewise it may be that ordinary troops in the military establishments may be issued carbines with the understanding that if a situation arises where skill is required, another sort of organization, equipped with rifles, will be called up.

The Pistol

The pistol — the "sidearm" — is completely and conceptually a *defensive* weapon. It is a reactive device with which to stop a fight that someone else starts. It is unlike any other smallarm in that it is *worn* rather than *borne*. If you know there is going to be a fight you will acquire something bigger and more powerful than a pistol. But if you do not know there is going to be a fight, a pistol, in proper hands and guided by an alert brain, can accomplish miracles in short-range, sudden actions which occur without warning.

The advantage of the pistol, which it shares with nothing else, is readiness. It is there on your belt. You do not have to go fetch it.

The range of the pistol is short. It is normally used at conversational distances, within which you can talk to your enemy. This is important because the typical pistol engagement is brought on by conversational confrontation. If a bandit orders you to put up your hands, or turn around, or give him your wallet, or lie down on the floor, you can draw and kill him before he has discovered that you are not going to do what he told you to do. You can thus work inside his response time, and that is the great virtue of the sidearm.

Because of the need for concentration and a high degree of careful practice, it may be that the pistol is no longer, strictly speaking, a military instrument. It may be that its proper niche in today's society is completely civilian. Certainly soldiers *like* pistols, and carry them whenever they can. If they are not issued pistols by their own side they will acquire them from the enemy, as has been noted throughout the 20th century. Whether they can use them or not is another matter, and it seems that the armies of the world simply cannot spend the time to train soldiers to use them well. Thus it is that all the military and law-enforcement men that I know who can use the pistol expertly are hobbyists who shoot for fun. As a line-of-duty instrument it may be just too difficult for troops at large.

The Shotgun

The shotgun, which originated as a fowling piece, has

come into increasing popularity in law enforcement circles in recent decades. When police in America find themselves embattled they invariably go for the shotgun, if one is available. This is only reasonable, since the combat shotgun is measurably more powerful than the police pistol and also easier to use. (Curiously, it is regarded as unacceptably brutal in Europe.)

To be used most efficiently the shotgun requires certain technical and training factors that are not widely understood. Those who criticize the shotgun for lack of range and lack of precision are talking about the wrong sort of shotgun, used in untrained hands. The shotgun is capable of astonishing precision at the very short ranges at which it is often used, since the shot charge does not begin to open inside five or six paces, at which distance it can be used like a rifle. Furthermore, skilled shotgunners generally prefer to use the single-projectile, which turns the shotgun into a very powerful short-range rifle. To those who insist that the advantage of the shotgun is its dispersed pattern it should be pointed out that in order to achieve a solid stop on a human adversary the pattern must be centered, and a centered charge of shot is no more, or less, effective than a centered single projectile.

The combat shotgun must be equipped with a proper set of sights. Without sights its reach is about 35 paces, whereas with a good set of sights and a good single projectile it can add 100 paces to that distance.

Training with the combat shotgun need not be elaborate, but it must be complete. It is unfortunate that very few of the people who are issued shotguns for combat duty, both in the law enforcement and the military establishments, have anything resembling proper training in the use of the weapon.

The shotgun comes into its own after dark, when ranges are short and speed and power are paramount. A shotgun delivers a terminal blow — which cannot always be said of a pistol, a machine pistol, or a carbine. For this reason the

magazine capacity of the shotgun is not a particularly important consideration. A man who cannot handle a personal confrontation with two or three charges of buckshot probably
cannot handle it with anything.

I was interested to find that the single-barrel, nonrepeat-
ing shotgun is very popular for guard forces in Latin America.
A gateguard armed with one load of #00 buckshot must be
taken seriously by intruders. If, on the other hand, he is killed
or robbed, or if he defects, the enemy has not gained as much as
might otherwise be the case.

The shotgun can never match the pistol as a defensive arm,
since you must go and get it. Neither can it match the rifle, since
it cannot reach. On the other hand it has great usefulness in
situations where the user is not quite sure of the situation, such
as entering a confused bickering in which there probably will
be no shooting, but may call for it if things go wrong. Thus it is
attractive for police entry into questionable buildings. Its
drawback of large and bulky ammunition is not serious since it
is hardly ever intended for sustained combat operations.

Probably its ease of use remains the most conspicuous
asset of the smoothbore. Most men can be trained to use the
shotgun effectively in less time and with a smaller expenditure
of ammunition than with any other smallarm.

The Machine Pistol

The machine pistol is a medium-sized, two-hand weapon
capable of fully automatic fire, *and shooting a pistol cartridge.*
It is very popular all over the world today, and yet when
considered carefully it is a weapon of limited utility. Often
called a "machinegun" by the unenlightened press, it is about as
much like a machinegun as a Cessna is like an intercontinental
jet. The difference, of course, is power. The rifle cartridge of a
machinegun will smash the block of a gasoline engine, or blow

a man almost in two, whereas it takes a well placed or continuously repeated blow from a pistol cartridge to take an adversary out of a fight.

As with the shotgun or the carbine, the machine pistol is something you have to carry for an anticipated purpose — it is not something you wear on your belt. If a skilled marksman has to go and fetch something in anticipation of a fight he will almost always choose a rifle. If the fight comes to him without warning he will use the pistol on his belt. Under what circumstances he would go and seize a machine pistol is moot.

There are certain specialized jobs for which the machine pistol is best.

1. For the point man on patrol in thick cover, faced with third-rate troops, it is comforting to be able to spray when the enemy starts shooting at the wrong man. A skilled enemy will let the point man through and attack the main body, but if the point man is alerted by a lot of badly-directed close-range fire, an instantaneous counter-blast of pistol bullets is often enough to cause the ambushers to drop their weapons and run. This situation is, of course, not to be counted on.

2. For anti-piracy action where boats bump together in the night the machine pistol is an excellent means of neutralizing a cockpit full of ambitious pirates. It can be handled with one hand while the helmsman maneuvers the boat with the other. It is also useful when responding to an emergency distress call on the high seas. Pirates often simulate distress in order to lure a victim into reach. Under these circumstances the machine pistol has much to recommend it, since the action commences practically at arm's length and the enemy will necessarily be compressed into a small space.

3. The machine pistol has evident utility in penetration attacks against buildings occupied by known hostiles. It is probably not as good as a shotgun if the inhabitants of the building may or may not be enemy, but if a group of trained men penetrates close space in which all of the inhabitants are presumed to be hostile the machine pistol may be an ideal choice.

The principle problem of the machine pistol is lack of power. By far the most common versions today take the 9mm Parabellum cartridge, which has been proven unsound over a very long period. For this reason the most sophisticated American tactical response teams are trained to control the machine pistol very carefully in two or three-shot bursts, on the premise that one round of 9mm is very unreliable, but a burst of three, properly-placed, will do the job. Clearly if the machine pistol were made for a more powerful cartridge this problem would not exist. On the other hand one might say that if the power of the cartridge is radically increased, one no longer has a machine pistol but rather an assault carbine. This argument is easily countered. One can use a powerful and effective automatic pistol cartridge in many machine pistols without going either to a full-sized rifle cartridge or to the reduced rifle cartridge of the carbine. The obvious choice is the new 10mm auto pistol cartridge, which is decisively more potent than the Parabellum, and outreaches the 45.

Both the assault carbine and the machine pistol are capable of fully automatic fire, and hand-held full-auto is an equivocal feature. I have talked with a good many battle-wise fighting men — men with deep personal experience in close combat —and about three out of four reject it. This being so, one may wonder why it is almost universally available. One reason might be that the people who design, manufacture, sell and buy military smallarms almost never have had occasions to use them. Another might be sheer fashion — "Everybody's doing it."

There may be some uses for hand-held automatic fire, which, contrary to common belief, *can* be controlled. An experienced hand, shooting a machine pistol that is both low-powered (9mm) and heavy (10 lbs.), can write his name on a barn door. He can also keep a long burst on a man-sized target with an assault carbine, if the range is short. But why should he? One well-placed rifle round will do what needs to be done — more economically and without giving away one's position.

One twice-seasoned Marine officer told me that a long burst from an M-16 was "a ticket across the street" in Viet Nam. It might not hit anything but it kept heads down while he sprinted to a new position. The same man also said that if the gooks were on full auto he could approach with comparative safety to within fifty meters. If they were on semi he might expect to take casualties at 150, or even beyond.

The question remains open. At Fort Benning recently I suggested that the Army canvass its experienced infantry veterans in order to settle upon a policy, but I have not heard that this has been done. I did get the impression at the Infantry School that if one needs full-auto at all, he needs a lot of it. This would make the three-shot burst option (a French notion) a step backward.

Hand-held full-auto is imprecise. With a powerful cartridge it is not necessary. It is wasteful. And it discourages the sort of ice-cold concentration that a man needs in order to control himself under fire. Military scholars should investigate it more deeply.

Thumper

When I was privileged to attend a portion of the Lebanese War of 1982, it seemed clear that no infantryman with any of the many opposing factions was carrying a respectable personal weapon. By "respectable," I mean a true *battle rifle*, by means of which to impose one's will upon an enemy. I saw M-16's, Galil's, Uzi's, SKS's, AK47's, and a few other miscellaneous types which I could not readily identify at the distances involved. All of these weapons shared the handicaps of excessive bulk and weight, the capacity for hand-held fully automatic fire, and essentially underpowered ammunition. Each, moreover, while fully capable of spraying an ill-defined target at short range, was difficult to shoot carefully.

It had been a long time since I had seen an infantry action close at hand, and it seemed obvious that the world's armies have been "progressing backwards" in the matter of infantry smallarms.

The United States provided its soldiers with a truly Jovian instrument in World War II, and we used it again in Korea. But "progressive military thought" has since decided that such a weapon was not the answer to "modern conditions," and the world has settled upon what many commonly now refer to as poodle-shooters. It does no harm to us if our enemies insist upon using such equipment, but when we use it too we hand them an advantage which our technology need not grant.

We can and should do better, and I therefore propose "Thumper" as one means by which we might.

Thumper (which exists at this time only as a concept), is a small, light, powerful, controllable, infantry weapon. It is about 18 inches long with its stock folded. It weighs 4½ pounds unloaded. It is equipped with strong, simple, ghost-ring sights, and comes over-the-counter with a clean, light trigger pull. It fires the 44 Automag cartridge — which utilizes the basic 7.62 case blown out straight, to take a 240-grain bullet to a starting velocity of about 1800 f/s from a ten-inch barrel. It utilizes an advanced muzzle-braking system which both unlocks the action and pulls the weapon forward on discharge, mitigating the recoil of a powerful cartridge in a light weapon. It takes a twenty-round box magazine, and fires semi-automatic only.

Thumper is so compact that it frees both its user's hands for nonshooting tasks, and yet it is so easily controllable, and so powerful, that it needs only one round to take out an armed adversary at any range up to 250 meters.

The fact that Thumper is essentially a short-range weapon is no drawback in modern war. The day in which infantry soldiers won battles at long range with rifle fire is past. In our era of instant communication, enemies detected at any distance are taken under fire by support weapons, and even if they are engaged by personal arms no modern army spends enough time on marksmanship to teach its people to hit enemy soldiers reliably at any great distance, when under pressure. The trajectory of the 44 Automag cartridge is flat enough to enable Thumper to thump conclusively out to a distance beyond which modern infantry cannot hit. Any talk of 400- to 600-yard hits with a poodle-shooter is based upon unrealistic targets, such as large black spots on large white sheets of paper. At Gunsite ranch we have been working with a variety of military units for many years, and we find that troops armed with the standard 5.56 cartridge of the Western World pose very slight hazard to individual, indistinct, intermittently visible human targets at 300 meters — under battlefield conditions. We also find that the tiny bullet of the 5.56 loses its capacity to inflict damage radically as its velocity drops off with range. Thumper, on the other hand, fires a large, heavy, blunt bullet which maintains its effectiveness by means of mass rather than velocity; and mass is constant while velocity is evanescent.

Thumper's primary sights consist of a square-front post and a large-aperture rear sight with a thin rim, known as a "ghost-ring." It can, of course, be equipped with various types of night sights or laser pointers. Its trigger breaks clean and crisp at 3½ pounds, making it easy to use well. It may be fired with the stock folded, but it is normally used with the stock in its extended condition in the manner of a rifle.

Thumper features the "flash-loading system," by which the entry of the last cartridge in the magazine into the chamber discharges the empty magazine to a halfway point, informing the shooter that he has one round left but must reload in order to get more. Thumper does not encourage sloppy shooting, but rather is designed for a one-shot, one-hit method of employment. Unlike a poodle-shooter, its one hit is decisive.

Thumper does not fit into any current category of small-arm. It is neither a battle rifle nor a machine pistol. It might be referred to as a carbine, except that that term has, in recent decades, come to denote a weapon of reduced power, whereas Thumper is extremely powerful.

I have shown Thumper to two major arms manufacturers, but have been able to arouse no interest. Arms manufacturers are interested only in large contracts, and since Thumper goes contrary to our aforesaid progressive military thought, no large contract would seem forthcoming for its manufacturer. Thumper is indeed "a better mousetrap," but the world has not yet seen fit to beat a path to its door.

After working extensively with all five of the combat smallarms over the last several decades, I am often confronted by the skilled shooter who asks me why he has any need for anything but a rifle and a pistol. He maintains that he can handle any sort of defensive situation with his pistol, and that if he needs more he will use his rifle. The point here is that these questions come from highly skilled marksmen. For the really good man the rifle and the pistol, balancing attack and defense, will truly do the job. It is when the user is less skillful that the other weapons attract attention.

Nothing can replace the pistol as the primary defensive arm, simply because of its availability. The pistol is *there*, within reach, and that is rarely true of any long gun. Therefore, despite its relatively low power and the high degree of skill needed for its proper use, the pistol cannot be supplanted by anything else. The novice may say, "Well, if I need something to protect myself I am going to get a shotgun," but what is overlooked here is the fact that he may not have the privilege of going to get it when the flag flies.

If one does have the luxury of going to fetch out a long gun, the highly skilled man will choose a rifle, but not everyone is highly skilled. The shotgun has great merit in house defense after dark on the part of people who are not basically shooters. The carbine is essentially "a substitute rifle" to be issued to people in uniform who cannot be counted upon to shoot well. The machine pistol is a specialty weapon to be issued to specially trained troops on special missions. It is in no sense a general purpose instrument and should never be so regarded.

If you are a dedicated "shottist," you will probably not select the same tools for the task as either the novice or the common soldier. If you are not a hobbyist and do not wish to study the arts of marksmanship, certain compromises are in order. Obviously the master shot is safer in today's turbulent world — if he is properly oriented — than the unschooled non-combatant. That is why the Left excoriates skilled weaponry — it is *inegalitarian*.

THE MACHINE PISTOL - CON

Our era has been justifiably denigrated as "The Century of the Common Man." In weaponry we might call its second half "The Age of the Machine Pistol" — equally true and equally depressing. The machine pistol — the "submachine gun" — so often miscalled "machinegun" by the police — is the ubiquitous smallarm of the current scene, quite appropriate to a time of massive mediocrity and ineptitude.

It is my profound conviction, based upon a great deal of experience with it, that the MP is a silly weapon — clumsy, wasteful, puny for its bulk, over-prone to run dry at the most inconvenient moment, and a source of frequently lethal over-confidence. This is currently a minority view, but that may be more of a credit than a debit. In specialized disciplines the majority view is almost automatically wrong.

For those who can afford its extravagant appetite the MP is an enchanting toy. In firing so many rounds through a wide selection of these pieces that I am embarrassed to think about it, my range work was enormous fun. (Imagine being paid to demonstrate with the taxpayers' ammunition! Something like being a ski-bum.) The MP makes a glamorous racket, it is hard for a novice to control but a cinch for an adept, it makes a brave show — in short, it is made to order for a "snow job."

But it hits no harder than its cartridge. That cartridge is most often the 9mm Parabellum, of dubious repute; and even when it is the 45 ACP nothing is accomplished that cannot be done as well with a handgun — in almost every case.

There are situations in which the MP can be a serious weapon, but they are very rare. "Housecleaning" — a military euphemism for interrupting a staff conference and totalling the conferrers — is better done with a MP than almost anything else. Point response to a badly planned ambush is often best handled with the squirt gun. But these are very particular sorts of actions, in no sense common enough to justify the procurement of a specialized weapon which is good for little else.

As I write this I have just returned from a consultation in one of the world's teeming hot-spots. The many MP's in evidence when I appeared gradually vanished as operations got more businesslike. The word became "For defense, the pistol. For attack, the rifle. For showing off, and using up ammunition, the submachine gun."

On my return, a new client with much experience in Sir Gerald Templar's Malaya told me that his people had used many MP's — Stens, Austens, Owens, and Sterlings — and that their doctrine was "Always semi-auto, and always from the shoulder!"

I asked him why, in that case, a rifle would not have been better. He answered that it would indeed have been much better, but that MP's were available and there were not enough rifles to replace all of them.

"But a rifle kicks! And a pistol is too hard to use well!" Just so. If we are stuck with third-rate troops the MP may be what we want, and that is the point. Good troops are not impossible to come by, though certainly more difficult all the time. The U.S. "Uniform Code of Military Justice" (U.C.M.J.) is more of an obstacle to a good military establishment than even our current "volunteer army" policy. Until both these things are changed we are unlikely to produce good troops. It is not that we are lesser men than our fathers but that we are, as a political entity, not serious about our future. Americans make marvelous soldiers, as the world has seen, but on a basis different from today's. We can be taught to use good weapons expertly, but probably not just now. For the present a slob's tool may be all we can manage, but that condition is not beyond correction.

The machine pistol, by definition, shoots a pistol cartridge. A pistol cartridge is necessarily underpowered since handguns are too small and light to handle anything more. Handguns (in good examples) do their primary job — providing instantaneous disabling response to unexpected close attack — very well. However if one is to go armed in expectation of big trouble he wants more power than any pistol can provide. If he is ready to pack around anything as cumbersome as an MP he certainly wants something that hits harder than a 9mm P — *or* a 45 ACP. This is why the Germans came up with the "MP-44," which was not a machine pistol at all but what we now term a "battle carbine," as exemplified by both the Kalashnikov family and the dismal American M-16. The battle carbines are hybrids — neither rifles nor pistols — and while they are universal with the major powers today we may note wryly that the Afghans sell the Kalashnikovs they loot from the invaders and keep on killing them with real rifles, which are, in the right hands, much better tools for the task.

Some may feel that the big thing about the MP is its burst effect, and we will admit that a burst of eight or ten rounds of 9mm P in the region of the wishbone will do a decisive job. But two rounds of 45 ACP, similarly placed, will do it every bit as well with less fuss. So will *one* round of 308, delivered from way out beyond the range of any MP, or, as to that, of any battle carbine.

I have talked to people who have used this hose-down technique with the MP, and seemed rather pleased with themselves. They were somewhat crestfallen when asked why they didn't just fire twice, carefully, with a pistol.

The great majority of MP's are "slam shooters" — they fire from an open bolt and chamber with a disturbing clank that is no help to good placement. Thus even in the semiautomatic mode they are difficult to use with precision. It may be true that precision usually does not matter in modern fighting (remember we are in the Century of the Common Man) but there are still cases in which it might, and it seems orkish to dismiss it altogether. (The MP-5 from Heckler & Koch fires from a closed bolt and is thus the only current MP that permits

·KIRCHNER·

shooting-gallery finesse. It thus risks "cook-offs" in sustained action, but sustained action with an MP is a gloomy prospect at best.)

In a recent training operation we were conducting a version of the venerable F.B.I. duel, with MP's. The students naturally could not draw so it was not a "Walk 'n' Draw," but the principle was the same, starting cocked-and-locked at high port. Advancing side-by-side from thirty meters the two duellists reached a tie, two points apiece, at perhaps twelve meters. For the deciding point I let them close right up to where the need for speed seemed overwhelming — and blew the whistle. Both men were using M-3's and each had reloaded after the last point, with twenty rounds available. Such a clatter you would not believe! But no hits. The man on the left went dry, dropped his grease gun, stroked his 45 and won with one center hit. Consternation!

It is easy to say that with more or better training on the MP that could not have happened. Perhaps, but why bother perfecting one's technique just for its own sake? To what end? The blow is the same.

This is just an echo of the early days of the Modern Technique, when I was working for another chief of state. On the final day of training, the great man dropped by in person, accompanied by two henchmen carrying MP's. We set up a demonstration to show how much his boys had learned, and he seemed impressed. As a finale I matched the best of the pistol class against the better of the two MP men (as selected by the president). They were placed at fifteen meters and given six silhouettes apiece; the pistolero holstered in Condition One and the squirt-gunner cocked-and-locked at port arms. On the whistle the handgunner placed six nicely centered hits in about nine seconds. The MP went dry in twelve, having hit one target four times, two others once (with one edger), and missing the other three.

The president thereupon asked if I could train his MP people as well as his handgunners. I said that I certainly could, but that it would take some 2000 rounds per man instead of 400 and that the tactical effect would be about the same. "Because, Your Excellency, the two weapons strike the same blow."

Tactical efficiency aside, there is the matter of false confidence. Hand a duffer an MP and he suddenly thinks he is an assault brigade. He's got a *machinegun*, man, and look out for him! (We codgers recall Jimmy Cagney demonstrating this in *The Public Enemy*, back in 1492, or was it 1066?) He shoots too soon, he shoots too fast, and he shoots too much. And he often gets himself killed, if his antagonist is dangerous. (I know of two such cases, personally.) For this reason I much prefer that my enemies, if they have any firearms at all, have machine pistols. With a rusty old Mauser a man knows he has to hold and squeeze. With a nice new Uzi he feels that all he has to do is spray.

A man can become highly skilled with a squirt gun. In those dear dead days when I had access to warehouses full of ammunition I used to put on some pretty fascinating shows for the front office types. This is not to brag — anybody could do the same in the same circumstances — but only to establish that it is not personal incompetence that causes my negative view of the weapon. There is a place for the expert squirt gunner in the special forces, and you may believe that if our leaders would unleash some of our young lions upon the creeps who find joy in brutalizing unarmed hostages the machine pistol would probably play a useful role in the festivities. It would, however, be a very specialized role, and even then it would not actually be necessary. Even in those rare situations where the MP is indeed the best arm for the job it is only slightly ahead of a good pistol, in good hands — and it can never be as handy.

Fully automatic fire can be fearfully effective — off a tripod or a vehicular bracket. An honest-to-God *machinegun*, shooting a full-sized rifle cartridge and handled by a team of experts, can win battles — not just fights. But *hand-held* automatic fire is generally a drag. It is great fun, but to be taken seriously only if fun is the object of the exercise.

My son-in-law tells of his unit's policy on night guard alarms. The phone to response center rings:

"Lootenant!"

"Yes?"

"We got a problem!"

"Is everybody on semi-auto?"

"Sheese, Lootenant, the gooks are through the wire!"

"I said, 'Is everybody on semi?'"

"I dunno."

"Find out!"

"Lootenant, everybody is on semi."

"Okay. Now what's your problem?"

I think perhaps the nicest thing about fully-automatic hand-held weapons is the way they fascinate our BATmen*. Our local sociopaths would be much more dangerous if they stuck strictly to aimed fire, but it's not for a bureaucrat to reason why, only to pry and spy. As long as he concentrates on *machineguns*(!!) he has that much less time to harass our marksmen.

---

*Bureau of Alcohol, Tobacco, and Firearms.

·KIRCHNER·

UNDERSTANDING THE SOCIAL SHOTGUN

While the shotgun has been used for a very long time as an anti-personnel weapon, it is evident that scholars have not approached its technique in that mode, being concerned entirely with its other and primary use — that of a fowling piece. A good many people know a great deal about shooting birds or clay targets with a shotgun, but while many others have used shotguns for combat almost none of these latter have given that use any penetrating study. A shotgun may be an excellent instrument for home defense (especially in the hands of one who does not choose to study weaponry in any depth) but its technique when employed in this mode has been insufficiently explored. The art of the skeet, trap, and bird shooter is only indirectly connected to the "social" use of the piece.

Here at Gunsite we have been studying this matter for five years, and while we do not claim to have all the answers, we at least have posed a number of rather pungent questions, and have come up with some unconventional ideas. The fact that we do not have any scatter-gun champions on our staff can be considered more of an advantage than a disadvantage, since shotgun champions are naturally wing shots, while our students are largely interested in other matters. Our staff can bring a good deal of active combat experience to bear upon the problem without the handicap of preconceptions brought over from the sporting field. We do not teach sport shotgunning, because that is best left to the champions of that art. We teach the shotgun as a defensive weapon, for use against people, and we believe that we can make more progress in a shorter time if we do not clutter up the student's learning process with irrelevancies.

The first question, then, is in what way does the defensive use of the shotgun differ from its sporting use? The two main considerations here are the nature of the target and the range at which it will be engaged. An armed enemy does not have the characteristics of a pigeon, either live or clay, and the range at which he may be engaged varies from inches to as far as the weapon may be put to effective use. A wing target is engaged within a narrow range envelope, but this is not true of an armed enemy.

The weapons commonly thought of as "combat" shotguns used to be known as "riot guns," and are, for the most part, slide-action repeaters with reasonably short barrels, and mostly in 12 gage. About half the examples we see come with some form of open sight. The term "riot gun" has fallen into disuse and the current slang for the instrument is "rehabilitator." The pump guns are generally quite serviceable, but we have discovered that other types can work well, too. A good many pieces are now showing up with extension magazines, allowing for longer periods between loads, and some come with military handgrips and folding stocks. As yet we have seen few equipped with "ghost-ring" rear sights, and we find that a good part of our gunsmithing in the shotgun course consists of fitting large ring, thin rim, receiver sights to students' shotguns. To those who are amazed at the thought of putting any sort of rear sight on a shotgun, we can prove that the ghost-ring really works, and few people leave their training sessions with anything else.

It is doubtless true that the master wing shot does not need any sights, since he accommodates the stock of the weapon to himself and merely points, keeping his eyes on the flying target and allowing nature to take its course. This is one of the principle areas in which sporting shotgunning differs from combat shotgunning. It has, like other considerations, to do with range.

We refer to that range at which the shot pattern has not had a chance to open up, as the "A Range." Up to seven or eight paccs the shotgun must be used like a rifle. It cannot be simply waved at an adversary, but must be handled so as to place its small-diameter shot charge exactly on target. This can be done without sights but it is easier and faster with a ghost-ring.

We call that range at which the shot charge is about right for a maximized pattern strike the "B Range." At this range, extending from perhaps eight paces to twenty, a good shotgun with good ammunition can place all its buck shot into the stop-zone of a human target, providing more reliable stopping power than almost anything else that can be hand-carried. In the "B Range," a shotgun need not be used with sights, but sights do not inhibit its efficiency if present. The "C Range" is that beyond which the weapon may be counted upon to place the majority of its pellets on a human target. At these ranges the single ball comes into its own, and here the weapon is much more efficient with sights than without. A good shotgun, with a good barrel, using a good grade of rifled slug, can consistently place all of its hits on the palm of a man's hand at 50 paces. It can usually keep all of its hits in the chest area at 100 — but not without sights.

Thus it is that while we can take extension magazines or leave them, and that we find collapsible stocks uncomfortable, we discover a good set of sights to be a primary *desideratum* on any social shotgun.

As noted, practically all of our shotgunners use the twelve-bore, but we have been speculating that for the recoil-shy the twenty might be a wise choice. Some people are offended by the recoil of a full-charge twelve and, while this blow is considerably less than that taken by every member of a touch football team every time the ball is snapped, it is still true that a shooter who is afraid of his gun is not going to do well. We have been suggesting, particularly to our women students, that there is nothing unsatisfactory about a 20-gage shotgun in the house-defense role. When we have seen a couple of dozen in action here at the school we will be better able to assess their utility.

The majority of our students seem to favor the 870 Remington slide-action weapon, though I believe this is as much a matter of marketing as anything else. The Remington line got to the police establishment first, and it has the edge in popularity. That should not be taken to mean that the self-loading shotgun is in any way unsuitable for the home-defense assignment. My personal view is that the self-loader is slightly *more* reliable than the slide-action weapon, if both types are kept equally clean, and that the fixed forend of the semi-auto is quite a bit more satisfactory to use in single-ball delivery, as well as giving a steadier base for an arm using a loop sling. Again, it may seem somewhat odd to think of a loop sling on a shotgun, but results are what we are after and one can deliver that rifled slug with considerably more confidence — way out past Fort Mudge — when his arm is locked solidly to his piece.

We have seen very few doubles so far here at the school, but that does not mean that the double is unsuitable for the defensive assignment. To begin with, a double is necessarily shorter and more compact than any repeater, since there is no loading mechanism incorporated into the action. Secondly, the double permits instantaneous selection of the rifled slug without any operation of the weapon if a long shot should suddenly present itself. (It is well to remember that multiple shots from a shotgun are very seldom a tactical requirement. The great majority of shotgun actions which are reported to us in the police files involve the use of one round only. As with any sort of fighting tool, it is extremely important to be ready for the next action, but one does not need to hit a man more than once with a full charge of 00, or a single rifled slug, to take him effectively out of the argument — and speed loading the double is somewhat simpler than with the repeater.) The major disadvantage of the double shotgun at this time is its exorbitant cost. No police department can afford to equip its people with doubles, but this does not necessarily affect the individual householder.

In selecting a repeating shotgun some thought should be given to the location of the cross-bolt safety. It is much more easily operated if it rides in front of the trigger rather than behind it. This is a matter which designers have not addressed for awhile because one does not carry his shotgun in "Standard Ready" on the skeet field or at a duck pond.

Shotgun ammunition is both heavy and bulky, and this affects the utility of the weapon in the combat role. When one goes hunting or takes his place on the trap line this matter does not intrude, but in a defensive action a man may have to grab his gun and run without time to stuff shells into a shell vest, or sling a box around his waist. This poses a problem for, though it is probable that the action will be terminated with one round, we still wish to prepare ourselves for anything subsequent which may come up without going back to base. The extension magazines of the repeaters handle this problem part way, but they do make the weapons clumsy and give rise to doubts about the strength and durability of magazine springs. Of course a bandolier may be slung around the barrel of the shotgun as it is left in its ready condition in closet or rack, but this may require the user to open doors and switch on lights with both hands full. We have found here at the school that the "butt-cuff," carrying six or seven spare rounds and laced onto the butt stock, is a good solution to this problem. Our "school solution" for ready storage with a repeater is one trap load in the maga-zine (one round will not give the spring a set), two rounds of 00 in the first two loops of the butt-cuff, and two rounds of rifled slug in the two rearward loops. The piece is racked with the chamber empty and the hammer down. From this condition, on a Red Alert, the weapon's action may be racked as it is seized and made ready for an indoor confrontation with one round of number sixes. If the action leads us outdoors, it is simple to rack the action a second time and load quickly with buck or single ball, depending upon the nature of the terrain outside the house.

Possibly the ideal house-defense configuration is the short-barreled, side-by-side double, with exposed hammers (affectionately known as the "*Lupara*" by the Sicilians). This piece may be racked above the kitchen door with one round of shot and one round of single ball, with all springs relaxed and safe — and left that way indefinitely. (Scotch tape may be used to cover the muzzles to avoid wasps' nests over the long haul.)

RIMFIRE IN RIOT CONTROL

The study of the control of rioting mobs is complicated by the sociological and political factors involved. The uninvolved are likely to opine that weaponry of any sort has no place in the suppression of mob violence, but the people who are given the mission of keeping order have to look at the subject with a more military eye. One is reminded of the anecdote from Vienna in 1848 in which the Emperor was told that the people were rioting in the streets. His Majesty considered this at length, stroking his beard, and then asked mildly, "*Ist das erlaubt?*" (Is that allowed?). Such a serene view of matters is doubtless commendable, but the men given the task of defending the realm will eventually come to grips with the problems of riot weaponry, if only because they have no choice.

As with all forms of human violence, it is clear that the primary aim of society should be the speed of its suppression. Speed! The *sooner* any sort of scuffle — from a family quarrel to a major war — can be stopped, the less damage there will be to all hands. It will be even better if the incipient violence is aborted before it starts. However, the powers of the state are rarely called out for the purpose of suppressing mob violence until such violence has become difficult to obviate. By the time the state police, or the National Guard, or the Cossacks, or the constabulary are mobilized, the action usually has become sufficiently alarming to make speedy suppression unlikely.

When a thin line of uniformed men is confronted with an angry mob, the chances for a happy solution are not good. The authorities are naturally most reluctant to use serious weaponry against people in masses, since there is no presumption of guilt in the mass itself, but only in those agitators who have instigated the action. To use strong measures against a mob in general is, often as not, to increase both its sense of purpose and its public image. For this reason, mass suppressors, whether they be harmless like high-pressure water hoses or tear gas, or dangerous like gunfire or shock-vehicle action, are nearly always a mistake. "Browning" a mob is never the answer.

In recent times we have seen the increased use of rubber bullets fired from conventional weapons in mob control. In my opinion this measure is unproductive. It is true that rubber projectiles are less lethal than those made of lead, but because they are they encourage further violence on the part of those receiving them. One need only look at the films taken in Ulster to see that the adolescents attacking the armored cars take positive pleasure out of being struck by a rubber missile. They can wince and howl and run back to their friends holding up their wounded arm as a badge of courage. It is easy to stand up to gunfire that does not kill, even though it may hurt. Suffering for the cause — as long as one does not die for it — is a great boost to one's self-esteem.

Neither are intermediate measures such as bayonets, rifle butts and truncheons very helpful — principally because they are *indiscriminate*. Most people in a mob do not deserve violent repression, but some do. What means may be used to separate the one group from the other? At Kent State (according to Michener) two of those killed were active instigators, while the other two were simply standing in the wrong place at the wrong time. It would seem desirable to devise a system which would make sure, first, that the riot would stop; and, second, that only the leaders would feel the weight of social disapproval.

Let us consider such a means — the 22-caliber rimfire rifle. This weapon, properly sighted and equipped with a noise suppressor, may be used with surgical delicacy to neutralize mob leaders without risk to other members of the group, without noise and with scant danger of death to the subject. A low-velocity 22 bullet in the lung will not knock a man down, and in these days of modern antisepsis it will almost never kill him if he can get to a hospital in a reasonable time. It will, however, absolutely terminate his interest in leading a riot. This instrument must be used by a man very carefully trained in marksmanship, target selection, anatomy and discipline. And, above all, a man who is in complete control of his nerves.

Naturally, the rifle must be used with extreme care and only as a last resort since, despite the best efforts of the user, it *can* kill. It should only be ordered into action when it is obvious to the commander of riot police that if something does not happen quickly the situation will degenerate into a blood bath. It should be regarded as a specialized instrument, and its use should be very carefully controlled, but it will absolutely deprive any mob of effective leadership at its most critical time.

In use, the troop commander will do well to keep the 22 out of sight and out of mind until, in his opinion, serious bloodshed is about to be initiated by the mob. During the period of confrontation it will be the troop commander's duty to select those people in the mob who are leading it and to point them out unmistakably to his riflemen. During this period, they should be given both code names and priorities.

"Wilson, see the big one with the checked shirt, bald head and gray beard. He is 'Red One.' Stand by to take him out on signal. Ortega, see the thin one without the shirt, with all that black hair. That's right, he's wearing cutoff jeans and sandals. That is 'White Two.' Stand by to take him out on signal."

In general, firing over the heads of a mob is a mistake, since it produces the impression that the troops are not going to use deadly force. This was apparent at the Winter Palace in St. Petersburg in 1917. However, if the troop commander is going to employ such techniques, he can easily use the noisier manifestations to cover up the use of the 22 suppressor. If armored cars advance using high-pressure water hoses, there will be sufficient disturbance so that the employment of the 22 will not even be noticed — even, in many cases, by the person hit. He may not even know what has happened to him — only that he urgently needs a doctor. *But no one else need be so much as scratched.*

By choice, the 22 rifleman should not even be visible to the crowd and his control is best maintained by radio.

It may sound as if this technique is excessively cold-blooded and brutal, but we emphasize that it is only to be employed when the lack of its employment is judged to be more deadly, more dangerous, and the cause of greater loss of life. We don't like the idea of mob violence, but we don't like the idea of the Cossacks charging into the crowd blindly cracking heads. We would prefer to do without either, but we live in the real world, and in the real world many unpleasant things happen. If the glass-sighted, silent 22 rifle is regarded entirely as the lesser of two evils, its utility in mob suppression may be seen in its true perspective.

IV. THE HUNTER

ELG

The Englishmen who colonized the eastern seaboard of North America were neither woodsmen nor scientists. What learning they possessed was largely theological, and hardly suited to the systematic study of their new environment. When they saw the Virginia Whitetail they simply called it a "deer," neither knowing nor caring that it was basically different from the roe, fallow, and red deer hunted by the nobility in the land they had left behind. When they subsequently encountered a much larger beast of the same order they recalled that in Northern Europe there was a very big kind of deer, which none of them had ever seen, called something like "elch" or "elk." So they named this one, which was a scaled-up version of the hart, or "red deer," an *elk*. Finally they discovered a huge, black creature with a bulbous nose and palmate antlers, which was also a sort of deer, but for which they had run out of names. This was indeed an elk (Greek $\alpha\lambda\kappa\eta$, meaning "bodily strength, force, prowess, might." Latin *alces*), but the colonists, having used that word for the giant hart, had to come up with something else. They asked the Indians, and got "moose." Hence today a moose is an elk and an elk is a moose and neither is a wapiti, which is a deer. Have you got that? (The Russian word for old bulb-nose, by the way, is *losl*. It is the wrong word. The Russians seldom have the right word for anything. That is one reason why they have to steal technology from capitalists.)

Alces alces, which is the object of this exercise, is circumpolar in habitat and is now held to be a single species by the taxonomists, though racial characteristics differ. The European variety, no longer found south of the Baltic but flourishing in Scandinavia and Siberia, is about the same size as the Canadian "moose" but with much smaller antlers and sporting four elegant white feet. The Alaskan race is the giant of the species, bigger in body and enormous in antler. The great trophies come from Alaska, but there may be more action nowadays in Norway and Sweden. Game management has really succeeded in Europe since WW II, and hunting has perforce become harvesting in many areas in order to forestall what the biologists call a "crash decline." Try explaining that to the bambiists, if you have time to waste. As the Germans put it, "*Ohne Jäger, kein Wild*" ("Without hunters, no game") but the point escapes many indoor types.

So it came to pass that I was invited by Per Høydahl, director of the Norse Region of the International Practical Shooting Confederation (of which I am past president) to come and hunt with him in Norway. He explained that the Norse woods were crawling with *elg*, which were eating back country farmers out of pocket. Something like 30,000 had to be taken out this season in order to (1) ease population pressure, (2) protect the grain supply, (3) fill the freezer, and (4) provide a bit of shooting. This all gave promise of a Jolly Good Show, and I accepted at once with handclapping and glad little cries.

I am no "mighty hunter" in the Boone & Crockett sense, but I love to explore the sport to see how it is performed by colleagues in distant and exotic locales. Utah mule deer are a far different proposition from German roebuck. Yukon grizzlies are nothing like African buffalo, and chasing the bighorn is doubtless very unlike hunting the Norse elg. This was the chance to find out.

One thing did seem odd. Per had said that the elg were thick, but he had also said that in two seasons he had not had a shot. How come? I enjoy hunting for the experience itself and I do not have to kill to be content, but Norway is a long way from Arizona and the apparently good chance of getting skunked loomed perplexingly. Nothing ventured, nothing gained, however, and in due course I came whizzing over the Atlantic, properly equipped with rain clothes, rifle, and high hopes.

The weapon was, not surprisingly, the Super Scout, a Remington 660 carbine in caliber 350 "Fireplug," fitted with a Bushnell 2¾ Scopechief. This little jewel has been my companion all over the world for many years and is practically ideal for the Norse task. It is short, light, perfectly balanced, completely reliable, and has a glass-smooth action and a superb trigger. It starts a 250-grain, semi-spitzer bullet of ample impact area at some 2500 foot-seconds. This is more than enough power for anything in the world, short of buffalo, and in a neat, handy package. Everywhere I go people want to buy it, but I cannot oblige because all its elements — action, cartridge, and sight —have been "discontinued." The Remington 600 series of compressed bolt actions, together with their innovative "short magnum" 6.5 and 350 cartridges, were obviously way ahead of their time and did not sell. Fortunately those who knew got theirs while they could, and hunting rifles do not wear out.

There was no trouble at customs, though I did not anticipate any. The first girl approached at the counter did not know the procedures for weapons and ammunition, but the O-in-C had all the right papers and I was quickly legal — at no charge. Passing guns properly through customs is a study in itself, as those who travel know. The thing seems to be to pick the right countries. Stay away from England, for example.

In Norway every big game hunter must qualify with his weapon system just before the season opens. This arrangement not only assures a modicum of marksmanship in the field but also requires the applicant to bring his current rifle, ammunition, and sights into some degree of harmony — an excellent idea. (In Germany one's shooting is tested once, but annual zeroing is not required. I know of no place in the U.S. where any qualification is necessary for a hunting license.) The test is simple: five shots freestyle (no rest) at 100 meters, on a dark green deer silhouette. The pass/fail ring is vast — some ten inches in diameter — but it is invisible to the shooter, who can see only the silhouette and must thus shoot for where he thinks the vital zone lies.

When Per and I showed up at the test range it was raining — as usual. If anything was unusual it was that it was raining harder than usual, and blowing the rain briskly across the range. Conditions were not of the best, but then conditions in the field are sometimes difficult, too.

I was offered a bench rest for zeroing but declined with thanks. One of the lucky few who owns his own range, I can be pretty sure of my sight settings. The Super Scout had been set to print three inches high at 100 meters, so my task was to keep the vertical wire on the foreleg and the horizontal wire a handbreadth below the forward curve of the throat.

The firing point was covered against the rain and the target was softly visible through the slanting water. Naturally I chose prone, and looped up. On signal I fired the five shots, loading singly. The report of the fat little cartridge from its short barrel was emphatic inside the shooting shed. I called the last shot a bit out to the right.

So it proved. The group was larger than I had hoped for but still quite satisfactory. It was centered almost exactly in the scoring ring and strung out vertically to 4½″ due to my difficulty in finding an elevation index on the silhouette. Lateral dispersion was 1¾″, excluding the shot called bad — the last —which was 2½″ out as expected. The range personnel made complimentary remarks and filled out a license for me and the carbine, certifying that the pair of us were "go" for reindeer, hart, and elk for the 1981 season. So far so good, and ahunting we could go.

In Norway, as in all of Europe, the game belongs to the land rather than to the hunter. Beasts shot on public land belong to the state and those on private land to the landowner. This pretty well eliminates the slob hunter from the scene, and it sets up some interesting economic considerations. A prime bull ("*ochselg*") will weigh around 500 kilos. The meat sells for — brace yourself — $10 a pound. Five-hundred kilos is about 1100 pounds, which will dress down to perhaps 600 pounds of marketable meat. No matter how you tally that, there are few ways in which you can earn as much with one shot! But you, the rifleman, do not own what you shoot. Financial arrangements must be set up in advance between you and the landlord. In Norse practice this is a private matter.

Per's hunting contact is a successful lumberman who owns a piece of countryside on the Swedish frontier about an hour and a half by car due east of Oslo. This holding measures about 5 Km by 10, comprised mainly of rolling, well watered, spruce forest reminiscent of eastern Canada. It houses enough elg to be assigned a quota of 28 for the '81 season. Twenty-eight animals had to be taken out or the game license (which cost $1200) would not be renewed. Obviously the owner could not do this by himself, so he called upon his friends. For him there was the very considerable value of the meat, if he could get it to market in good condition. For his friends there was the hunt itself, plus choice cuts to take home at a rate of $1.50 per pound, the minimum allowed by law. For all there was open air adventure in beautiful forest, hard work, and good companionship around the fire in the evenings. Trophies, if any, went to the fortunate hunters who did the shooting.

And fortune it was, for the Norse system is different — a group effort in which individual skill, while necessary, only matters if the dice roll right.

It works thus: The hunt master, in this case the landowner, counts the available hunters and selects a patch of forest that is of the right size for them to cover. They are spotted around the perimeter in stations which offer some sort of field of fire. This is a problem since the forest is thick and no stands are used because in each period a different piece of terrain is searched. When all is in readiness a dog is released into the forest. He is, reasonably, a Norwegian Elkhound; an attractive little fellow who looks equally at home on Park Avenue or in the troll-woods of Scandinavia. He comes in black or mouse grey, chunky in build, with sharp muzzle, pointed ears, tightly curled tail, and thick coat. He hunts at a trot, nose up and silent. One dog is normally used, though pups are often apprenticed to seniors for training. If there is an elg in the search area the dog will pick up its trail and run right to it. Elg and elkhound are instinctive, mortal enemies. The dog attacks and the elg counters, trying to stomp the pest into the mud. The dog sets up a shout. The elg, who usually misses, becomes frustrated and runs off. The dog stops barking and takes up the trail again. Elg are fairly surly and will frequently attack a man if surprised at short range.

The hunter on station hears the dog. Then silence tells him that quarry is running. But which way? Then more barking —nearer or farther. Then more silence. Tension. Concentration. Depending on screen density and fields of fire, the elg will often run between hunters and that will be all for that period. But if he happens on harm's way he will burst into view at a dead run and be gone again in seconds. The range will be less than 100 meters and a bull is bigger than a horse, but the target is always moving and the shot must be quick.

This procedure explains why any individual hunter may fail to shoot for many seasons in succession, even though the elg are thick and the freezers are kept full. When I saw it working it was clear that I might well have come a very long way for very little action.

During the season, which is late September and early October, the hunters in our group come and go as they can spare the time, but the hunt master works at full throttle the whole time since meat recovery is his principle responsibility. His property is divided up by the game department into "bull only" and "any elg" zones. Yearlings are valued for both hides and meat, but in my own case a calf seemed something less than a prize. As a guest, of course, I was bound to observe the wishes of my host.

Shelter was available in an abandoned farm house without utilities — a sort of Norwegian "hooch." Per and I raided a market in Oslo and came away with bread and cheese and prepared meats, with which one can be well content for many days without cooking, but there was a fire night and morning and various "chef's specials" were whomped up. Scandinavians are powerful drinkers and there was no shortage of grog, and no need to avoid the draconian drunk-driving laws in force in both Norway and Sweden.

The drive out from Oslo was lovely, with the autumn colors blazing through the misty rain. On arrival at the meat shed we were introduced all around and it was clear that the season was well underway, as two big bulls were already hanging, plus a couple of cows and calves. Everything was ordered, and within an hour I was sitting by myself on a log in Peer Gynt country, awaiting the appearance of a troll — or something.

(I should say right here that I never did meet a troll. They cannot abide full daylight, of course, but I thought one might venture out in the constant overcast. According to Per trolls vary in disposition from wary to downright hostile, but you can often talk them into helpfulness if you are clever. You must be uncommonly clever, however, for trolls speak only Old Norse.)

There were also bears, roe-deer, foxes and Swedes abroad. I was told solemnly that if I shot a Swede I would get five extra points. Chauvinism is alive and well and living in Europe.

This was an "any elg" zone and a cow was killed within earshot that first afternoon. I was treated to the sounds of the contest, first far off, then much closer, then farther, and then a shot. A minute later another shot. (Old Indian saying: "One shot — game. Two shots — maybe. Three shots — heap dung.") In this case the second shot was the *coup*, which is normally necessary with these beasts. One can very rarely "ice" an American moose except with a brain shot, and neither his European cousin.

Homing on the sound, I found the working party hard at it. Processing was admirably swift and efficient, as these were old hands used to working together. While the carcass was opened and cleaned a nifty little tractor, complete with chain saw for obstacle removal, came growling up through the trees. A log drag had the game down to the road in minutes, where a transporter was waiting. The tractor winched the carcass aboard, climbed on with its own power, and the whole arrangement rumbled off to the shed where the meat was skinned, washed, and hung up before it had time to stiffen. Anyone who has ever downed a 1000-pound beast and then wondered what to do next will appreciate the neatness of this operation.

The next day was Saturday and I spent morning and afternoon periods on different stations, admiring the scenery and eating blueberries, profuse and dead ripe. The kill is the climax of the hunt, and without it the sacrament is not complete, but the hunting itself is an end in itself, and even if it is not complete it is always successful. The common question at day's end, "No luck?" is properly answered, "Much luck! I was hunting all day."

Nothing was taken that morning, but a bull and another cow in the afternoon. As before, the processing was absolutely first rate.

Saturday night in the farm house was noisy and cheerful, but I retired early because I had acquired a nasty cold on the airplane, and also because my lack of the language rather kept me out of things. Most Norsemen speak some English, but when nine out of ten sportsmen speak one language the tenth man is naturally outside the conversational circle. I did provoke some jests about "moose" hunting. In Norway a *müs* is a tiny, grey rodent hunted with housecats.

Sunday was the day. I was on station at eight and promptly at nine I heard the dog. My position was better than usual, in a blueberry bog halfway between two stands of thick timber. I could cover the edge of the forest for perhaps 100 meters left and right, from about 100 meters out.

Silence. Then contact again, closer. Then still closer. *Coming this way!* Sitting on a stump, sling loop in place, finger straight, safety on, I tried to cover the full sector.

And here it is! A huge cow crashes out of the trees to my right and down the low bluff, running hard, target angle about 280°. This is a "bull only" area. Not to shoot a cow!

Through the glass, the thick cross hairs track her. The dark brown hide gleams wet as the big muscles ripple beneath it.

To the right! Behind her! Another! *This is a bull!* The dice have rolled right, and you have been elected. *No mistakes.* Will he stop? Certainly not. He's breaking from cover to cover, with the cow leading. He won't stop. Why should he stop? *You've got to take him running.* All right, you can do it. Hold a little low. Don't bother to lead, with less than a tenth of a second's flight time. Swing with him, and keep on swinging as you press. There — the bulge of the big shoulder — right there. Gently. Swing. Press gently! Swing! CRASHwhap! The *Kugelschlag*, the unmistakable sound of the bullet striking home, comes instantly behind the explosion. That was a solid hit, but he pounds on.

Snick the bolt. He's staggering. Press again. CRASH —and he's down. Well, well, well. The little dog comes full tilt along the trail, but does not stop for the bull as the fresh cow trail is first priority.

Life is measured in episodes, not years. Those who note and appreciate its important moments are the truly affluent, because they live truly rich lives. A talent for appreciation is the greatest gift one can give one's children, for it constitutes wealth beyond measure. So the bull was down and I luxuriated in the accomplishment of the mission. It was no great triumph, but it was a job carried out as assigned and intended, with a full measure of luck capped by proper technical dexterity. Well, well.

The elg was a big, prime animal, but with freakish antler development. There was a full if modest palm to starboard but only a heavy, double tine to port. Spread and beam diameter were quite good for the district but nothing to hang in a museum.

The range was eighty-four paces. The bullet had entered the shoulder at the extension of the foreleg, about a third up from the bottom of the brisket. It went into the angle of the shoulder bones without touching them, struck a rib on the near side, and drove through the lungs to leave a half-inch hole on the far side. The rib was shattered, leaving a lesion the size of a softball at the entrance to the chest cavity. Secondary bone fragments in the lungs brought almost instant death. The second shot, for insurance, broke the near humerus just below the joint and pulled the rug from under him. Hung by the hocks from a 10-foot overhead beam, the elbows of the mightly carcass rested on the ground. Protein aplenty!

It was noteworthy that the 250-grain "Corelokt" bullet was the only missile in the party that went clear through to open air.

We ate fresh tenderloin that night, and it seemed both finer in grain and tastier than the moose meat I have eaten. Without aging, it was amazingly tender and juicy. Apart from eland, it was the best venison I can remember.

When we left on Monday night, twenty of the allotted twenty-eight animals had been taken, with another week to go in the season. Sad to say, nothing ran in Per's direction on Monday so he logged another season without a shot. But the hunt was still his, and as much meat as ever. Maybe next year!

And that is the way it is done in Norway. It is not trophy hunting, and it is neither luxurious on the one hand nor backbreaking on the other. Scoring depends heavily upon luck, but at the moment of truth a full measure of marksmanship is necessary. The land is beautiful, the fellowship is warm, and the prize is well worth the effort.

Besides which, you now have added to your list an excellent crossword puzzle item — "Norwegian moose," in three letters.

TEXAS MOUFLON

The mouflon (*Ovis musimon*) is the native wild sheep of Europe. It was found in early historic times all the way around the Mediterranean, and up into the central mountains of Europe, also extending eastward through Asia Minor and farther into what are now Iran and Afghanistan. In recent times, however, it has been killed out, except for the islands of Sardinia and Corsica, which two spots were its only surviving habitat at the beginning of the twentieth century. It has now been re-stocked into some of the mountain ranges of Europe, and additionally into North America. After some sixty years, it has proliferated and may now be hunted on private land in the Western United States.

Mouflon is an attractive beast, about half the size of a North American Bighorn, and somewhat more colorful in aspect, usually sporting a chestnut back and an ivory belly. He is a true mountain sheep, with the legendary agility of that tribe, together with the telescopic eyesight that makes sheep hunting demanding.

In West Texas the massif that forces the Rio Grande south into the Big Bend extends northward, perhaps 150 miles, before petering out as it approaches the Panhandle. The northernmost block of this chain is called the Davis Mountains, and these afford some of the handsomest scenery in the entire state, rising from flat low-country plains to heights of eight thousand feet or more. In these Davis Mountains a veteran cowman named Darrell York maintains a hunting *revier* on which one can pursue both the wild sheep and a variety of other exotic game.

Mr. York's terms for hunting on his property are very attractive. There is a nominal accommodation fee for quartering in his cabin. There is a trophy fee for each taken, but if you get nothing you pay nothing. There is no charge for the services of a guide (one for two hunters), and non-hunting guests are free. The hunters furnish their own equipment, bedding, and food, but no license is required and no game tag. This all works out to a total which is gratifyingly low compared to that for out-of-state hunting in any other part of the U.S., and the hunting itself is good. No sheep hunting is ever easy, since the mountain sheep are creatures of the crags, but the game is there, and if the hunter is willing to climb and knows how to shoot, his chances are good. When we asked around about hunting in the Davis Mountains, our responses were uniform in that we could expect beautiful country and long shots. This was true on both counts.

We hunted in the second week of October and the climate was perfect, with the days cool enough to be pleasant for hard walking, and the nights chilly without freezing. We arrived about the time that hurricane Wanda was breaking up, and spent much time in the rain. But a Scotch mist is no hardship to a mountain hunter, and actual downpours were spotty.

On this occasion both hunters used 308 scouts; one a fairly standard Remington 600, and the other the prototype Scout II, which was as close to the "state-of-the-art" as any weapon then in use. Ammunition was the Nosler "Greenpoint" 150-grain boat-tail bullet, propelled by 43 grains of 3031. This combination has proved highly satisfactory for all light four-footed game, shooting quite flat enough to avoid trajectory problems out to ranges where the difficulty is not drop, but group size. Both rifles are feather-light, and most comfortable to handle even under the most severe climbing conditions. We never actually had to hang on by our fingernails, but, if we had, the conspicuous handiness of the scouts would have been most comforting.

Mouflon hunting, as all sheep hunting, is a spot-and-stalk proposition. One glasses the high grass just below the rocks until something is discovered, and then works out a method of approach which is both feasible to the hunter and acceptable to the ram. It must be acceptable to him because he will almost certainly see the hunter before the hunter spots him. One of the challenges about sheep hunting is the regularity with which the spotted animal is first seen looking directly at the hunter. Any attempt to approach from below will usually be frustrated by the quarry's miraculous eyesight. The plan is thus to move away and out of sight, discovering some track by which the rifle can be placed above the target. Even when this is possible the results can be disappointing, since a ram spotting a hunter approaching from below will usually rise leisurely and move away to some other mountain, whereas if he glimpses something above him he will panic and be gone in a flash.

We had time for only a short hunt, so it is impossible to say whether the Davis Mountains teem with flocks of mouflon. In two days we saw two acceptable rams, each with a full curl, and nothing else. That is to say we saw no other sheep, but the mountains abound with mule deer and Catalina goats, which have also been imported. There is also a full measure of cougars, to the annoyance of the cattlemen.

The countryside was indeed beautiful, as the intermittent misty rain gave the rocks a well scrubbed look and avoided any sense of aridity or heat; and the shots were indeed long — longer than a sensible hunter can enjoy.

It took us four spotting posts to locate our first target. He was about three-quarters of a mile away across an impassable canyon. Benito acquired him first, but dismissed him as a goat due to his uncharacteristic color. He was feeding, and when he turned sideways I was able to make out the full curl of the characteristic ram's head. Naturally he knew we were watching him, and paused now and again to stare at us. No approach was possible from this direction.

We retreated off our own ridge, got aboard the hunting car, and proceeded in a large circle over extremely rough terrain, going around the mountain to the right. While we followed a two-rut field track, I was gratified that we were not moving in a car that I owned. Mountaineering in a four-wheel vehicle is hard on the machinery. The circle was directed by Benito, who knew the terrain, and in due course we found

·KIRCHNER·

ourselves topping out over the far mountain, with the prospect of coming down on the ram from above, if he was still there. As it happened, he was, and had decided to bed down for the morning. Our final approach led us straight down the ridge above him, and he presented a stationary target, lying down, and at about target angle 235. The shot was well beyond Townsend Whelen's sporting maximum, but since the ram was stationary — and I was not blown — and there was no wind —and I had time to acquire a rock-solid sitting position with CW loop — and since I knew *exactly* where my zero was —and since Scout II is quite phenomenally accurate — I took the shot. I held well up into the top-third of the brisket, and the bullet entered the armpit. The "Greenpoint" fractured on a rib, expanded, passed into the body cavity, and took away half the heart. It did not exit. Such a hit is painlessly fatal, and the ram did not even know he was hurt. He stood up, suspecting that something was wrong when he heard the shot, and bled to death on his feet.

I paced the distances best I could, and it came to 334 steps. I am never unequivocally proud of a long shot, because I know how many things can go wrong, but I rendered due thanks to the gods of the hunt for the success of this one. All went well, and, apart from the loss of half the heart tissue, no meat was spoiled. There may be those who hold that a short-barrel 308 may hardly be considered a sheep rifle, and yet I cannot see how a flatter-shooting or more powerful weapon could have done a better job.

Mr. York has a ground rule forbidding the use of the 6mm rifles on his ranch on the grounds that he has seen too many sheep escape when hit with a 243. I would have thought that the 243 should be an ideal cartridge for this junior-grade mountain sheep, but such does not appear to be the case.

There is also a ranch rule forbidding movement with a loaded chamber. This may be a bit restrictive in some views, but remember that this is mountain hunting, and the chance of an unexpected snap-shot is almost nil. When shooting from crag to crag there is always time to work the bolt as one goes into firing position.

Our second contact was different. We topped a small saddle and another solitary ram, somewhat bigger than the first, spotted us instantly. Again across a canyon, and again too far away. Nonetheless we attempted a direct approach, but were forced to engage too soon — at a distance which is better left unstated. In the classic words of the mountain man, "We was shootin so blamed fur we had to use salt bullets to keep the meat from spoilin afore we got thar." This time the Greenpoint took the ram forward of the shoulder near the top of the brisket, and passed diagonally through the upper portion of the boiler room without either expanding or exiting. Despite this, the ram was instantly killed, presumably due to shock transmitted through the skeletal system. The fact that the Greenpoint did not expand at all, despite its reputation for fragility, suggests that the terminal velocity was so low that the rupturing effect of the ballistic tip was not initiated. Again no meat was spoiled, and this time the heart was untouched.

And that was it. Two rams sighted, and two rams taken —with two hits. *Ganz waidgerecht*, as the Germans say. I repeat that I am a little embarrassed at attempts at unreasonable distances. The rule is: "If you can get closer, get closer. If you can get steadier, get steadier." We might have got closer on the first shot by a laborious crawl through broken rock. On the other hand, we might have made such a fuss that the ram would have spooked and departed, especially since our approach was from above him. And at that the first shot was within feasible shooting distance, if just about at its far limit. In the second case I have no real excuse. The nullah between us prevented our pacing the distance, but I feel quite sure that it was great enough for my own field-group to be greater than the shoulder of the target. In Thell Reed's dictum, "There is no such thing as luck." However, when your working group size is about two feet, and your shot takes the center of it, somebody is on your side. The renowned Major Maydon told us years ago that luck will be with you if you have been playing fair. That is an optimistic view which may not be supportable philosophically, but it is what I must fall back on in this case.

Everything seemed to work out on this day. I was experimenting with a new ripple-blade knife from Japan that floated through those two sheep as if they were butter. The saw on the Swiss Army knife neatly took care of the pelvic arch. We even had *two* string bags for viscera, and both were necessary. I have rarely seen matters click so neatly into place on a hunting trip.

The fact that we were all fairly soggy was nowise disheartening after a successful pursuit.

That night we feasted on fresh kidneys and fresh liver with onions. The following morning, we dressed up our scrambled eggs with sweetbreads. By early afternoon we had completed skinning and butchering, and had packed our coolers with venison for the return trip.

There are those who may feel that "ranch hunting" is unexciting, unsportsmanlike, and unchallenging. To each his own, of course, but sheep hunting is never easy. The climbing, spotting, stalking, and shooting are a true test wherever a mountain sheep is found. It is unwise to characterize the whole concept of mouflon hunting in the Davis Mountains on the basis of two experiences, but my own feeling is that it should not be undertaken by a casual marksman. The game is there, and it can be had, but do not expect success if you cannot shoot up to your rifle.

AFRICA CIAO!

A general of distinction, for whom I once had the honor of working, maintained that there were two transcendent experiences a man might have in a lifetime — the two great ones known only to the fortunate. First was hearing the idolized girl say "yes"; and the second was watching brave, strong, well-armed men flee in terror from one's presence.

Perhaps. The "sexual revolution" has largely eliminated the first as it has debased romantic love; and the increasing predominance of gadgetry in war has made the second even less likely. But there may be others. The African Experience has indeed faded in many parts of the continent, but some of those fabled "golden joys" are still available. And believe me when I say that they really *are* golden. Honest to God!

Back once again from Africa I can reflect upon the great good fortune that kept me reading and dreaming for many decades before finally getting there. The African bush is not what it was (what is?) but it is still "the greatest of the world's great hunting grounds." Everything else is a step down, and it is not good to top out too early in life.

Much of the Africa we have read about has now been abandoned to the so-called Third World, and its boondocking possibilities are very nearly forbidden to the traditional sportsman. However we can still prowl the Africa of the *fourth* world — the Southern Constellation, as its people are beginning to call it — and it is big enough and wild enough (in the right parts) to afford a full measure of the delights our Victorian ancestors told us about. You can still confront a testy tusker or a belligerent buffalo. The crocodile, the rhino, or the mamba will still get you if you don't watch out. Lions thrive anew in the war zones, for obvious reasons. And that hippo snorting in the pool hard by your camp is nobody's pet. This is *rifle country* — like unto no other — and there is a zest here for the rifleman that he cannot match elsewhere. The hunting rifle is the queen of weapons, and in the African bush it is never out of easy reach — twenty-four hours a day. It is a luxurious experience to live thus intimately with a queen.

Much of the game country is embattled at this time — not as Iwo nor Stalingrad — but thinly, as in the pioneer American West. Hunting under such circumstances has a curious attraction. If one is careless he may be mangled by something far more savage than any lion, whereas if he is careful he just may acquire a trophy far more significant than any elephant.

Some three months prior to my last visit, a German sportsman arrived in Salisbury all booked for a bit of hunting. His hosts told him clearly at the airport that things were unsettled — even a bit dangerous — in the game country, and that if he wished to cancel they would fully understand. He considered that and elected to go ahead with his holiday. One dislikes to turn back from a long-planned adventure simply because of the possible presence of a paltry pack of pernicious piddlewits. As it came to pass, however, he actually did make a contact. There was an ambush within hearing, and he and his host were able to enfilade some goblins who had set upon a supply truck. Using a regulation R-1 auto rifle and a 375 Mauser sporter, the two of them iced five of six — to the European's mild consternation. "I should not do this kind of thing!" he spluttered. "I am a sportsman, not a soldier. Why, I have never even been in the *Bundeswehr!*"

A thing that is noticeably different from the old days is that one now sleeps in semi-permanent camps rather than in a temporary outspan. No more tents and sleeping robes, but barbed wire, sandbags, and indoor plumbing. What wilderness atmosphere is lost is made up in convenience.

Nothing has changed the legendary meat-hunger of the Bantu. The locals still love to go along on hunting trips because of the guarantee of all the *nyama* they can hold — which amount is almost beyond belief. There is a lot of game in the African bush. It may not be just the type you are after, but game of some sort is always there; and since you have a kind of extended family to support, you take it. If your entourage had its way you would take *all* of it — that being the reason why it has vanished where the Third World has its way. (This delights certain people. If there is no game there can be no hunting.)

The situation occasionally leads to complexities. One is that your local boy will urge you to shoot anything, of any size or sex. To him all bulls are of trophy size because they are all equally good to eat. Another is his insistence that, if the beast does not fall in its tracks, the shot was a miss. If you can be convinced of this you will go after another target, allowing him to come back later and gather up an extra full helping of *nyama*, which may be only a few score paces off in the under-brush, and which need be neither reported nor shared. You cannot blame your man — he's just "looking out for number one" — but you do learn to make your own decisions.

It is reassuring, of course, to have qualified local help available for tracking in thick bush. I could never have found my Zulu nyala without it. The hunter insisted that I had missed, as there was no drop of blood to be seen, but I had heard the *Kugelschlag* and I knew he was down — and not too far off at that. Extra trackers were recruited, and though the bush was thick as a hedge they went right to him. The bullet had not exited, and the entrance wound was entirely bloodless, yet the lads followed the track like hounds into vegetation so thick they could not see the ground — to a target a quarter-mile distant. It was all very impressive.

Without the background of a Selous or a White or a Taylor it is presumptuous to preach about rifles and cartridges, but gun-talk is excellent entertainment in Africa and one cannot avoid forming opinions. So let us have at it.

As a boy I was a great devotee of the "mediums" — rifles of about 9mm caliber taking bullets of 250-300 grains. The idea of an "all around cartridge" was appealing, and the consensus was that proper placement of the bullet was all that mattered.

Proper placement is truly the most important single element in shooting, but it is not the *only* thing.

On my first venture I carried a very nice medium — 36 caliber, 250 grains, 2400 f/s. It did fine on all the light stuff, but it fell way short on buffalo. Now we all know that buff have been downed with light (30-caliber) rifles. For that matter Graham Whistler has taken two buffalo with a *357 revolver*. A lot of deer have been killed with 22's, but that does not make the 22 a deer gun.

All the small game I shot with the medium was cleanly taken, but I believe that a light rifle would have done every bit as well. On the other hand prudence and humanity indicate a heavy for dangerous game. My own limited experience leads to the conclusion that a medium is unnecessary for 90% of African shooting and inadequate for the other 10%.

The disconcerting thing about African hunting — to an American — is the vast variation in bulk that the normal game displays. It is quite possible to engage impala (100 pounds) and eland (2000 pounds) on the same afternoon's walk. You cannot employ an ideal cartridge for these two extremes, so you must try to select a proper compromise in bullet design. I fancy the 308/180, using Silvertip or other slow-expanding bullets. With that you can deck a duiker neatly without blowing him up, and at the same time obtain adequate penetration on a big kudu or wildebeest. Ranges are mainly short, in the seven places I have hunted, so one need not bother much about minor increments in velocity or trajectory.

For my money the 30-06 is still king — backed by a sound heavy (500 grains +) if you attempt dangerous game. The 308 is almost as good as the '06, as is the 7x57. The 375 is a splendid cartridge, and if you own a rifle of this caliber by all means use it, but it is an exaggeration on reedbuck and risky on buff.

If you are lucky enough to contract for dangerous game a heavy rifle is best, but good heavies are not common. The doubles have much in their favor — handiness in particular —but those of us who have grown up with bolt actions may prefer a magazine rifle. My own 460 is a true six-shooter (one up the spout and five more in the ready room) and this gives me a nice friendly feeling in thick thorn. One shot *should* be enough. We all know that. But twice now I have needed three in quick succession. This was my mistake, of course, but it was still pleasant to have three more rounds all set to go if necessary.

Today the standard heavy cartridge is the 458, so obviously it must suffice. It is nonetheless a poorly designed round, with inadequate case capacity, no shoulder, and out of balance. The 460 Weatherby, on the other hand, uses a case so big that its magazine capacity is two rounds, in order to reach for a problematical and needless 2700 f/s. Hence the 460 on the Jeffery case — a happy compromise.

Probably the best heavy cartridge for magazine rifles was the 505 Gibbs (ballistics much like the 460 G&A with one-sixth more frontal area) but the guns must be strictly handmade now and proper 50-caliber bullets are difficult to organize.

Telescope sights are nice but not generally necessary, and they can cause confusion in the thick brush which is so common in much of the African wilderness. This is not to recommend primitive open sights, but a sound aperture — of the "ghost-ring" variety — is my own first choice.

Actually I get more satisfaction from a shooting sling —which helps my holding, than from a scope sight — which helps only my seeing. A scope helps you see the target but it does not help you hold nor squeeze. Unless the target is very small or very distant (both rare conditions in Africa) you won't have trouble seeing it. Hitting it, once you have seen it, is a more pressing matter. I'd rather have a rifle with good aperture sights and a shooting sling than one with a scope and nothing but a carrying strap.

The pistol has long been disdained in Africa, and certainly it is no charge-stopper, but this attitude may be changing. First, if he hunts in a war zone a qualified pistolero wants his sidearm handy for unexpected company at odd moments.

Second, I know one young man who got into a wrestling match with a shot-up lion on a "photo safari," and he claims that a sound pistol on his belt could probably have obviated a long stay in the hospital. Crocodiles and leopards — both common — might be equally well diverted with a belt gun. Third, there's a lot of short-range small-game hunting in Africa (ranges under 50 meters, animals under 200 pounds) which lends itself ideally to handgunnery. The warthog in particular is ubiquitous, diurnal, fast on his feet, and very good to eat. It is possible that warthog hunting is the best pistol game anywhere.

For me there are two kinds of hunting — buffalo, and "other." I love them both, but the "joined-horned infidel" (*Syncerus caffer*) must be given pride of place. The mood of the buffalo hunt is different. With other game the approach is everything — with the buff it is only the introduction. Sometimes the stalk is hard and sometimes it is easy, but the "moment of truth" — far from being a foregone conclusion —offers a 50-50 chance of mortal hazard. No matter how well you place your shot, nor with what, you can't be sure your bull will drop. If he doesn't he will do his very best to kill you, and his best is very good indeed.

The other day one of the unenlightened said to me, "But no animal has any chance against a rifle!" Well, statistics do favor the rifle, but to say that the beast has no chance at all is not quite correct. Nor is it relevant. Peril, not variety, is the spice of life, but few people can stomach a half-and-half mixture of chile pods and beans. The fact that I cannot be sure of dropping a buffalo, and that if he is not dropped he can quite possibly squash me like a bug, is spice enough for me.

I use a heavy rifle. I get close. And I shoot carefully. My wife would not like it any other way.

For dangerous game your best bet is Botswana (all types except rhino). There is good lion hunting around the Etosha Pan in South West Africa. Buffalo may be had — if you know the right people — in the N.E. Transvaal. You can even take a rhino — for a sheikly fee — if you feel the need.

But dangerous game is expensive. If it is not your prime goal you can proceed much more economically in Southern Africa and still encounter more species in one visit than any place else can show you in a lifetime. In one 10-day sojourn you can take eland, kudu, gemsbok, wildebeest, nyala, impala, blesbok, bushbuck, reedbuck, and zebra. (Zebra heart is a rare delicacy known only to a discerning few.) If you fancy the scattergun you can also have your fill of waterfowl, guineas, and francolin. And there is some splendid fresh water fishing!

African hunting is still there and still very good, and it will probably remain so for a long time. The political situation is clearly difficult but we may bear two current axioms in mind:

"Gold is going up."

"South Africa is *not* going down."

Despite the best efforts of the Russians, the Chicoms, the Fidelistas, and their multifarious camp followers in the remaining free governments of the world, the Southern Constellation is not cowed. Among other things it offers, and will continue to offer, superb hunting to the connoisseur.

The point is this: Don't write Africa off as down the drain just because the Kenyatta family has closed Kenya to all but photographers, poachers, and terrorist conscripts. Hunting in the south is great, and it is as expensive — or as cheap — as you want to make it. The golden joys are still there — for those wise enough to appreciate them.

OKAVANGO ADVENTURE

Let us dream of legendary places. Let our fancies conjure up Tintagel and Tahiti, Samarkand and Cíbola, Mandalay and Machu Picchu. And Okavango. Okavango — the garden in the heart of darkness. Okavango — the water world in the desert. Okavango — the remote, the magic, the mystical.

It is there. I have been there and I know.

Water runs down to the sea, as everybody knows. But not always. There are places where it runs into a lake with no outlet, such as Baikal, the Dead Sea and the Great Salt Lake. But there is only one place where a mighty river system, a thousand miles long, decides abruptly to fan out into an enormous delta at the base of which it simply disappears into the desert. This place is Okavango, certainly one of the wonders of the world, lying almost dead center in the lower lobe of the continent of Africa.

Okavango is most frequently referred to as a "swamp," but the term is misleading since it creates visions of stagnant mud puddles and dysgenic exhalation. The Okavango delta is nothing like that. It is green and blue and gold, a maze of running waterways, mighty forests, crystal lagoons and water so pure that every drop is potable. It is also vast — some 160 by 120 miles in extent, making it larger than the delta of the Mississippi or the Nile, about the same size as the delta of the Ganges, though smaller than the delta of the Amazon. A European might visualize it as extending from Paris to the sea and there covering the coast between Boulogne and Le Havre.

Politically it is now located in the northern extremity of Botswana — once known as Bechuanaland. Its drainage system begins far to the north in eastern Angola and adjoins those of both the Congo and the Zambezi. It is economically uninhabitable, since its water level is in continuous fluctuation, and its very remoteness has kept it clean — even up to the present day. Africa is still "the greatest of the world's great hunting grounds," and this pocket in its heart is the Garden of Eden for those hunters who can put out the very considerable effort to reach it.

All hunting in the delta is strictly controlled by the government of Botswana, which grants concessions to a small number of expert outfitters. The surrounding population is sparse and the area is not an easy one in which to poach, so it now constitutes a pristine, Arcadian park, with plenty of game of most kinds and in no danger of overpredation by man.

(The exception is the elephant, which was opened to native hunting some years ago and heavily reduced. This mistaken policy was terminated and the elephant may come back. Certainly the vastness of the delta remains one of the few places in Africa where the destructive feeding habits of the elephant do not constitute a danger to the environment.)

The area abounds in most of the common antelope of southern Africa, with the exception of eland, sable, oryx and waterbuck. Lions are present but rare, as are, surprisingly, crocodiles. One would think that a place of this type would be crocodile heaven, but such does not seem to be the case. The cheetah and the wild dog, rare in most places, are comparatively common here. The main sources of camp meat are wildebeest, tsesebbe, impala and lechwe.

The prize of the Okavango is the sitatunga — the water antelope related to the nyala, the bushbuck and the kudu. This beast is a specialty — both rare and difficult. He lives among the waterways deep in the reeds and hunter success on a 28-day safari runs to about 25%. This discourages some people and entices others.

For ornament there is an abundance of giraffe, ostrich and hippo.

As everywhere, there are great numbers of leopards but, as everywhere, they are unseen.

I am a buffalo hunter, and to my mind everything else is secondary. There are plenty of buffalo in the Okavango delta and their heads, while not the fifty-inchers of the great safari days in East Africa, are still very impressive. But any buffalo is impressive. It is not how big his horns are but what he can do with them — and often does. The buffalo is an antagonist rather than a quarry, and we went to Okavango to hunt buffalo, with everything else as a side dish.

The experience was magnificent. As Winston Churchill said of the Grand Canyon, "It exceeded my expectations —and they were very great."

In April when we were there the rains had stopped and the water was rising about an inch a day. Weather was perfect —neither hot nor cold. The scenery was magnificent. The camp was almost embarrassingly comfortable. The company was witty and the hunting was superb. It was truly a hard act to follow.

My partner was Dr. Werner Weissenhofer of Austria, and our outfitter was Ian McFarlane, whose main office is in Gabarone, Botswana. Mr. McFarlane operates in three general hunting areas so as to be able to provide his clients with Kalahari lion and gemsbok in the south, and sable, eland and elephant in the north. Since we could spare only ten days we spent them all right in the heart of the delta at a camp called, rather spectacularly, Khurun!araga. That exclamation point is not a mistake, it is the phonetic symbol for a click. If you cannot click, you can get by by substituting a "k" sound. To reach Khurun!araga one flies first to Johannesburg. From there AirBotswana can take you to Gabarone, where you pass Botswana customs. Thence there is scheduled service across the Kalahari Desert (which goes on forever) to an odd place called Maun. At Maun it is necessary to take a charter airplane sixty miles northwestward to where a new airstrip has been scraped out for the camp. This strip proved difficult to find, for the delta country viewed from above is bewildering. One can also drive from Maun to Khurun!araga, but while it is only sixty miles it takes half a day. As you might suppose, the road is not a fast one.

It's a long, long way to Okavango, but it is worth every bit of the trouble. The camp was quite lovely, located on slightly high ground and shaded by enormous wild olive trees. A particularly attractive extra was a clear, crocodile-free pool whose gentle current kept its water absolutely sanitary, day in and day out. (There was also a field shower which I suppose is more useful in cold weather later in the year. With that pool so handy and so inviting, however, we never used it.) The reedbuck around the camp were almost pets, and of course we did not shoot them.

The object of the exercise was buffalo, and for this Werner and I brought heavy rifles. They are siblings — "Baby I" and "Baby III" — made up on the ZKK 602 action and taking the 460 G&A Special cartridge designed by Tom Siatos. They start the standard 45-caliber 500-grain bullet of the Winchester and the Weatherby at 2400 feet, splitting the difference in velocity between the other two. They thus provide almost perfect balance between power and controllability while remaining compact, relatively easy to shoot, and with a full capacity of six rounds each. I tend to favor solids for buffalo but the advice from our outfitter was to load with one soft point in the chamber and to keep five solids in reserve in the magazine. This arrangement avoids overpenetration on the first round when the animals may be standing in a bunch. Thus we used both solids and soft points, and we both used Hornady bullets.

As secondary battery, Werner brought a Ruger Mark I in 300 Winchester, loaded with Speer 180-grain spitzers. I carried a Remington 660 Carbine in 350 RM, featuring the scout elements of a long-eye-relief two-power telescope and a CW sling. I had used the 350 in Africa before with excellent results, but always with the original Remington Corelokt 250-grain spirepoint bullet. Since that ammunition is no longer made I brought hand loads this time with the 250-grain semi-spitzer steel-jacket Norma soft-point, in an attempt to find out what to do about feeding the "super scout," as we call a medium carbine, in the future.

We both carried the heavy rifles at all times, with the secondaries in reserve for camp meat, though Werner hoped for a trophy kudu if it came his way.

From our first day's outing it became apparent that ranges in Okavango could be quite a bit longer than those usually encountered in the Mopane forest and Jessie thorn that covers so much of southern Africa. The timber islands are separated by broad, grassy floodplains and if the hunter keeps to cover of the trees he may find his target far off across a dry pan or on the far side of a lagoon. I had never encountered long shots before in five African hunts, but the first round I fired on this trip was at a wildebeest at the extravagant range of 319 steps. Using a tree rest, however, this was a feasible shot and it struck solidly home. The animal ran, as animals so often do in Africa, and presently we were involved in a long, hot walk through the tall grass. By an ironic coincidence, when our chief tracker decided that it was finally time to give up pursuit the animal was permanently down within a couple of hundred yards of our position. This was a most annoying way to commence the adventure, but the hyenas found the animal in the night and we came to the conclusion that the Norma bullet was not holding together. This idea was corroborated by subsequent experience.

This failure on k'kong (the Setswana word for wildebeest, which I think is a better word) upset me somewhat since I am used to having things fall when I shoot at them. I had never met wildebeest before and was anxious to log one for camp meat, as I had been told that they are particularly good eating. It was apparent at once that, of all the beasts in the area, the k'kong has the best sight. When he runs in packs there is always a first-rate visual alert in all directions. I would estimate that he has eyes fully equal to those of an American prong-horn antelope. Thus when I was able to take one a couple of days later in a spot-and-stalk situation I was well pleased.

It happened thus: We were out at first light, chilly on top of the car and grateful for a down shirt, when we spotted the bunch nearly half-a-mile away in an open floodplain. As we

·KIRCHNER·

approached they spooked, crossing the plain into a somewhat smaller bay separating two islands of timber which offered some cover. We drove as close as we dared while they kept us under continuous observation. In the glass it appeared that the herd leader and some others were distinctly shootable, though the difference between a big wildebeest and a small one is slight.

Leaving the hunting car in plain sight, Allistair McFarlane and I moved directly away from the herd, defiladed by the car itself. As soon as we were out of sight we cut left and described a large ¾ circle, which in about twenty minutes placed us on the far side of one of the timber islands. We moved up on this, hoping that the herd had not vanished in the meantime. From a tree Allistair could see that they had started to move away from the truck but veering to the right in the direction of the timber island which now covered us. This was the luck of the chase, since from a small hillock in the island I was able to cover the passage through which the herd was about to pass.

Looking dubiously at my carbine, Allistair asked, "How accurate is that?" My response was, "As accurate as I am," which was the simple truth. Contrary to popular myth, a short barrel is no bar to precision.

It was indeed a long shot (later measured at exactly 220 steps) but from my firing point I was able to achieve a solid, textbook, sitting position, using the CW sling. The herd leader went down with one round and never moved out of his tracks, a rather uncommon event with this animal.

When we dissected out the bull we found that the bullet had shattered completely — the core separating from the jacket without sufficient integrity to exit the far side. Since a good k'kong will weigh about 400 pounds, and the 350 is designed to take animals up to 1500 pounds, this cannot be considered a satisfactory performance.

The episode on the second k'kong, however, was completely satisfactory — "*Ganz waidgerecht*" as Werner put it.

Werner had his own share of complications over the first few days but was able to bring off a very successful stalk-and-shoot on a lechwe which turned out to be absolutely sensational in size. In this case Werner made the original contact, organized the stalk, wound up with a low crawl through the high grass and killed with one round at about eighty yards. Also *ganz waidgerecht*. This bull looked larger than anything I had ever seen — even in a photograph — and when we checked the records we found that it indeed is well up amongst the top few lechwe of this type.

As day followed delectable day we never forgot that our primary objective was buffalo. They were located in bunches, mainly to the south between our camp and Maun, and each day we would take off looking for tracks or visual contacts. When we spotted a bunch we would attempt to make an approach close enough to determine whether the heads were shootable. Sometimes they would spook before we could get a clear sighting, and sometimes prolonged observation led us to conclude that we should not shoot. But each contact was an adventure in itself, and successive failures only increased the zest of the pursuit.

Werner was inclined to fill his license and thus took impala, lechwe, tsesebbe, warthog and zebra. This kept us well supplied with meat, so the only pot-shooting I did involved one impala and two k'kong. Werner did want a kudu, of which there were several prime specimens around, but the high grass made kudu hunting very difficult. In Mopane forest one can get fairly good shots in cover, but the uniform high grass of Okavango in April made it impossible to see anything except the great twin spirals above the intervening foliage. Shots under those conditions are hurried, taken from offhand, and rarely successful.

We took two pan-sized impala because I am particularly fond of impala venison, and the legendary bantu appetite for meat at the camp kept us alert for opportunities. I fear I shocked our hostess at one point by cutting a thick chunk of impala tenderloin and slicing it up to eat raw. Fresh impala tenderloin really is that good.

Making quick approaches in the tall grass can be hard on machinery. There are no rocks in Okavango but there are logs and stumps. There is also grass seed which fills radiators very quickly. We spent some of our time afield removing the radiator from the Toyota and rinsing it in lagoons. Ian opined that motor maintenance is 20% of the duty of a hunting guide in the region. He said that 50% of his job was public relations, 20% motor maintenance, 20% camp management and only 10% hunting. With competent clients the last segment fairly well takes care of itself. This is just as well since Ian's backup rifle is a double 475 for which ammunition is both scarce and expensive. The fact that he never had to shoot it was gratifying to him.

One day my granddaughter and I were poled upstream in a dugout canoe typical of the area, ostensibly looking for sitatunga and crocodiles but actually as much to see the country as anything else. We glided between palms and snaked in and out of inlets most of the day, seeking contact with "scaly wisdom hidden under lily pads." On another occasion we tried to assassinate a crocodile known to inhabit a particular pool, but he was not in at the time. The crocodile is not a game animal but rather a loathesome brute who takes as many as ten human lives a day throughout Africa — besides which I rather wanted to eat one since I had never done that before. No luck.

Our daily wanderings were a continued delight. Each morning about five, as I began to lace up my boots, my wife would ask sleepily, "What are you doing up at five o'clock?" The fact is I simply could not wait for dawn to get dressed. My feelings were those of a child on Christmas morning.

We did some catfishing by hand. Many of the floodplains had receded into mud pools as we moved southward, and while the water was rising in them daily they were still small enough so that eight-to-ten-pound cats could be heaved out onto the shore. In this we were supervised by the gorgeous fish eagle of Okavango, certainly one of the most magnificent birds in the world. He resembles the American bald eagle except that the white extends farther down his body and his shoulders are a rich russet color. His scream is the call sign for Okavango, and I recall it as I write — knowing that I will never forget it and that I must go there again.

I looked over the warthogs with some care but found none big enough to justify a shot. Allistair told me that warthogs lead a hard life in Okavango since there are so many leopards that few of them grow to a size permitting very much ivory. The giraffes were, as always, simply fantastic. No matter how many you have seen, you retain the nagging conviction that there just cannot be any such animal as that. On one occasion we were able to approach within a few feet of a baby who was strictly out of Walt Disney. It is said that only one in four giraffe young reach a size to escape further attention from predators. One can well believe it as the little creatures are stupid, innocent and clumsy all at once. This is the way of the wild.

We saw the cheetah on several occasions and once we actually saw him attack. As a bunch of impala bounded away in front of us I suddenly saw several of them change their gait from that typical floating leap into a sudden overdrive, stretched out flat and low to the ground. In the glass we could see that the form in the rear was no impala but the long, greyhound shape of the "flash-cat." It is commonly assumed that the cheetah is the fastest thing on four legs, but in this case he could not overtake the impala which, in fifth speed, was able to maintain his distance. Ian said that in all his years in the bush he had only seen the cheetah charge once before.

The great day finally came, as we had expected that it would. We were out early and made contact just before 7 a.m.

We saw them coming down a shallow draw from the right, a bunch of about sixty lunging along like a black avalanche, two hundred meters out. Tsetebbe called first but we all saw them within the same second. A squadron of running buffalo is not inconspicuous. The earth seemed to tremble under their hoofs with the sound of distant thunder.

We stopped the cruiser as quickly as we could, but the master bull had glimpsed our motion and swerved in our direction. In the glass there appeared to be at least two —possibly five — trophy bulls. As I scrambled down from the spotting seat the herd kept coming, following the leader. At a hundred meters they stopped, the master a bit to one side, tail lashing.

There it was! There was the famous buffalo glower. No sort of ox has mobile features, and this one's face is set at maturity into an expression of stolid, sullen hostility. But when he snaps that terribly armed head high and opens his eyes wide on the *qui vive*, the effect is one of unspeakable malevolence. I don't think his eyes flash red, as Stigand claims, but they might as well.

"That one on the right!" hissed Ian. "He's the biggest."

Baby swung up, the square red post of the front sight bright against the great black chest.

Too far. Too far for offhand. What to do?

> Rule: *If you can get closer, get closer.*
> *If you can get steadier, get steadier.*

No chance to do either. He is looking right at me, and any movement at all will trigger him. The shot must be taken as offered. Offhand. It can be done. He is a big target, but you can't hit a buff just anywhere. You have perhaps three seconds — and the clock is ticking.

Steady. Target angle about 300°. Shoot for the near shoulder joint. Focus on the front sight, not the target, and press the trigger *gently*. Easy now — *there*!

We speculate about an irresistible force meeting an immovable object. Something like that happened now. The 500-grain, 45 caliber bullet slammed into nearly a ton of the world's toughest muscle, sinew and bone at over thrice the speed of sound, and the *Kugelschlag*, coming back half a second later, seemed to ring louder than the explosion of ninety grains of rifle powder.

The bull reared high, and his colossal bellow almost blew my hat off. As he came down he stumbled and fell, but was up instantly so I flicked the bolt and shot again. Again came that fearful smash. He lunged to his left, impacted a twelve-inch tree, and fell. I dropped my hat to mark the shooting point and slipped two big cartridges into the piece, eyes on target.

We advanced with due caution as his cyclopean roaring continued. He tossed his head above the grass and I tried to brain him, but the shot was an instant too late and went only where the target had been. I shot again, close on his portside quarter, and again. One takes no chances with buffalo. Each of those shots was enough to kill an elephant, but he died only as the blood gradually failed his brain. *Mbogo. Nyati. Syncerus caffer* — the "joined-horned infidel." The killer ox. What a beast!

That first shot, placed as intended, killed the bull. But I didn't know that, and neither did he. As Jack Lott puts it, "With buffalo the problem is not killing them so much as giving them to understand that they have undergone a change of status." The bullet had hit the bottom of the heart and smashed the starboard shoulder, taking out both fuel pump *and* transmission. I could not have placed it more precisely with a chalk mark, but there was chance in that. At a hundred meters I will promise to hit a coffee can — given enough time and under no pressure — but not a silver dollar. And there was little time, and there was much pressure.

"I've never heard one roar like that," I said.

"It's not usual," said Ian. "They will often give a long groan as they die, but that is a different sound. I think this one wanted you. He was full of juice, probably just newly in charge of the herd and feeling very macho. You saw how he ran out in front. When you hit him he wanted to get you but he couldn't. Those bellows were pure rage."

The head was no record but still very satisfactory, classically molded with an almost solid boss and stylishly swept-back tips. Meat hooks! It looked well over forty inches but the steel tape insisted otherwise. There are bigger buff in the bundu, but this one will do very well.

One cannot "ice" a buffalo except with a brain shot, regardless of caliber. If elephant were as tough they could not be hunted with any hand-held weapon. Experienced buffalo hunters estimate that a heart shot incapacitates in about twelve minutes. Unless you can stay out of his way for twelve minutes you must break his major bones. Baby did this as intended. It was not technically a one-shot kill, but all shots after the first were physiologically superfluous.

Werner got his buff shortly thereafter, but as I was not with him at the time I cannot render a firsthand account. It was, however, a one-shot kill, broadside, delivered at about 12 paces, the 460 soft-point driving through both shoulders and bringing the animal down on his nose without dramatics.

The heads are two of a kind, Werner's being a little more massive and mine being slightly longer in the curl. They are beautiful trophies and I don't think either one of us would be disappointed if there was a mixup and we got the other's horns by mistake.

I do not care for a full head-and-shoulders mount for a buffalo since, in the first place, the trophy is too big for anything but a museum and, secondly, a buffalo is not pretty. I have various skull mounts displayed around the house, and I will now have to make room for one more, but I still haven't got a 45-incher — and that gives me leave to dream about future hunts.

It is a rule of life that anything that anyone does for long enough, no matter how pleasurable it may seem, will eventually grow wearisome. I do not doubt that this is true but I can say that a ten-day buffalo hunt, no matter how successful, will always be too short. Werner has a Spanish friend who spends sixty to ninety days annually on safari. Naturally such a man must be immensely rich, but there are a plenty of rich people who do not know how to enjoy life. I think our Spanish friend does.

Elvira, our hostess, remarked that the only thing wrong with Okavango is that it is too easy to get to. In this air age that is sadly true. It is a long, long flight but it is still accomplished in a couple of days. In justice it should take weeks of walking to reach this marvelous place — as it did when people had to hike across the Kalahari Desert with ox carts. It should remain fairly clean for some time as long as the present system of concessions is maintained. The danger on the horizon is not from over-hunting but rather from the march of civilization. Southern Africa is an arid country and its population is expanding rapidly. The scientists are already thinking up ways to move all that crystal water from the Okavango delta to places where it can be used for irrigation and the other needs of settlers. The delta may last in its present form — the same form it has had since before man walked erect — for another twenty, thirty or fifty years, but unless the population growth of the world is violently arrested by nuclear means it will not last another lifetime as long as mine.

The Okavango adventure is by no means inexpensive. In fact its cost is intimidating to people of average means. Nonetheless it is perhaps the only luxury that I deem worth borrowing money to obtain. Only a few can afford it, and only a few can appreciate it, but those few had best make their plans while they still can.

The experience is as close to paradise as one can get without dying.

RIFLE HANDLING
UNDER HAZARD

The hunting of dangerous game is addictive. After having become hooked on (fortunately not by) buffalo in these my later years, I have taken to re-reading all the old sources that I can locate — between trips to Africa. Some of this writing is superb. Some is passable. Some is inferior. And quite a bit is downright egregious. All is interesting — one way or another. While many adventurers who have made a hobby of dangerous game seem to be telling the truth, others are misinformed, or overly credulous, or inferior observers — and some are just liars. Having now been in at the death of a dozen buffalo and three elephant, I have just enough experience to understand what the old hands were writing about, and the comparison of the works of these men has been a revelation into the mind of the adventurer. One could prepare a fascinating doctoral dissertation on "buffalo writing" alone, and preparing it would be an enjoyable piece of research.

The subject of this present piece, however, is gunhandling. It is an important subject, for a close study of episodes in which hunters and others have been killed or seriously injured by dangerous animals suggests that faulty gunhandling is a major part of the problem.

Hunters seldom fall to a dangerous beast, but when one does it is a newsworthy event. We hear all about these incidents (not "accidents," for the beast was usually doing it on purpose), so we have a good bit of information with which to work.

There are several reasons why a man may be caught by a game animal. He may be a bad shot. He may be using an inadequate weapon. He may lose his nerve. But, in a surprising number of cases, it seems to be *because he does not know how to manage his rifle*. His marksmanship may be good enough, but his gunhandling is completely unsatisfactory.

What shall we say of the hunter who cannot work his safety correctly? What shall we say of the hunter who attempts action with an unloaded gun? What shall we say of the hunter who fires by mistake when he steps in an ant-bear hole? What shall we say of the hunter whose weapon fails because it was improperly cared for? Above all, what shall we say of the hunter, professional or amateur, who takes after a potentially lethal beast without having troubled to educate himself in the management of his weapon?

It may be that this curious situation exists because hunters are by definition "sportsmen," not warriors. The hunter who is both is something of a rarity. The normal precautions taken by an experienced fighting man — especially one experienced in this current World War III in which we are engulfed — sometimes seem onerous to an inexperienced man who is simply trying to enjoy a pleasant vacation. Such a man is unlikely to prepare himself for unexpected action. He feels that life should be orderly, and one should not involve oneself in conflict except on those occasions where everything is prepared and in order. The fact is that something deadly may come to you at any time, either on the streets of a big city or in the African bush. One is no more justified in dropping his guard in one than in the other.

I notice a strong tendency among experienced African hunters to do just that. I have seen them wandering around camp *without their rifles*! A careful perusal of writings on dangerous game will reveal an astonishing number of cases in which a man was mauled simply because he was unarmed.

One such incident came to my attention just last year. A friend had been successful on wildebeest and had, after taking pictures, handed his rifle to one of the crew to be placed in the rack on the hunting car. Then, while he was admiring the scenery, he was blind-sided by — of all things — a hippopotamus. He is lucky to be alive, but he will not walk again.

Part of this problem lies in the lack of awareness of the situation on the part of the hunter, and part on his lack of understanding of what he should do to protect himself when he is aware.

I offer the following suggestions, therefore, as a means not only of staying out of trouble, but also as a means of staying out of embarrassment, which may, in some cases, be worse:

a) Learn how to operate the safety on your rifle. There are a number of old hands who have given up on safeties, and simply do not use them under any circumstance. This is probably not the right answer. When I am preparing for an African hunt, I sit every evening for a time in front of the televisor, with my rifle across my knees, safety on. Whenever a printed announcement or advertisement appears on the screen, I engage all the O's in the inscription as rapidly as I can. The safety comes off as the rifle moves into battery. I press the trigger on the first O, snap the bolt, and engage the second O before the inscription changes, trying for a clean, precise sight picture and a surprise break on each press. I do this for about half-an-hour a day for the best part of a month. In the field, I do not miss the safety, and my bolt work is rapid.

b) I note that a good many hunters of dangerous beasts seem unaware of Rule Three, which is "Keep your finger off the trigger until your sights are on the target." A man creeping into dense brush after a wounded buffalo or a lion, with his safety off and his finger on the trigger, is a classic example of "an accident looking for a place to happen." You cannot mount your rifle as fast as you can take the safety off and engage the trigger. Try it! But you must practice safety operation and quick mounting enough to make this operation automatic.

In a recent anthology of buffalo stories, a professional told of a time in which he fell down an ant-bear hole in an action, and simply fired his rifle into the air by mistake. He wasn't even embarrassed.

c) For the man who uses a bolt action rifle (and that includes most of us) the instantaneous, smooth, dependable operation of the bolt is essential. When this is done correctly, the weapon is reloaded by the time the front sight gets back on the target after recoil. This dexterity does not come naturally. It must be cultivated. It calls for a powerful stroke, which must be practiced powerfully. I know one hunter who very nearly came to grief when facing an elephant at a distance of eleven steps, because, after having placed his first shot too low, he worked the bolt gently and did not pick up the second cartridge. His backup saved his life. Not only should the bolt be withdrawn with great force, it must be closed the same way. A bolt handle which is not fully depressed on loading may cause a misfire.

If the second form of reloading is used, which is known as the "shoot-one-load-one" technique, the butt will come out of the shoulder as the bolt opens, and the weapon will be reloaded manually with a spare cartridge, *while the shooter keeps his eyes on the target.* This is not the usual action when confronting something which is trying to kill you at close range, but the occasion does arise — and especially on buffalo. Modern bolt action rifles tend to have reduced magazine capacities in the major calibers, and buffalo are so tough that it is quite possible to hit one several times and still be in need of more ammunition. The prospective hunter should practice the shoot-one-load-one system — using his big rifle and keeping his eyes on the target — until this action, too, becomes reflexive and automatic.

d) Not many people understand the proper ready position for the rapid mounting of a heavy rifle. The most efficient system is derived from the shotgunner, and in it the rifle is carried with the butt at the waist, the safety on, the thumb on the safety, and the trigger-finger outside the trigger-guard, while the muzzle is placed exactly where the eyes of the hunter are searching. As the hunter shifts his gaze from right to left, that muzzle stays right with it, so that if something turns up, the only motion of the rifle will be straight forward and not sideways. On this quick mount, the front sight slides directly ahead as the butt comes to the shoulder. As the butt leaves the body, the safety is pushed off and the finger is inserted in the trigger-guard, so that at the very instant that the shooter can pick up his sight picture against his target he is ready to go. A reasonably good shot can learn to deliver his bullet into a four-inch circle at 25 meters in one-and-a-half seconds, using this technique. A particularly good man can cut that down by a half second. This stroke should be practiced until perfect, with a heavy gun, before the hunter takes the field after anything which can kill him.

e) Many African hunters of wide experience disdain the sling — and many experienced African hunters hand their heavy rifle to the hired help to carry until they think they have a problem. The two attitudes are related. In almost half the cases we can research in which a hunter was mauled, somebody *else* had his gun. This should tell us something. The careful hunter carries his own gun at all times, and if there are two rifles available — the second a light gun to be used for camp meat should the occasion arise — the hunter carries the heavy, and lets his henchman carry the light — never the other way around. There is no problem in swapping your heavy for a light if you suddenly want an impala or a wart hog, but there may be considerable trouble swapping the light for the heavy when you are suddenly confronted with something huge, black, and angry, just a few yards away.

This is why I fancy the sling. It is most convenient on that long walk back to the car, and remember that just because you have tagged out is no reason to think that the campaign is over. The modern CW sling, with its flush detachable mounting system, is ideal for your heavy rifle — there when you want it and instantly removed when entering thick brush.

f) Regardless of what anybody may say — professional, amateur, or blood relative — do not become separated from that big gun! The heavy stays with you while you hike, while you stalk, while you crawl, and while you take pictures. It also stays with you going to and from the hunting car, going to and from the bushes for the call of nature, and going to and from the fire circle for the evening sundowner. A friend once told me that he had seen a full-grown lion come right up to the edge of the fire circle, apparently for cocktails, only a year previously. *As he told me this, his rifle was in his tent.* Mine was leaning against a tree about eighteen inches from where I sat.

Perhaps you remember the story about the tycoon who, when asked the secret of his success, replied: "Well, when I was twenty-one years old, my father called me into his office and said, 'Son, here is a million dollars. Don't lose it!' " In parallel we may say that when you are afield or in camp after dangerous game, "Here is your heavy rifle. Don't lose it!"

g) I recently read of a professional who met with near-disaster because when he and his client fired neither could force open the bolt of either rifle. It turns out that this hunter had handed the rifles to the hired help the night before for cleaning, and the bolts had been interchanged. Both rifles were of the same make, but they were of different calibers. The bolts fit, but the cartridges did not. Lesson: Do not give your rifle to anyone else to handle, maintain, or clean. Do it yourself. The colonials were always great ones for giving such menial labor as cleaning a gun, or carrying a gun, to a servant. Innumerable mishaps can be laid to this foolish custom.

h) In the field your heavy rifle should be carried fully loaded, with a round in the chamber, magazine full, and the safety on. Your light rifle may be carried with a full magazine but nothing in the chamber. Spare ammunition should be carried, by choice, in a butt-cuff on the stock, except with the Mannlichers, in which case it is carried in full spare magazine in the pocket. Do not count on any help. Spare ammunition carried by someone else is a weak reed indeed.

In camp, the light rifle may be unloaded, but the heavy rifle should be kept with its magazine full, with the chamber empty and the striker forward. A good place for your heavy rifle in camp, while you are yarning or dining, is hung by its sling strap, muzzle down, on a tree limb or a heavy nail. In some climatic conditions thought should be given to keeping the muzzle protected against water, sand, or small varmints. (A 45 or 50 caliber muzzle is big. All sorts of things can crawl into it if you are not careful.)

i) For the hunter using a double rifle, and who prefers to unload his weapon in camp, one good place for those two spare cartridges is inserted into the muzzles as the rifle is leaned against a tree. This means that in an emergency a hunter can grab the rifle with one hand and two rounds with the other and be fully ready. This system can also be used, of course, on single-barrelled rifles, but for them I rather prefer one of those rubber thumb-caps available at any stationery store for use in sorting papers.

The foregoing admonitions are the result of a lot of reading, plus some personal experience. In most cases, they are self-evident, and hardly to be controverted by any amount of erroneous adventure. Napoleon is said to have remarked about one of his generals, who had a great deal of experience, that his kitchen mule had been through forty campaigns — but he was still a mule. A man may have killed a hundred buffalo, but if he hands his rifle to a henchman who scuttles off with it in an emergency, the hundred-and-first may very well kill him. As Bismarck put it, "A fool must learn by his own experience. I prefer to learn by the experiences of others."

The great safari days are indeed over, but the hunting of dangerous game is not so esoteric a pastime as some may think. Just now, for example, the buffalo are still plentiful in Africa. There are also lions and elephants — and leopards are all over the place. Tigers may be nearly extinct in India, but not over east across the Bay of Bengal. There are *tak-san* tigers in Thailand still, and there are also the great bears of the North. It may even be said that the pursuit of dangerous game is experiencing a sort of comeback in this decade. It may not last forever, but it is there now, and a man who has followed a wounded buffalo into thick brush knows several things more about life than a man who has not. The best advice remains, however, "If you are going to do it, do it right!"

LION

On this trip I did not score on lions, so there can be no talk about color, configuration, shooting exploits or impact ballistics, but I was in intimate contact on three different occasions, and I can truly say that playing tag with the king of beasts, in thick bush, is an exhilarating experience. I did not shoot because I never got a viable shot, but the hunting was great fun. The trophy collector may call it sour grapes, but there are those of us who really do believe that the thrill is in the chase itself rather than its conclusion. Naturally I would have preferred the drama of the shot, but I cannot consider the pursuit as time wasted. Just as every general election is a *qualified* failure, every hunt is a *qualified* success. And of course, I have an excellent excuse to go back and try again.

Now why should anyone want to shoot a lion? Good question. He is not much of a trophy, and I am told he is not good to eat. He is no longer the actual hazard to human life that he has been throughout the ages, though that element has not entirely disappeared. Lions do kill and eat people with fair regularity, and more frequently now than fifty years ago due to the proliferation of bush wars in their habitat. Such wars are apt to leave the forest cluttered with dead or dying soldiers, and night security posts place troops out there on the line where the lion has every advantage. Nevertheless one does not now set forth to shoot a lion because of the fear that if he does not the lion will eat him. He does not often shoot lions to protect his stock, because in those parts of Africa where stock-raising is successful the lions have gone the way of all things which interfere with the march of man. I believe that one pursues the lion because of the legend. The lion is *king*. He is strong and terrible. His roar proclaims him, and makes even rifle-wielding man feel humble. His arrogance is intimidating, and his courage is such that even in the space age an extraordinarily brave man is referred to as "lion hearted." He is not cute, and he is not a friend. He is fearfully savage among his own kind as well as to his prey. He is one of God's mightiest killing machines, and he constitutes a noble adversary. Even in our current blasé era the killing of a full-grown, wild lion by fair means, on the ground, is an event to quicken the heart and raise the spirit. The elephant is majestic, the buffalo is grim, the leopard is sinister, but only the lion rates champagne.

Lion stories are part of our heritage, dating back to the ancient world. Hercules wore the skin of a lion as his official uniform, and the terrible kings of Assyria boasted more of their skill at killing lions than of their conquests of nations. Today the best campfire stories are lion stories, and each good one seems to produce a better one to top it. One of my own favorites is that of John Gannaway, whose tale is very modern in that it involves the lion's assault on a four-wheel vehicle. It seems that John and his professional hunter were cruising along looking for other game when they spotted a large prime male moving off into a clump of brush. John had no lion license, but he thought this might be a good chance to get some pictures. The lion apparently thought so too since, as the car approached the clump of brush, he took strong umbrage and roared. "Too close" was the idea that occurred to both John and his hunter at the same time, as they stopped and attempted to turn around. As the car was broadside the cat came on. This was not in accordance with the planned scenario, and no rifle was ready. Before the driver could shift from reverse into low the lion was in the truck-bed. Between the truck-bed and the front seat was the spare wheel, and this is what the lion chose. As the car picked up speed he tore the spare tire to shreds, bending the wheel and breaking a couple of teeth in the process. John, unarmed, watched him do this at a range of eighteen inches.

"Pretty big lion?" I asked him later.

"Oh, I'd say about twenty inches."

"Twenty inches?"

"Between the eyes!"

Having disposed of the spare wheel, and making his mouth sore, the lion bounced out and ran off, cursing under his breath. Said John, "I wouldn't take a million dollars for that experience — *but let's not do it again!*"

The Tamafuta country, in the extreme northeast corner of Botswana, is flat, dry, sandy, and shadeless. It is covered mainly with Mopane scrub from six to eight feet high. Full-sized trees are not the rule, and visibility at ground level averages between five and twenty paces. In such country the only hunting method is tracking. Baiting is illegal in Botswana, which is all right with me for I dislike sitting up at night. The brush is too thick for spotting, and still-hunting is out of the question. As everywhere, there is a chance of just happening on to a lion, but this is not something to be expected. So the system is to ride the trails in the hunting car until a track is picked up, and then to follow it with a Bushman.

I suppose there are people who can track a lion as well as a Bushman, just as those who can speak French as well as a Frenchman, but such are most unusual. The Bushman's tracking skill is legendary, and as far as I can tell the legends are true. The Bushman does not move from sign to sign the way I have to, but rather he senses the passage of the beast through the bush in a way that is part physical and part spiritual. His cultural tradition is to understand the wild, and when he picks up a track he seems to put himself in the mental condition of the animal he is following, and to move as he thinks the animal should. He occasionally loses a track completely, and from time to time he actually sees a paw print, but for the most part he slips silently through the bush at a walking pace with the apparent assurance that his quarry is doing what it ought to do. All hunting for lion and buffalo in the Tamafuta country is conducted this way, and it is remarkably productive. The fact that I struck out on lion is just one of those things, and should not be taken as representative. The lions are there, but as in all hunting luck is a vital force.

The best time for this sort of pursuit is mid-day, since that is when the beasts tend to seek what scarce shade there is and sleep off their morning meal. Since distances are necessarily short, and the lion's senses are keen, walking him down when he is on his feet is nearly impossible — as we found.

My own first contact was not nearly so dramatic as Gannaway's, but it seemed stimulating enough at the time. We picked up the prints of a big prime male, and a somewhat less impressive male companion. The Bushmen read these things instantly, and I found out later that as the lion grows bigger he walks increasingly on his toes, leaving a track broader than it is long. A lioness, by contrast, leaves a round foot-print. The excitement of the Bushmen was quite evident, and it increased as the track led us right through the middle of a scattered herd of about thirty elephant. At this point Ian, my host, exchanged the soft-points in his double rifle for solids, since we were close enough to the elephants to exasperate them if the wind blew suddenly wrong. I could not back him up since I had no solids for the 360. Threading our way through this bunch of elephants, on the very fresh track of a big lion, was invigorating. I had time to reflect that this sort of thing was exactly what I had come for, and that I should take pains to soak it up emotionally.

We continued the march for about an hour, and then they spotted us. We did *not* spot them, but the Bushmen showed us, by easily decipherable hand signals, where they had been when they saw us, and what they had done. The element of surprise had been lost, along with any chance of catching them asleep, but we followed anyway in the hope that some sort of unforeseeable circumstance might give us a shot. About our only chance from that point forward was to annoy them sufficiently to provoke an attack. I was hoping to hear the warning growl of a lion who knows he is being followed, which says so unmistakably "Back off!" — but none came. The beasts obviously did not want to leave the vicinity, and so we commenced a game of "figure-eight," by which they could always pick up our scent from some direction no matter which way the wind was blowing. The Bushmen would point now and then very much like a bird dog, but I must admit that though my eyesight is still quite keen I never saw anything that I could identify as lion skin. Twice the Bushmen pointed out large wet spots in the sand where the cats had just urinated. Several times they pointed out with their hands "They saw us from here," or "They winded us from here." More frequently they signaled "They are just there!" And so they were, but at a distance of thirty paces when visibility was confined to about ten.

We kept this up all day. I find it hard to believe in retrospect, but we stayed something over eight hours on that trail. According to everything I had heard, the lions would lose patience before we would and charge. I kept my thumb on the safety and my finger straight, just outside the trigger-guard, and was careful to keep the muzzle pointing wherever I looked. On one occasion a bunch of sand grouse burst out from just underfoot, and the butt hit my shoulder even though I had no target. It was delightful to see how marvelously those Bushmen could disappear. I did not see it happen, for I was thinking of other things, but I do believe that they both were flat on the ground before my rifle moved.

Finally the two took a straight line downwind and away from us, and as it seemed clear, after a whole day of this activity, that we could neither spot them nor provoke them in that terrain, we gave up the chase. I feel sure that both Ian and the Bushmen could have kept it up until full dark, but I am not embarrassed to admit that I was bushed, and we were a good two hours by car from camp. I was tired, but not depressed. This was only the second day of my hunt, and I had weeks ahead of me. What a way to spend a day!

We stayed for a full week in the Tamafuta country hunting buffalo, and during that time we picked up another lion contact which led us straight into the Chobe National Park, where hunting is forbidden. Close, but no cigar!

There was always the hope of a "pop-up," and we never dropped our guard — even in camp. My practice of keeping my rifle at hand while in camp may seem somewhat affected to some people, but I have heard too many camp stories to take a chance on being caught with my trousers at the dip. As a very junior Marine I was strongly impressed, by a distinguished officer who later became Commandant of the Marine Corps, that there is no forgiveness in this world or the next for being caught by surprise. I would rather look foolish than be damned.

Having done very well in the Tamafuta country on buffalo and sable, we moved the hunt to the Okavango Delta, where the country is much prettier and the chances for lion are just about the same. In the Delta I made another contact, and had another excellent hunt without a successful conclusion. We called this one off on purpose because we found as we proceeded that we were involved with a family — a prime male, a lioness, and three cubs. Again we were in very thick brush and the situation became very tense, but our only chance was for the male to separate from his dependents, which is not an uncommon move. He did not choose to do this, and we became more and more concerned lest the lioness opt to charge. If she had done so it would have been necessary to shoot her, leaving the cubs at the mercy of the old man — who would doubtless have eaten them. We glimpsed the lioness and the cubs, but not the boss. Since a lioness is about twice as likely to charge as a lion (according to Kipling, among others), we elected to disengage and let the matter drop. Another splendid day with no score.

I only picked up one more track in the Delta, and this was that of a large solitary male with whom we could not close before he entered the marsh that was the main channel, and scraped us off with ten feet of water which was home to a good number of both crocodiles and hippos. The lion was evidently unconcerned about crocodiles, but I could not say the same about myself.

As luck would have it, the only pop-up lion of this excursion was met in the Tamafuta country the day after we left it.

This lion — a very big one — was just suddenly there right in front of a client with a professional hunter who were looking for buffalo. There was no time to get organized, and the client, using a 375 Model 70 with solids, socked the lion in the ribs at a range of about thirty-five yards. He was understandably annoyed at this and came right up the gun, breathing fire and smoke according to the client, who worked the bolt as fast as he could, and in so doing threw the three-position safety to mid-point — rendering the gun inoperable. Ronnie, the professional, terminated the lion with his 416 at a range of a few feet, leaving the client more than somewhat shaken. He told me later that he never intended to hunt lions again with anything but a double-gun, which viewpoint does not make a lot of sense to me but apparently satisfied him. He was almost killed, not because he was using a bolt action weapon, but because: (a) he did not place his first shot properly, and (b) he was not properly familiar with the action of his own gun. Ronnie's 416 was, of course, a bolt action weapon, and it was that which saved his client's life.

If I am fortunate enough to hunt lions again I will continue to use the 360 with the 250-grain Swift "H-Mantle" bullets. I am determined to place my first shot properly and if — perish forbid — I fail with that first shot, I feel that I can brain the beast as well with a 360 as I could with a heavy rifle. If something goes wrong with another hunter, and I am invited to back him up on a wounded beast, I will, of course, take Baby and use soft points.

Lions are great, and I will hunt them again if luck is with me. As our family is a hotbed of cat-fanciers my daughter took some exception when she learned that I was going to take after lions on this trip. I handed her a copy of Capstick's "Death in the Long Grass," and when she returned it she told me that she now understood and would therefore forgive me. She did not have to, of course, because I did not score, but, as they say in the sporting world — "Wait till next year!"

CROCODILE

"All creatures great and small: The Lord God made them all." Indeed. But the ways of the Lord are beyond our understanding, and when He made the rabies virus and the hagfish — and the crocodile — He was being even less understandable than usual.

The crocodile is a singularly unpleasant beast. He positively radiates evil, whether lying in prehistoric sloth on the mud, growling and snapping in rage, silently watching at periscope depth, or streaking to attack. In Africa he kills about ten people a day throughout the continent, and his total in India, Southeast Asia, and Oceania may well be greater. There are those who warn us that he is an "endangered species," though they do not seem to have been to the same places I have, but to a good many people it may appear that he is not endangered enough.

No death is pleasant, but the death dealt by the crocodile is particularly horrifying. His jaws are so arranged that he can neither shear nor masticate. They are tongs, serving only to seize. His gullet is relatively small, and he cannot chew, so he must reduce his prey to gulp-size portions. He does this by rotting it. He grabs his victim and drowns it, then he stacks it somewhere under water until it is putrid enough to pull apart. Thus his victim dies in terrible pain and utter despair: there is full consciousness, and there is no escape. He will not let go. This is the end. Nothing can save you.

The absolute finality of the crocodile attack is shocking. Witnesses all tell of an awful feeling of helplessness. There is a splash, a cry, and that is it. Your companion is still alive, knowing that he is about to die, and you can do exactly nothing to save him. You cannot shoot. You cannot call for help. You cannot dash into the water and swim after him. (Actually you can do those things, but to no purpose whatever.) All you can do is finish your coffee.

Anyone who has experienced this is unlikely to worry much about a dwindling crocodile population.

The crocodile grows quickly to a length of six or eight feet, and then begins to slow down. Beyond ten feet his length increases very slowly, but his girth and bulk enlarge for the rest of his life, which can be long. You hear talk of eighteen- and twenty-foot giants, but these are seldom actually measured.

Probably the best system for gauging a croc's length is the Dinwiddie Method — also used for the weight of Alaskan bears and the height of the surf. You divide your first guess by two and add one. Thus a recently reported twenty-four footer would come on at thirteen — half of twenty-four plus one.

The saltwater crocodile of Oceania is reported to grow distinctly larger than the African variety, but from the standpoint of his victim this hardly matters. A ten-foot croc can kill you. A fourteen-footer can just kill you more easily. On my last visit to Africa I saw no very big crocodiles, but I saw the hand-print of one that was exactly twice as broad as those of the one I shot.

Oddly enough, crocodiles do quite a bit of overland traveling in the Okavango Delta when the water is low. They move from channel to channel straight across the country, guided by some sort of water-homing sense that is not at this time understood. Their tracks are unmistakable, with curious demon-hand prints straddling the sinuous groove of the tail.

The BaYei — the water people — live with the crocodile, and because they are more careful than other tribes their casualty list is not high. When a particularly big crocodile becomes an intolerable burden they have a curious way of dealing with him. They cut a buffalo hide into one long continuous spiral strip. ("First catch your buffalo.") This strip is about one-and-a-half inches broad and perhaps sixty feet long. To one end they tie a couple of pounds of spoiled meat, and leave it in the water's edge. If the plan works the croc swallows the meat and eight or ten feet of the hide strip, but he cannot get the rest of it down. He cannot bite the strip off because his teeth are not arranged that way, and he cannot close his gullet because the strip holds it open. Thus when he submerges he drowns. As with all best laid plans, this one does not always work, but the BaYei feel it is worth a try, assuming that they can organize that buffalo, which is no minor operation.

Early African travelers regarded the crocodile as a dangerous monster — in no sense a game animal — and today if you tell your professional hunter that you wish to gather one up he eyes you askance. While crocs are by no means scarce they are difficult to hunt, and even more difficult to secure once you have shot one. They offer nothing much in the way of a trophy, and they are not regarded as edible. They do provide excellent leather, but at the time of writing crocodile leather is considered contraband in the western world. One answer to this is to have your crocodile skin fabricated into artifacts such as luggage, boots, or clothing in the country where you take him, and to come back and use such things on your next visit.

Since crocodile hunting is time-consuming and generally unproductive — unless you jack-light and harpoon the beasts at night — I have done very little of it, but in Okavango in 1987 I secured a license and decided to give the matter proper attention. At that time the water level was down and pools could be scouted with care. These scouting visits were most interesting, and conducted with great stealth. The croc likes to bask mornings and evenings, and while he appears to have all the alertness of a dead tree, his senses are remarkably keen. You approach each pool under cover of bordering vegetation, and crawl to a position from which you can search the surface of the water with your binoculars. You are distracted by five- and six-footers, which are just as alert as the big ones and can spook the whole group if they sense your presence. When in the water their aura of evil intensifies. The still, blue surface of the pool is smooth as oil, and as you traverse your binoculars you notice at the edge of the field-of-view something that was not there before. There is no splash, there is no swirl, no disturbance in the water, but suddenly there is just this black protrusion. It barely breaks the surface of the water, but it is symmetrical, with a slight rise at each end. As you focus in on it it disappears. Again, no splash, no ripple, no sound. You scan, and he scans. The silence is deafening. You cannot engage the target he offers, but you can use it to estimate his size. If your spread hand will just measure the distance between his eyes you have got something worth noticing. Since you cannot shoot, you wait — and he waits. You can stick around as long as you wish, but usually you decide to go hunt something else and come back to try this pool again tomorrow.

The crocodile is hard to kill. His sluggish nervous system is not susceptible to shock, and a fatal body wound is not sufficient to anchor him before he gets under water. He must be shot in the brain or in the cervical portion of the spine. The brain is about the size of a walnut, and it is buried down there in the bony structure of that prehistoric head. A shot straight into the stubby neck from directly to one side may cut the spine, but the target angle must be exactly right. A heavy rifle is not necessary as long as there is sufficient penetration to traverse the beast through. A 500-grain bullet in his brain will kill him no deader than a 150.

We set out up the main channel of the Okavango River in two mocoros. These vessels are dugout canoes each hollowed out of one log and propelled by a pole. They are notably unstable and show about two inches of freeboard. One rides carefully. A certain zest was added to the venture by the presence of a good number of hippos, which can become highly excited if surprised in the reeds. A nervous hippo can quite easily bite a mocoro in half, and we saw the remains of one that had been treated just that way the year before.

We traveled this way for about an hour-and-a-half without sighting anything, and beached ourselves at an island where the heavy vegetation gave us the chance to approach the waterway on foot and under cover. From our third spying point we made contact. Across the river, at a distance rather too great for the type of delicate shooting necessary, two crocs were basking on the sand bank. One was too small, but the other was quite a lot bigger. Whether he was big enough was difficult to say, since he was lying almost straight away from us and no nearby objects gave us any index of dimension. Our observation point was constricted, offering a view to only one person at a time. As usual in that part of the world it was based upon the ever present termite castle, which offered a perch for one foot only where a fairly large tree grew up out of one side. By placing my left foot in the notch between the slope of the anthill and the tree I could rest my left elbow on my knee, loop the CW sling, and align the rifle through the leaves, with my right elbow steadied on the tree trunk. The problem was my right foot, which was more or less in empty air. I could touch the ground with it, but in no way provide any support on a slippery slope of forty-five degrees. An additional complication was the screen of vegetation between me and the croc, which moved gently back and forth, sometimes offering a shot and sometimes not. This was an essentially unsatisfactory firing position, and under other circumstances I might have passed the opportunity by, but this was my fourth try for crocodile, and I had no assurance that anything better would offer itself.

While I was waiting out the situation, and hoping the croc would turn a bit so I could see him better, Ian and Steve tried to move to a more satisfactory firing point. Since we could not make a sound I was unable to tell if their shooting position was any better than mine. As it happened Steve did find a point from which he could achieve a solid sitting position with loop sling in place, but he still could not see the beast well enough to shoot, and I was the one who had the crocodile ticket.

I do not know how long we waited. I did not look at my watch, but the croc did not move, and I suppose we could have sat there until sundown. The target angle was about 165 degrees, and though I was shooting from a somewhat elevated position the curve of his back rose enough to protect the spot down between his horns where I supposed his brain to be. It might have been better to wait it out, especially since he did not appear to be a particularly large beast, but finally my patience ran out and I hoisted the Baker flag.

I was using "Fireplug IV," an enlarged scout rifle taking the 360 Short Magnum cartridge, loaded with the 250-grain Swift bullet starting at about 2500 f/s. The shot (as we discovered later, of course) just skimmed the scales of his back, hit at the back of his neck and passed beneath the brain, exiting from the lower jaw. It did not touch the spinal cord nor the brain, so it did not stop him. He thrashed sideways, and as he moved Steve shot him through the barrel with the 270/150, a foot or so abaft the forelegs. And then he was in the water.

It is an axiom that if you do not anchor a crocodile he is gone. Once he gets to the water you will never find him again. But in this case it was Steve's shot that saved the day, since it took him through the lungs and ruined his diving system.

We crossed the river as quickly as possible in the two dugouts, without any great expectations. However, as we approached the far bank we saw bubbles. Now the pursuit took on the aspect of a submarine chase. At intervals swirls of bubbles would appear on the still surface of the river and we would steer toward them, exactly like two corvettes chasing for the oil slick of a stricken submarine. Finally there was a swirl in the water some fifteen feet away, and a long reptilian snout shot straight up, whirled once, and subsided. Not enough protruded to expose the brain, so we did not shoot again. In any case the croc was dead on the bottom in about four-and-a-half feet of water. Since we knew exactly where he was we were able to fish him out with hook poles and drag him ashore. He was no giant, measuring just a click under ten feet, but his jaws were murderous jaws, and he could quite easily kill a six-foot man.

It is traditional that crocodiles give off a foul odor, but this one was completely free of any scent that we could detect. It is probably the stomach of the crocodile, which he prefers to keep full of rotten meat, that produces the stench, so until he is cut open or regurgitates he gives off no smell whatever.

This was no special triumph, but still I found it satisfying, and I will try again for a bigger one when the occasion affords. The shot was particularly difficult, at an estimated 135 meters, because of the difficult target angle, the tiny target, and the unstable firing position. Though it did not hit the brain it went where I wanted it to go, and the error was one of anatomical analysis rather than marksmanship. The belly skin was in perfect shape, and is being made up into a briefcase which I will be able to use in Africa, whether or not I can import it into the United States later as "finished goods."

We took a portion of the tenderloin and ate it that night. As with most reptiles the meat was white and bland, with no particular flavor. As with frog, or lizard, or turtle, it tasted like whatever you put on it, from salt-and-pepper to chili sauce. The portion we had was rather tough, but that is to be expected of fresh meat, and I think that it would be quite good to eat if it were tenderized in some way such as pounding or pressure-cooking.

The crocodile is a challenging quarry, regardless of his status as vermin rather than game. He is harder to hunt than all but the most difficult of the antelope, and while he is not dangerous to the hunter he certainly is dangerous to the general population.

It is interesting to speculate about whether the crocodile attack can be forestalled by ready gunfire. From a study of recent cases reported in the press it appears that there is quite often some warning, if not very much. When the American model, Ginger Meadows, was taken in Australia in 1987, her companion is said to have shouted "Get out of the water!" twice before the girl was hit. If that report is true it indicates an interval of about three seconds, perhaps four, during which the croc could have been shot if a weapon had been ready. Other cases are parallel, and suggest that while a rifle will hardly be in hand, a pistol on the belt might be the answer. Since there are no such cases on record it is difficult to judge whether a crocodile would be deflected from his purpose by a bullet wound to his head, but I would guess that it might, since valor is not a characteristic of the reptilian brain.

The presence of crocodile is not an absolute bar to water-sports, but it definitely calls for precautions. If the water is clear, and can be scouted for some distance and riflemen are posted as guards, the situation can be kept under control. However, if you are not willing to take such precautions you had best bear in mind the injunction contained in the old pioneer jingle:

" 'Mother may I go out to swim?'
'Yes, my darling daughter.
Hang your clothes on a hickory limb,
But don't go near the water.' "

BIRTHDAY PRESENT

The thing that perplexes me about the whole episode is that I cannot remember it accurately. I cannot now, some weeks after the fact, and I could not at the time, either. There is a hole in my memory of the events at the moment of truth that I simply cannot fill.

We had started out looking for gemsbok, but a little after eight we cut the trail of a nice bunch of buff. There appeared to be about seven, and one in particular had enormous hoofs, which suggested, without promising, a splendid head. The terrain was not bad for walking, with visibility a little better than usual, but a light and shifting breeze which made walking comfortable made following impossible. We made visual contact in about an hour, but a shift in the wind gave us away, and the buff simply walked on ahead, downwind and just out of sight. Every time the wind shifted they changed direction, keeping it dead-astern so they could maintain a 200-yard interval without hurrying. After about two hours of this the Bushmen suggested we call off the pursuit. Tracking was easy, but the buffalo could keep up this routine forever, and we would never get a shot.

The walk back to the car would have taken us the rest of the morning so we decided on another plan. To the east lay a series of waterpans, mainly dry, but with just enough moisture to attract buffalo. In this area the wind had steadied down and now was holding firm at right angles to the axis of the water line. Thus we moved from pan to pan with the wind on our right flank. At eleven-thirty we cut the track of a large bunch of buff moving away from us at right angles and directly upwind. The Bushmen cannot lose a trail once they have picked it up, and the situation looked good, except that the cover had closed to zero visibility — five to ten paces. After no more than twenty minutes on this trail we made contact, but it was not a good contact. The buff had bedded down in dense Mopane scrub about eight feet high. At this time of day buffalo normally seek shade, but there is no shade in the Tamafuta country. It was clear that there was quite a number of them, but all that could be seen was a patch of black here and there, and the curve of a horn. We worked up with extreme caution to a small anthill, the base of which enabled us to get a little elevation. From this point I could make out, just ahead, the head of a very large bull, lying down at a target angle of about 315 degrees. He was the only animal I could see clearly, and I could not see any of his body. He was distinctly shootable, and I pushed the "Go!" button. The range was thirty-five paces, but my firing position was very unstable. It was sort of a "jackass offhand," since my feet were insecurely placed on the slopes of the anthill, and I could not stand erect because of overhanging brush. I remember telling myself to be instantly ready with the second shot if it were needed. I remember the red post of the front sight steadying just between the ear and the eye.

"Front sight, press. Gently! Press!"

At Baby's solid roar I snapped the bolt just as fast as I could. As the great rifle came back on target I saw the bull scrambling to his feet, and I realized that something had gone wrong with the first shot. The second shot took him in the ribs as he whirled away and vanished.

"Blew it. *DAMN!* "

But Ian and the two Bushmen were making all sorts of happy noises.

"You got him! He's a beauty!"

?????

Thoroughly confused, I ran forward with four more rounds still ready in the rifle. There at my feet, quite dead, was a very big bull, but he could not have been the one I saw getting to his feet because he was facing toward me, and I had seen him vanish in another direction.

The boys were shouting, "Numbah two! Numbah two!" and pointing off to left-front.

The light dawned. The buffalo I had shot at first was killed so instantly that his head simply dropped into the grass, vanishing in the brief interval it took me to work the bolt and realign. It was *another* bull, bedded down in the grass behind him, that I saw scrambling to his feet. I had *not* goofed. I had put my shots exactly where I intended, and both beasts were stone dead. The second bull was slightly smaller than the first, but still a nice trophy — especially in view of the circumstances.

What troubles me still is that I do not remember the sight picture on the second shot. I do not clearly remember even firing the second shot, but two shots were fired and two buff were killed. The whole thing, after the first shot, must have been done on reflex without any conscious thought, and without any clear awareness of what happened. The first shot took the buffalo just ahead of his ear, ranged under the rear of the skull, and cut the spinal cord at the second vertebra, going on out the other side of the neck. I suppose it is theoretically possible that I missed the second shot, and that the second buffalo was killed by the first bullet after it had exited the first bull. If we had recovered any bullets this would have been possible to determine, since the first was a soft-point and the second a solid, but the first hit exited into empty air, and no bullet was recovered from the second bull since it took him in the ribs and ranged forward out the other side.

Things were pretty tense there for a moment, and neither Ian nor Barry, who was along as backup, has a clearer picture than I. Both maintain that the two shots came so close together that they seemed to come from a self-loader.

This happened at high-noon on the 10th of May, 1987 —my sixty-seventh birthday. Two trophy bulls, with two shots, in two seconds. Some birthday present!

How do I know that it was two seconds? Well, I don't. Nobody was holding a watch, but I do know how long it takes me to fire a controlled pair with a bolt action rifle on the range, and I think I was probably a little quicker in the field. Perhaps it was 2.3. Perhaps it was 1.7, but it was close to two seconds, and "Two-for-two-in-two" sounds good.

By a curious coincidence I just recently happened to read an account by Stewart Edward White of one of his adventures in which he killed two lions. I was fascinated to find that his experience in recalling the event was very close to mine. He remembered firing his first shot, and nothing clearly after that. He knew that he had fired seven times, and that two lions were dead, but he could not remember how he did it. It appears that programmed reflexes take over in moments of intense excitement, blocking out both conscious thought and conscious memory. We all know how unreliable eyewitness action reports can be. This may be the reason.

That night my friends raised glasses. "Many happy returns!" said Ian.

"Now *that* may be difficult to arrange," said Marc.

I'll just have to think of something!

ANTELOPE IMPRESSIONS

The Africa of yesterday was the wonderland of the hunter. Karamojo Bell put it perfectly when he opined that he was surely destined for hell after death since he had already spent so much time in heaven. Even now, though much reduced, Africa is still the happy hunting ground. But attitudes change along with goals and objectives, and in reading Africana one can discern a very different outlook in the old-timers. Their Africa was different, and they held views about the beasts that they hunted, and why they hunted them, that were different from those we may hold today.

To the old-timers "big game" meant elephant. Lions, buffalo and rhinoceros were dangerous nuisances, though they were still considered game animals in opposition to such other nuisances as crocodiles, hippos, and hyenas. Leopards were not taken seriously because they were too furtive to be engaged often and, compared to lions, unworthy trophies. These old-timers shot everything in sight, but in general the only thing they considered worth talking about was elephant. The majority were professionals who made their living out of the sale of ivory, and in a sense they paralleled the early "buffalo" hunters of the American plains who shot for hides. This is not to say that they were not naturalists, in large measure, and they give us much fascinating information about the habits and behavior of all sorts of beasts, but to them the endless herds of antelope that covered the "million miles of bloody Africa" were not really very interesting except as an auxiliary source of meat for the troops when "real" game was not available.

Today elephant and lion are strictly one-per-trip operations, and many forego them because of the expense involved. Black rhino are out of the question, and white rhino are vastly expensive and, to my mind, rather uninteresting. Buffalo are plentiful, available, exciting, and probably the primary African trophy of the present day. And leopards, prolific and stimulating to hunt, have become another important goal. Regardless of these stars, however, the antelope remain in numbers enough to make their hunting both fascinating and rewarding, and as one gets to know them they begin to acquire generalized personalities of their own, each variety different from the other.

When I first took the field in Africa I knew the shapes and sizes and general descriptions of dozens of different antelope, but because the old-timers never made much of them I had no idea how interesting they were in their variety. After a number of hunts now I find every antelope to be a special sort of creature, charming in his own and different way. I have come to regard some of them as primary objectives, some as secondary objectives, and some as forbidden — not by law, but by my own viewpoint. Some I will hunt whenever I can, others I have hunted once and will not again. Still others I will not hunt at all. A personal matter, of course.

Eland
(*Taurotragus oryx*)

The eland is the greatest of the antelopes, taller than a man and sometimes weighing as much as a ton. The ordinary weight of a big bull will run about sixteen hundred pounds. The eland is a particularly gentle animal. If he had the disposition of a buffalo he would be a tough customer indeed, averaging somewhat larger in body-bulk, much more agile, and with horns better designed for goring. But such is not the case, and eland, both male and female, strike one as sort of Disney-like creatures, with soft brown eyes, long eyelashes, smooth, clean fur, and a rather playful disposition.

Their agility is astounding. I have seen a big bull eland leap clean over an eight-foot game fence, *without a running start*. I have also seen a full-grown male proceeding happily on his way, cavorting above the grass out of sheer high spirits, leaping and gamboling about like a spring lamb. "Those big cowey things that jump like hares" is how the wife describes them in Hemingway's Macomber story. "They are not dangerous, are they?" she asks. To which the response is "Only if they fall on you."

As a trophy the eland is somewhat disappointing, since a very big eland and a just average specimen look about the same until the tape measure is used. Those I have encountered were not particularly wary, and in no sense difficult animals to take, as they offer a very large kill zone to the bullet.

I do not intend to shoot another eland unless I am hard-pressed for food, as his venison is the very finest I have ever eaten. There is more fat in eland tissue than in that of any other African animal, and this enhances the flavor. Surprisingly, the fresh meat is very tender and moist, and may be served as steaks on the same day it is taken. It is hard to get most African cooks to treat it right, since the tendency, as in all frontier communities, is to slice meat thin and burn it brown. But I can testify that a two-inch-thick tournedo of eland tenderloin, individually wrapped in a strip of eland fat, is one of the great delicacies of the world.

The killing of an eland is an occasion of great joy in camp, providing, as it does, an enormous supply of the tastiest protein on the continent. If you want to raise the morale of your camp crew this is the way to do it. Still, in the future I will only take an eland when the circumstances are special, as his death is a somewhat sorrowful experience.

Kudu
(*Tragelaphus strepsiceros*)

Though less than half the size of the eland, the kudu, at six to seven-hundred pounds, is still a big animal, about the size of an American elk. He is the arch-typical *strepsiceros* (spiral horn), and his marvelous spiral horns constitute the most beautiful of game trophies.

The kudu has always been more plentiful in the south than up in Central Africa, and even in today's reduced hunting environment kudu are abundant and readily available in all of Southern Africa. Under controlled hunting conditions the kudu seems to be thriving almost everywhere, and trophies taken today tend to run larger than those of a generation ago.

The kudu is a very handsome beast, with his silver-gray hide striped vertically with thin white ribbons. His carriage is not his strong point, as his thin neck does not seem to match the massive hump on his shoulders or the great corkscrew horns above his head. He is a forest animal and moves furtively, something like an American whitetail. Since he is tricky to hunt and moves typically in cover he is far more of a challenge to the rifleman than the eland.

He almost never uses his horns for defense, though I have heard of exceptions to this.

I like hunting kudu, and though I have no room for any more sets of spiral horns in my house I will continue to hunt him with pleasure for as long as I am able. The meat is good to eat, and there is always room for one more such handsome trophy in club, sporting-goods store, or hotel.

Unlike many of the African antelope the kudu is frequently stumbled upon almost by accident, and ranges can be very short. On our last hunt together Werner Weissenhofer practically stepped upon his trophy, which was excellent, and on one occasion during the Rhodesian War I killed a smallish but still prime specimen with a headshot at seventeen steps with a 45 pistol.

Kudu are great. They are handsome, plentiful, widely distributed, and tasty. They come across as somewhat sneaky, which makes hunting them the more pleasurable.

Sable and Roan
(*Hippotragus niger* and *equinus*)

These are the two "horse antelopes" (*hippotragus*). Though not the biggest, they are the grandest of the antelope, and their carriage, bearing, and elegance are positively royal. The roan is bigger, running about six hundred pounds. The sable is smaller, but with longer horns, and handsomer in his jet black coat and white vest. (In Afrikaans the sable is called *svart-vet-pens*, which means "black with white belly." Exactly.)

The roan is not doing well today, and is thus completely protected almost everywhere, which is just as well. Though smaller, the sable is the nobler beast in appearance. Both sable and roan are tough-spirited animals, and quite ready to use their remarkable rearward curving horns for lethal purposes. These horns do not appear to be well designed for fighting since they curve sharply back over the withers and point almost straight down at the tips. This means that the beast must practically jam his chin between his forelegs to present the points in any fashion to do damage, but there are too many stories current in Africa about their efficient use to be ignored. The consensus is that a bull sable or roan is easily a match for a lioness in a fight, and hunters are advised to use extreme caution in approaching either beast after the kill. I have never heard of a specific case of a hunter being killed by a sable, but I am assured that such things have indeed happened.

On a farm near the Lundi River I once met a young bull sable who was a pet. The game was to toss pebbles at him to watch him catch the rocks on the tips of his horns, a pastime which he appeared to enjoy. I know of few fencers who could duplicate that trick with a foil.

In the Tamafuta country I was treated to the splendid sight of two bull sable in confrontation over a cow. Their behavior was very stylized and formal — clearly not intended to draw blood. The bulls stood about two feet apart, nose to tail, and strutted slowly round and round each other. On some sort of signal they would separate, go to their knees, and close in with their heads down. They would then rattle the forward curve of their horns fiercely against each other, with no attempt to use the points. After a few seconds of this rattling-on-the-knees they would arise and continue the circling behavior. Nothing seemed to be accomplished, and when I approached too closely they broke the engagement and trotted off into the Mopani.

The trouble with the sable as a game animal is that he is just too princely looking; too noble and arrogant to shoot. He is not furtive. He just stands there in the open and stares you down. To hit him with a rifle at that point is rather embarrassing, and I do not intend to do it again.

Sable are not common in most of Africa, but when you get to country where they are fairly plentiful, as in the Tamafuta, they are not hard to hunt. A big bull sable makes a very grand trophy, but he is difficult to mount because the backward sweep of his horns requires more room than is generally available on the wall. Taxidermists overcome this by turning the head ninety degrees to one side, but somehow this does not do justice to the lordly carriage of the beast on the hoof. A really good sable is one of the few animals which calls for a full body mount, rather than a shoulder mount.

The sable is grand. I for one will let him be.

Nyala
(*Tragelaphus angasi*)

The nyala is a close relative of the kudu, and belongs to the same genus. Carriage and general behavior are similar, and while the nyala lacks the spectacular spiral horns of the kudu, he makes up for it somewhat in his gaudy coloring. A mature bull nyala has a body of charcoal grey, topped with a silver mane and striped with vertical white ribbons. All four legs, from the knees down, are a rich russet, and he wears the same white chevron on the nose that the kudu does. The horns make just one full turn, and when the tips begin to flare outward rather than pointing in toward each other you have a shootable bull.

The nyala is a forest-loving animal and shows the same furtive carriage as the kudu. He is smaller, running to about three hundred fifty pounds.

This antelope inhabits the east coast of Africa, and I have encountered him in Zululand. He is also found to the north in what used to be called Mozambique, and up into Malawi. There is said to be a much larger race, far up to the north in communist Ethiopia, called the mountain nyala.

Few people other than residents of South Africa care to make a special trip to the country where the nyala is found, but he is good hunting and good eating, and everything that is said about the kudu can be said approximately about the nyala as to his desirability as a quarry. His head makes a beautiful trophy, and one is less likely to encounter him in American collections than his larger cousin. He is readily available in Natal, where hunting can often be arranged for quite reasonable rates as compared with Botswana or the Transvaal.

Gemsbok
(*Oryx gazella*)

The gemsbok, which used to be called the "giant oryx," is certainly the most dapper of the antelope. He is a creature of the open plains, and is immediately distinguished by his long, almost straight horns, carried by both sexes. He is about the size of a donkey, and vividly patterned. He runs in bunches averaging around twenty, but sometimes much larger. In a running herd it is nearly impossible to tell the bulls from the cows at any distance. Cows' horns tend to be longer, while the bulls' horns are heavier in the beam.

It has always seemed to me that a gemsbok horn would serve well as a prefabricated weapon for primitive man. The rings around the base would furnish a nonskid grip, and the long sharp point would serve as a neat stabbing spear. I have never, however, seen any evidence that this was ever attempted by any of the local people, either now or in ages past.

Gemsbok are runners of the grassland, and offer very demanding shooting at medium to long range. They are especially wary, but they do love to run, much as the American pronghorn, and their excellent eyesight enables them to pick up an intruder at considerable distance.

In southern Africa today the giant oryx is not as common as the kudu, but moreso than the sable. A representative trio of sable, kudu, and gemsbok make up into a handsome decoration for a living room wall, especially if lesser trophies are placed elsewhere to avoid cluttering.

Wildebeest
(*Connochaetes taurinus*)

The wildebeests, black and blue, are the clowns of the African antelope. They are so different in their appearance and behavior that they almost do not seem to be antelope at all.

The black, or whitetailed, wildebeest is a creature of the south, and was first encountered by Europeans who called it the "gnu." As exploration pushed farther north its larger relative, the blue wildebeest, was then termed the "brindled gnu." Both beasts suggest the silhouette of an American bison when seen at a distance, but whereas the horns of the true gnu hook down and straight forward, those of the blue wildebeest are shaped more like those of a buffalo, curling out and up to the side. Additionally the blue wildebeest is generally of a blue-gray color with a darker mane on the shoulders and neck, whereas the true gnu is jet black and sports a pure white tail.

The wildebeest is different. In contrast to other African antelope he is ugly. Beauty is, of course, a subjective consideration, but only a gnu is likely to admire the physiognomy of another gnu. These beasts are wary, and have very keen eyesight. Since they move generally in herds there is always someone watching while another is grazing, making them the most difficult of African antelope to approach in open country. Neither makes up into much of a trophy, though the forward-curling horns of the black variety do furnish a splendid rifle-rack. The big ones are hard to tell from the small ones, and the cows are hard to tell from the bulls. They love to run, and while they run they are fond of hooking at each other with their horns. This is acceptable behavior amongst other wildebeests, but it is dangerous to try on the zebra with whom they are often found grazing. A wildebeest who hooks a zebra while running may fatally regret it, as zebra are irascible and fierce. So, for that matter, is the wildebeest. He is another antelope which is quite dangerous to approach when wounded. I have only heard rumors about the ferocity of the sable and the roan, but I have first-hand accounts of incidents with wildebeest, one of which was captured on film.

The gnu will frequently enter into running contests with the hunting car, offering excellent opportunities for photography.

The wildebeest, though common, can offer some very hard hunting, especially so in large bunches which spread out enough to invalidate the cover of an ant hill. This is mitigated somewhat by the fact that the big old bulls are inclined to wander off morosely by themselves, and are thus able to keep a lookout with only one pair of eyes.

This animal is exceptionally and notoriously bullet-resistant, and is seldom dropped with one shot. From my own experience I would say that one is more likely to lose a wounded wildebeest than any other game animal in Africa. Ian McFarlane, who has taken me out twice in the Okavango, once remarked that he had seen a bull blue wildebeest absorb eight rounds from a 300 Winchester Magnum, well-placed in the boiler room, before losing his footing. "You can break your heart on those," he said.

The blues and the blacks are rarely found in the same region, which usually means two separate hunting ventures to acquire both. Ordinarily the blues are common in areas where you might be hunting something else such as buffalo, kudu, waterbuck, or impala. The blacks are more likely to be found down to the south in company with nothing other than springbok.

The wildebeest is great fun to hunt, and should not be scorned because he is relatively common. He is a fine and challenging game animal, and even if he does not make up into much of a wall decoration he is a worthy antagonist. I will continue to hunt him with pleasure whenever the opportunity affords.

(Incidentally, wildebeest is pronounced "vil-da-be-est." The two e's in Afrikaans are pronounced as two syllables, as "ee-est.")

Waterbuck
(*Kobus ellipsiprymnus*)

The waterbuck is an odd sort of beast, with very distinctive characteristics. He is a short-coupled, compact and hairy antelope who is, as you might suppose, partial to aquatic environments. Just how he manages to make out in company with the crocodiles I am not sure, but there he is, and he is not uncommon. He is a handsome creature, with erect posture and long powerful horns shaped like the two halves of a parenthesis. The cows do not carry these horns, and identification is easy. One of the outstanding features of the common waterbuck is a brilliant white ring around the rump which has been inelegantly referred to as the result of sitting upon a freshly painted toilet seat. His color is a generalized dove grey, lighter below. Where I have found him he is less wary than the kudu and the nyala, but quite a bit more so than sable and roan. He is, oddly enough, an animal about whose edibility there is some discussion. Selous ate him with relish, whereas Hemingway said he was inedible. I made a special point of eating the tenderloin of a waterbuck that I killed up near Kariba, and I found the meat quite tasty, though tough since it had been killed the same day. It is said that there are skin glands on the waterbuck, which if not carefully removed in dressing will taint the meat, and this may be so. It is also possible that being a water animal the waterbuck eats certain kinds of vegetation which may lend an unpleasant flavor to the meat in certain times and places. I can testify that this is not true everywhere. I will hunt waterbuck in the future if he is available, and if it is established that he is eatable. I would not again kill him for his trophy.

Impala
(*Aepyceros melampus*)

The impala is the ornament of Southern Africa. His beautiful soaring bounds have become legendary, as described in Fitzpatrick's marvelous work *Jock of The Bushveld.* He is a delicately-formed, small antelope rarely exceeding one hundred twenty pounds in weight, and where circumstances permit he breeds like a rabbit. In the places I have hunted he constitutes the primary meat supply for Europeans. He is not particularly hard to hunt, and he is generally common, so he does not pose a great challenge to the rifleman. He is ordinarily found in thin orchard bush rather than deep forest or open plain, which makes his approach normally rather simple.

Impala herds come in two forms. The first is a large gathering of bachelor bulls, with no cows and no calves. (As to that, impala are normally called rams, ewes, and kids, in the places I have visited.) In these bachelor herds most of the horns are of the same size, and there is little to choose from.

The other grouping will consist of a breeding herd, always with one herd bull and an astonishing number of cows, anywhere from twenty to fifty. One need have no qualms about killing the herd bull because with that many breeding cows available you may be sure that there are plenty of other lads nearby — ready, willing and able to take over the job of the head man the moment he falls — and the girls will not know the difference.

If you want the meat you take the one nearest to you who is not in line with another beast. Impala heart, liver and kidneys are delicious, and the tenderloin may be eaten raw as it falls, perfect in texture and savor.

The unique thing about the impala is his marvelous leap. He does not just bound, he flies. He flies so high and so far that he frequently leaps clear over another animal in full bound, forming a sort of living arch over an obstruction. Fitzpatrick tells of an occasion in which he intervened between a bunch of impala and the direction in which they wished to go, and rather than flowing around him they simply flew over his head, out of reach. This is one of the astonishing and beautiful sights in nature, resembling more of the play of dolphins than that of any four-footed, earth-bound beast.

Impala do not always run this way, and when they seek maximum speed they do not leap. I was once privileged to see the charge of the cheetah, and when the impala knew that the cheetah was close behind he stopped bounding and leveled off close to the ground in top gear and actually outran the cat. The cheetah is said to be the fastest four-footed creature on earth, but *this* cheetah was not fast enough for *this* impala on *this* occasion.

The impala is a beautiful creature, but I have no qualms about hunting him. He is plentiful, prolific, and his social life is such that one never feels guilty about interfering with it. There is no sense of bonding about impala, and to take one out of the pack for food never seems environmentally destructive — especially when he is so good to eat.

Lechwe
(*Kobus leche*)

The lechwe is a cousin of the waterbuck, as both are included in the genus *Kobus*, but he does not look nor act very much like a waterbuck except in his addiction to wet environments. He has the same coarse hair, but he is much smaller, and given to running in larger herds. He also has a splayed hoof which enables him to make progress rapidly across semi-liquid environments. The lechwe comes in several races, but is found principally around the shores of Lake Victoria and in the Okavango Delta. He is a nice enough animal, but somewhat undistinguished, offering neither an ornamental trophy, nor particularly hard hunting, nor rarity, nor exceptionally good meat. He rates about a C+ on all of those counts. It may be said that in the Okavango he is likely to offer long and difficult shooting out across partially inundated meadows and lagoons. In this connection I should caution those who take after him to be careful about trajectories and sight settings. He is a respectable quarry, and I will hunt him again when I return to Okavango, but I would not put him at the top of the list as a specialty.

Sassaby
(Also spelled *Tsessebe*)
(*Damaliscus lunatus*)

The sassaby of southern Africa is a relative of the hartebeest of central Africa, and shares many of the same characteristics. He is ungainly, ugly in the face, sexually indistinguishable, plentiful and good to eat. In Okavango he may be a better source of meat than impala, since he is somewhat larger, running to about two hundred pounds. Sassaby are very territorial, and the same animals can be found in the same places day after day as one comes to recognize them. They are said to be the fleetest of all African antelope, but I must wonder how such a fact can be ascertained. It is true that they run very fast, but then so does everything else in Africa, with the possible exception of the hippopotami.

One of the good things about the sassaby is his excellent leather, which makes up into very handsome artifacts of a dark red color. Sassaby hides are possibly the finest that can be obtained for this purpose. The bulls are hard to tell from the cows, and a big one is only an inch or so bigger in the horn than a small one. I do not consider them to be prime game animals, but they are a fine source of camp meat and leather, and they serve as an excellent warm-up for a hunter new to the area. One has no particular sense of responsibility about shooting them (always in accordance with the law) because they have little or no individuality nor discernible personality.

Bushbuck
(*Tragelaphus scriptus*)

This is another most attractive little beast, running about the same size as the impala. The biologists list him in the same genus with the kudu and nyala, but to the layman this seems very odd since the bushbuck shares nothing with those two except for a full turn of horn.

The bushbuck, as might be expected, is a creature of thick vegetation and will almost never be found out in the open. He is dark red in color, with vivid lighter markings, and carries two straight sharp horns twisted once upon themselves. He has a reputation for using these horns with skill, and there are many stories of hunters' being mortally stabbed by this little creature.

Personally I think this stems from the days when settlers used to hold large drives, in which a long line of beaters pushed everything from rabbits to guinea fowl into a line of guns. These hunters used shotguns, and one can readily see that the attempt to bring down a one-hundred-pound antelope with a charge of birdshot might not be successful. If the unfortunate beast was then followed up on foot, the chances of a novice hunter leaping upon the downed animal and receiving a dagger thrust through the gizzard would not seem unlikely.

Bushbuck bark, as do various other African antelopes, and I have cheerful memories of hearing that bark in deep forest, and looking along its evident direction to see the elfin head of a handsome little bushbuck staring at me through the trees.

Bushbuck have curious affinity with baboons, and where a troop of baboons inhabits a thickly forested pile of rocks or kopje it is normal to find bushbuck in residence along with the apes.

I have never shot a bushbuck, nor do I intend to, but I passed one up once which might have been some kind of a record, while hunting buffalo. (At that time I did not realize that you cannot spook buffalo by shooting. I also did not realize that in Africa one is unwise ever to pass anything up that is offered, from a trophy elephant to a lobster dinner.)

Reedbuck
(*Redunca arundinum*)

Reedbuck are pets. Though they are very good to eat they are such charming little camp ornaments that I do not believe I could bring myself to shoot one unless I was *very* hungry. They live, as the name implies, in marshes and reed beds, and they are distinctly family-oriented. It is quite common to see mamma and papa and junior in a family group. They have a quaint habit of taking cover simply by crouching, regardless of any lack of grass or reeds that may intervene between the beasts and their presumed hazard. It is quite funny to see a reedbuck hiding from you fifty yards away in plain sight, with his ears carefully turned downward so as to lower his profile.

Though they are about the same size and equally toothsome, I do not feel at all the same about impala as I do about reedbuck, because of their apparent family dispositions. To shoot an impala disturbs nothing except the impala himself. To shoot a reedbuck is frequently to break up a family. I shot a solitary reedbuck once, primarily for leopard bait. I do not think I will do so again.

Bontebok and Blesbok
(*Damaliscus dorcas* and
Damaliscus dorcas albifrons)

The "pied buck" and the "blaze buck" are southern relatives of the sassaby, and were nearly exterminated, along with the springbok, by the taming of South Africa. Today they are on the way back, as ranchers discover their value as sporting attractions. This is more true of the blesbok, as his larger cousin is still not common.

Ranch hunting lacks the glamor of the wilderness, but it is a lot better than no hunting at all, and on a ranch or in the wild the buck still have sharp eyes and fleet feet.

These medium-sized beasts have lyre-shaped horns, which they put to use in a very odd way that I have never seen mentioned in print. They use them as headrests! Glassing a bunch up in Zululand, I saw them all standing around with heads down. At first I thought they were grazing, but on closer inspection it was apparent that all of them had reversed their heads and planted the top curve of their horns on the ground. All bachelors, they may have just weathered a hard night.

As with all ranch game, blesbok must be culled to avoid overpopulation. Culling is not fun, and I do not recommend it.

Antelope Impressions

But do not scorn blesbok as a quarry if you stalk him legitimately. He is alert, wary, and good to eat.

* * * *

The foregoing subjective impressions about African antelope are certainly not inclusive and do not pretend to be universal. All the antelope are wonderful, but some seem more wonderful to me than others. Each hunter will, in due course, discover what sort of hunting gives him the most satisfaction, and which beast is his best quarry. Emotion ought not really enter into this, but it will, since hunting itself is an emotional experience. Hunting must always be conducted within the framework of existing game regulations, and always with a specific objective in mind other than indiscriminate killing. To those who insist that all hunting is immoral I insist upon the study of Jose Ortega y Gasset's *Meditations on Hunting*. To those who are not interested in the discussion I must say, "You go your way and let me go mine!" I hunt with enduring zest, and I do not damage the environment. The African antelope are a source of great joy to me and I make no apology whatever for hunting them. Among other things, the death that I offer them is a great deal quicker and more humane than that which they must expect at the teeth and talons of the great cats, the crocodile and the hyena. But non-hunters will be unlikely to read these works, and to my brother hunters I offer these suggestions and observations in the hope of sharing some of the earth's more delightful experiences.

AN AMERICAN SPORTSMAN LOOKS AT SOUTH AFRICA

In theory, politics should reflect the general will, but often they do not. This may be because the general will is not easy to determine — especially in large societies. If they accepted the news media without skepticism, readers in both the United States and South Africa would be led to believe that the generality of the American people regards South Africa with hostility. The reason for this hostility would be taken to be the institution of *apartheid* — that, and that alone. That this is a catastrophic over-simplification is something I will endeavor to discuss.

I am an American who has visited the Republic of South Africa ten times in the past fifteen years. I am much more familiar with the people and the ambience of South Africa than most Americans. Therefore I do not speak as a representative American, but rather as an American who knows South Africa somewhat more than superficially. My views may not be held by the majority of Americans but I have a feeling that they would be if the majority of Americans knew South Africa as well as I do.

It is never wise to generalize, and one cannot say that South Africa is thus and the United States is so, because there is great variety in both nations. Nonetheless we must speak in categories because our words work that way, and so henceforth I will have to qualify everything I say by the words "in general" or "for the most part."

It is very clear that the United States and the Republic of South Africa have a lot more in common than they have in conflict. This is especially so of the *western* United States, which is so similar to many parts of the R.S.A. that a stranger might not know where he was if the sun were not in the wrong place. Both lands are vast, and both tend to be dry. When our European friends visit us here in Arizona they marvel at the space, the openness of the sky, the uncluttered look of the land and the feeling of physical freedom that this engenders. Our South African friends find these things quite familiar.

A most striking similarity is the attitude which both peoples share toward government. In Europe, and unfortunately in the eastern United States, the general feeling is that what is not specifically permitted is forbidden. In the western United States and in the R.S.A. this is reversed — what is not expressly forbidden is naturally permitted.

A reflection of this is the institution of free enterprise, which was at one time the cornerstone of the American economic system and which made it the most productive on earth. Free enterprise is still largely the rule in South Africa, and it is one of the few remaining places where a businessman with an idea is encouraged by the state, rather than discouraged. The continued erosion of this attitude has seriously reduced this vital element in the U.S. economy, as can be seen from the fact that return on investment averages 10% in the United States and 15% in the R.S.A.

The settlement of the American West has curious and striking parallels with that of the hinterland of South Africa. The other empty lands of the nineteenth century were explored and developed by government agents. Only in the United States and South Africa were the pioneers free people, operating entirely on their own. The Great Trek itself took its inspiration from the insistence on the part of one farmer that the government should stay out of his business. The American pioneers likewise had decided that they needed no help and no supervision. Even the wagons in which the settlers moved were very similar in the two countries. This leads both the South African and western American to inherit traditions of self-reliance, courage, stubbornness, horsemanship, marksmanship — and strong religious faith. The ideals which join us are much deeper and stronger than those which separate us.

Clearly, however, we have problems to face in attempting to reach an emotional, political and economic understanding. The first of these is the provincialism of the majority of the American people. It used to be considered a snobbish joke on the part of the English to insist "But Americans are so provincial." Unfortunately, this is all too true. The majority of Americans tend to be interested only in those things which occur within a few miles of their place of residence, and many still feel that anything that takes place outside of the limits of the country is of no concern whatever. Most Americans cannot bring themselves to take interest even in the affairs of Central America — which is practically in our laps. So much harder is it then for them to notice the affairs of South Africa — which take place on the far side of the world.

Thus it is that an activist press can insist, and effectively persuade, that the Republic of South Africa is a pariah among nations because it maintains a separation of the races, and that decent people must have no dealings with such a country. The atrocities of the Evil Empire, directed from Moscow, seem trivial to these people compared to the institution of *apartheid*. Knowing little or nothing of the problem, they simply mimic the sheep in Orwell's *Animal Farm* — bleating "Four legs good, two legs bad."

The race problem is a very serious one, and all of us — in the United States as well as in the R.S.A. — would be happy to be presented with a good solution to it. Many of my South African friends have told me that they would welcome a good policy to pursue if I had it ready to suggest. They always add that — looking at the United States — they do not wish me to suggest *our* solution. While very few will admit it in this country, the breakdown in social order in our big cities, the absence of public safety, the decay of public education, and the appalling social irresponsibility in the major population centers are the direct results of our racial problem. We have essentially "one man, one vote" in the United States — and it is not leading to the solution of our social conflict. The elemental barrier to social harmony lies in the fact that our "black" population —or at least those who presume to speak for it — refuses to accept a man on his own individual merits, but only as he is a member of a racial group. The leaders of this community will not regard themselves as Americans first and blacks second, but rather the other way around. There is justice in the claim that the American white community has forced this attitude upon the American black community, but recognizing that an evil exists does not necessarily propose a satisfactory solution. From my personal view it would seem that about 60% of the American white population expresses a willingness to let bygones be bygones and to abandon the entire concept of race. No black leader will accept that view, and since there is great pressure upon blacks of ability to reject the elimination of race as a consideration, it is doubtful if even 10% of the American black population feels the goodwill necessary for true social harmony.

When it is considered that nine out of ten Americans are white while perhaps four out of five South Africans are black, it is clear that the problem facing South Africa is much more serious than ours. There are some whites in South Africa who do not wish to solve this problem, but most do, and I advise my American friends to encourage South Africans of all races to adjust their problems gradually, because any attempt to do so precipitately will result in chaos.

We have made racial progress in the United States over the past fifty years, but it has not brought harmony. On the contrary, those who presume to speak for the American black community are for the most part sowers of discord rather than pioneers in social equality. When one considers that a nominal candidate for the presidency of the United States (who makes a big issue of his being "black," when his skin is quite a bit lighter than that of a good many Caucasians) has stated for the record that when he was a waiter he was wont to spit into the food he served to white patrons, one can see that he is no standard bearer of political and social peace.

South Africa also has made much progress. That this has not brought the millennium overnight seems to annoy those who do not understand the problems. It would be nice if people would hold their tongues until they knew what they were talking about, but that may be too much to expect from a free press.

The United States is sadly polarized at this time. Once in our history we could assume that people of opposing political views had the same overall objectives in mind — the general good of our country. That does not seem now to be the case. The American Left has been behaving in the past few decades as if the demise of the United States was its principal aim —and the Left controls the press. That is why the majority of the American people are never told that the strategic security of South Africa is absolutely vital to the military safety of the United States. This is why it is difficult for South Africans to emigrate to the United States, and it is why raucous voices insist that American business cease investing in the economy of South Africa.

This "adversary press" does not represent the people of America. As a striking example of this truth I give you the last American presidential election. I could give you more instances in which the press was solidly on one side of an issue and the people voted against it when it came to a test. What I ask is that South Africans not believe what they read or what they hear without the most careful evaluation of the source. The Left excoriates South Africa for a social policy to which it has no solution, because it would like to see the Enemy triumph on that continent. The Right would be friendly if it knew more about the situation. Scholars have no trouble studying African history — but few of our people are scholars. Most derive their opinions from television, and our television is controlled by enemies of South Africa.

To those Americans who seem to feel that we must accommodate to communism but reject *apartheid*, I point out these things compare as cancer does to a sore throat. *Apartheid*, gradually being eroded, is no threat to the United States.

Communism is. And *apartheid* is being corrected, while the Soviets have no intention of "correcting" communism — even if that were possible.

My hope is in direct inter-communication between our peoples. My hope is in travel — increased travel and tourism on the part of Americans visiting the land. A great encouragement of this lies in the popularity of field sports in both countries. My various visits to Africa have been conducted in conjunction with shooting sports, which happen to be my profession. If I had not been a competition marksman and avid hunter I doubtless would never have seen this great country, but as it is I know it somewhat and I consider myself a friend. I will continue to put out that word.

·KIRCHNER·

CRUMPLER!

Long ago and far away — in the great days of hunting before the rot set in — there existed an association of gentlemen known as the Five Seven Seven Club. A member in good standing never ventured out of doors without a cartridge in his pocket — a 577 Nitro Express cartridge, suitably engraved with his name. Upon meeting with fellow members, he who could not produce his badge of membership was honor bound to buy the drinks.

The 577 Nitro Express was quite something. It still is. It is a "super heavy": one of two hunting rifles in that category, the other being the 600. It fires a bullet that weighs seven hundred fifty grains at an initial velocity of two thousand fifty foot-seconds. It is not the most powerful hunting rifle ever built, but it was certainly the most popular, and probably the most effective, piece of this kind. It outshone the 600 during the era of big ivory by a considerable margin, probably due to its reputation for superior penetration.

The super heavies are very specialized instruments. They are not just "elephant guns"; they are guns for tackling elephants under the most desperate circumstances. They are useful only to the tradesman, not the sportsman. The sportsman who hunts elephant does not need such devastating power, since he hunts in the company of a competent professional who is also powerfully armed, he chooses his one bull with care, and he avoids any single-handed confrontations with an enraged herd. On the other hand the tradesman — the money hunter —hunted by himself, and his objective was all the ivory he could gather in one session. He went right in among them and he worked like a tight-end amid 12,000-pound linebackers. His shot had to work — every time — or he was squashed like a bug. Often shooting from the hip at ranges of a few steps, he needed all the power he could hold. Hence the super heavies.

An elephant's skull is made of spongy bone much like styrofoam, with the brain — the size of a football — situated deep inside that huge mass. Shooting at the head and hoping to hit the brain is like shooting at the Pentagon and hoping to hit the gymnasium. A brain shot with any gun will stop any elephant, *but the head shot with a super heavy will knock an elephant out.* With a super heavy all you had to do was hit the head, solidly. And you may have had to do that just as the trunk was reaching out to seize you. That is why you squandered a year's profits on a pair of rifles that only a duke could afford.

Jim Wilkinson, the renowned hunter from Prescott, Arizona, recently acquired a magnificent "Best Grade" Westley-Richards 577, and when he showed it to me I all but lost my composure. Here was a true work of art — from the zenith of the machine age — manifesting man's ultimate genius in steel. The concept is Euclidean, the design is Archimedean, and the execution is worthy of Benvenuto Cellini. Everything has been foreseen, nothing has been sacrificed to economy, and the workmanship is such as we will never see again. The action rolls open and shut with soft, silent precision and the seams, when closed, can scarcely be seen without a magnifying glass.

Such artifacts have never been cheap, and today they are very costly. Jim's rifle is worth about four times what I paid for my first Porsche (in 1953) and now you might buy its sister for half what a new, top-of-the-line, street Porsche costs. In the twenties, when this rifle was made, one of its cartridges was worth the price of a first-class dinner in a first-class restaurant. It still is today.

Despite the intimidating cost of such a piece, it was not conceived as a rich man's toy. While the very rich might buy it for display, it is a completely serious weapon. Such gold as it bears is not placed there for show, but rather to assure by bright contrast that a vital message will be unmistakably transmitted. "Safe" and "Bolted" glow on the tang, and "L" and "R" below denote which barrel will fire first.

The lockwork is instantly detachable, without tools, and the fitting of these parts can only be appreciated under glass. This is not mere affectation, for this rifle was intended for use months beyond the help of any gunsmith. It had to work. Your life depended on it.

Jim's example is fitted with a selective single trigger and automatic ejectors, both of which features were optional and debatable in the brave days of old. Barrel selection is an advantage if one lock has broken, but it does make for complexity — a thing to be avoided. Automatic ejection is fast but noisy, and it tends to lose brass in tall grass. (The noise of ejection always seemed irrelevant to me, in view of the immediately preceding blast, until it was explained that the beasts are not alert before the shot but are very much so immediately thereafter. The *bang* comes as a bolt from the blue, but any *clink* that follows is a dead giveaway. We American hunters tend to forget that the hunting of really dangerous game is often an arm's-length business.)

The power of the super heavies is enormous, just on the edge of controllability. "Pondoro," the famous John Taylor, states that they are really practical only for men of "quite exceptional physique." Such values are subjective. After shooting Jim's 577 at some length I feel that anyone who could play first-rate high school football — as a lineman, linebacker, or blocking back — could manage it with confidence, after a bit of conditioning. It kicks, you may be sure, but not so much that a strong man cannot control it. (I cannot resist the jibe that any lady who can shoot it — well — is no lady.)

At the front end, the 577 "literally crumples elephant" —John Taylor speaking again. Its striking energy exceeds 7000 foot pounds, but kinetic energy is a misleading measure of striking power. Momentum is better. If we use the "M" factor now in force in I.P.S.C. rifle competition a sampling looks like this:

Caliber	"M"
308	42
375	75
458	100
460 Weatherby	135
577	144
600	171

But momentum disregards impact area, which is not to be disregarded. The cross-sectional area of a 46-caliber bullet is .16 square inches. That of a 58 is .26. Thus on Pondoro's "knock-out" scale we see this:

Caliber	"KO" Rating
7 X 57	15.6
318	27.25
375	40.1
404	49.
470	71.3
505 Gibbs	86.25
577	126.7
600	150.4

If John Taylor is accepted, the super heavies are simply not comparable to the lesser calibers — not even to such old reliables as the 470. (I do not interpolate more recent developments such as the 458, the 460 G&A Special, and the 460 Weatherby, all of which fire the same 500-grain, 46-caliber bullet; but we can estimate the 458 at something between the 404 and the 470, and the Weatherby at about 95.

Ammunition for the 577 is scarce. The original English Kynoch is long out of print and thus a rather choice scalper's item. New brass may be had from B.E.L.L. (if you can get their attention) but the bullets must be handmade unless you wish to order a thousand or so. Jim does not have any shooting ammunition for his prize but I was able to impose on Ross Seyfried, who also owns a crumpler, to let us have fifteen test rounds. Fifteen is enough. After half-a-dozen I began to notice a certain lack of delicacy creeping into my trigger squeeze. All that is needed is a short breather, however, and the touch comes back.

Shooting Jim Wilkinson's marvelous rifle was a rare delight. I was admittedly a little intimidated by all this talk of unmanageable power, so it was a nice surprise to discover that the 577 is really not all that bad. The "Number One" Westley-Richards weighs 13½ pounds — no more than one of the heavy-barrel M1A's, scoped and loaded, and it is neither so heavy as to feel clumsy nor so light as to belt you around. And it is *short*, a characteristic of doubles that makes for fine balance and easy mounting.

The trigger is quite good enough for clean control, and there is no problem in hitting an apple-size target from offhand at elephant range. We found that we could keep our shots in the black if we concentrated on it. (This was a three-inch bull at thirty-five paces.) The requisite concentration did become more difficult as the experiment progressed, but then one does not shoot a 577 in long strings. Among other things only an Arab could afford to.

I noticed that it is wise to keep the thumb over on the right when hip shooting, since if the butt is not supported against the shoulder the locking lever may be driven back into the web of the hand. Held waist high, the rifle pointed very well for me, and it was apparent that this technique could prove very useful in various close encounters of the terminal kind.

Another thing that became obvious was that very strong hands are required to load and unload the piece. The moving parts fit so perfectly that they seem to glue together, and both opening and closing the breech takes force.

Stock fit is an individual matter, but the stock on Jim's rifle suited me very well. The day after shooting I felt no tenderness at all on cheek or shoulder, and only a trace of discoloration on the biceps due to one bad mount in which I dropped my right elbow. There was no abuse of the second finger, such as is common on bolt-action heavies with vertical trigger-guard backs.

Various commentators have held that the super heavies, while undeniably perfect as "back-up guns," are too cumbersome to pack around all day. On this subject it is unwise for one man to speak for another. What bothers Smith may not bother Jones. My own opinion is that exhaustion is exhaustion, and two or three pounds of rifle have little effect upon it. What is a "practical weight" is a matter of dispute among practical rifle contest organizers, but it would seem wiser to put up with 13½ pounds of 577 than to quibble about the questionable advantages of a 14½-pound 308. The two problems are not the same, of course, but I cannot credit the notion that a heavy rifle, at 11½ pounds, is appreciably handier than a super heavy, at 13½.

The prewar British gunmakers were justly proud of their work. They combined theory with practice in a way that can no longer be justified economically, even if the necessary skills still exist. Artistry in steel is strictly a function of free enterprise and does not fit into the catalogs of the welfare state. Jim, who deals in fine guns, is of the opinion that certain Italian shops might be able to make rifles of this quality, assuming they had a guide to show them what they were trying to achieve. I suppose there are people in Liége and Ferlach who might be able to do the same. But since there no longer is a demand there is clearly no need to meet it. "A thing of beauty is a joy forever." Indeed. And if that thing is a perfect instrument for a demanding task the joy is greater. And if that task is a matter of immediate life and death, the effect is inspirational.

Sinfully, I covet my neighbor's rifle. Not only sinfully but foolishly, for I have no earthly use for it. Even in the grand old safari days I would never have needed it, for the ivory trade is properly left to ivory traders. Wanting to possess what one cannot use is wicked, yet, being mortal, most of us have an occasional wicked thought. Trying to cover up, I cast about for a really good use for a Westley-Richards "Best Grade" double 577, and came up with one, to wit:

Most of my cop friends are fearfully harassed by nitwit regulations requiring female cops to serve right alongside men in the combat zones of the war against crime. (Why any sane woman would *want* to be a street cop is one of those questions best left to the Left.) No department can lawfully tell a girl that she can't be sent into a fight because she is by rule of God and nature unfitted for such work, but it can specify that every trainee, of either sex (or even some revolting mixture of the two) be required to qualify with weapons. I therefore suggest that we revive the super heavies as a test medium. Anyone who can put four out of six 750-grain 577 bullets, powered by a full charge, into a six-inch circle at 50 yards, offhand, may be deemed qualified in weapons. Put that policy into effect and the problem of feeble cops will take care of itself.

SUMMA CUM LAUDE

In Unstinting Praise of the World's Finest Rifle

Pretty strong statement, hey? Well, permit me to support and defend it.

"Baby" is just ten years old. She was built up on the best of the Mauser actions — the ZKK 602 from Brno. She was barrelled by Douglas, for the best of the heavy cartridges — the 460 G&A Special, designed on the Jeffery case by Tom Siatos. She was then assembled and enhanced by Georg Hoenig, true master of the gunsmith's art, who created the extended magazine, built the stock, and brought the parts into harmony. In the hands of three different marksmen Baby has now taken nine buffalo and an elephant, at ranges from eight to one hundred and seventy-five paces, and *she has never needed a second shot*! (Second shots were frequently delivered, at the behest of a professional hunter who quite sensibly wished to take no chances. But in no case was that second shot necessary. Given any reasonable sort of placement, anything hit with Baby goes down — immediately.)

As a naval air task unit is a combination of aircraft and carrier, a rifle system is a combination of cartridge and weapon. In Baby the two components are ideally matched, and the result is magnificent. If the adjective had not been beaten out of shape by the younger set, who use it to describe anything from diet pop to Elton John, I would say that Baby is *awesome*. The hunting rifle is the queen of weapons, and dangerous game is the highest goal of the hunting rifle, and Baby is the perfect instrument for dangerous game.

First consider the cartridge. The 460 G&A Special splits the difference almost exactly between the 458 Winchester, which is too little, and the 460 Weatherby, which is unnecessary. All three take the same 45 caliber, 500-grain bullet, but the powder capacity of the three runs about 75, 90, 105, and velocities about 2,000, 2,400, 2,700. The impact difference between 2,000 and 2,400 seems to be critical, whereas that between 2,400 and 2,700 does not.

The 458 Winchester was a jury rig decided upon when its parent, the 45 Watts, was found to be too long to be used conveniently in available domestic actions. In cutting the 45 Watts back from 375 length to make it short enough to work through standard length actions much was lost. The original 458 loadings were designed to start the 500-grain bullet at 2,150. But this was found to be possible only in very long barrels, and consequently the first 458's ran to twenty-six inches. Even so, the figure of 2,150 has long been optimistic. Today's 458 loadings in shorter barrels are lucky to make it to 2,000 f/s, which makes the cartridge a sort of hopped-up 45-70. While there is nothing wrong with the 45-70, it is not a true "heavy," and neither is the 458. Does this matter? I think it does. I have seen penetration failures with the 458 on heavy animals, and I have heard of many more. That starting differential of 400 f/s relates the 458 to the 460 G&A as the 30-30 relates to the 30-06. The edge in both cases is decisive.

Now if the 460 G&A has proved decisively superior to the 458, it might be assumed that the 460 Weatherby would be about that much better again. This does not seem to be so, however. The 460 G&A will shoot right through the skull of an elephant — in one side and out the other. Just this year it knocked an elephant out with a headshot that did not touch the brain, an attribute previously accredited only to the super-heavies — the 577 and 600. It has, on two occasions, killed two buffalo with one shot. With that much penetration (and, incidently, 6400 foot pounds), it is inadvisable to opt for the Weatherby cartridge simply because "more is better." The penalty one pays for the Weatherby cartridge is bulk. The case is very large, and Weatherby rifles chambered for it carry only two rounds in the magazine. One might think that with that much power a three-shooter should suffice, but I do not agree.

The G&A cartridge is a modern, compact item, and Baby is a six-shooter — with one up the spout and five in the magazine. The recoil of the Weatherby is appreciably greater, with its fifteen extra grains of powder, and most people feel that the recoil of the 460 G&A is quite sufficient, in a medium-weight weapon.

Amongst the older cartridges, the closest approximation to the 460 G&A in ballistics is the 505 Gibbs, which fires a 525-grain bullet at the same velocity. But the Gibbs, like the Weatherby, is a huge cartridge, requiring both an oversized action and an excessively long bolt-throw. The 460 G&A, on the other hand, nestles into the ZKK magnum action most handily, and the resulting weapon is positively svelte alongside its ancestral giants.

You may have noticed a recent increase in the popularity of what may be termed the "light-heavies" — rifles of 40 caliber or thereabouts, taking 400-grain bullets. These evidently work well, especially the neatest of the lot which simply necks down the short 458 case to 40 caliber, and is called the "416 Taylor." This case has enough powder capacity to start a 400-grain bullet at acceptable velocity, and thus effectively duplicates the performance of the enormous Rigby cartridge in a smaller action. Still, I will not choose to substitute a 400-grain bullet for a 500-grain bullet, especially since in so doing I also sacrifice some 25% in impact area. The only reason I think of for choosing a light-heavy over a heavy is decreased recoil, and that leads to some very subjective discussion.

How much recoil the individual shooter can control is obviously a very individual matter. I find that, personally, the recoil of the 378 Weatherby is disturbing — moreso than that of the 460 Weatherby. This may be due to the shorter time-thrust of the smaller caliber. Baby, weighing in at 11½ pounds, appears to me to kick a good deal less than the Weatherbys, though my primary reason for favoring her over the larger guns is compactness and magazine capacity. It must be admitted, however, that Baby is a man's gun — nothing you cannot handle, but distinctly enough. This is not to say that some women might not enjoy shooting her, but I think it unlikely. The Russians have some female shotputters who might not mind, but we probably will not find them afield after buffalo.

(If the foregoing annoys certain kinds of dull-witted activists, let me say right here that I believe the difference between men and women to be among God's better ideas.)

Baby's barrel is 21″ long, yet we can still clock an honest 2400 f/s with 90 grains of #4064. On my last buffalo hunt I was impressed again with the advantages of a short barrel for use in brush. Baby's short barrel is thick, and I specified it so in order to build up to the optimum loaded weight of 11½ pounds. If I had fitted it with a lighter barrel of the same length, recoil would have begun to be distressing, and if I had made the lighter barrel longer, to make up weight, the piece would have been clumsy in quick handling.

The extension magazine is a particular triumph of Georg Hoenig, cleanly hand-crafted with very smooth lines. One might ask why repeated shots are needful, in view of the enormous power of the cartridge and its proven record. I cannot establish that those extra rounds are really necessary, but I can say that they are comforting. I have never had proven need of a steel helmet or a life jacket, either, but I find them encouraging in certain kinds of situations. Likewise I like to have six rounds in hand when I swing down from the hunting car. I have never yet needed those six, but there may come a time when I do — and besides the extension magazine makes the completed weapon look better.

Baby's stock is of simple, classic style in selected California Claro walnut, and lovingly hand-checkered. More ornamental wood might have been used, but the piece is almost ostentatiously utilitarian, and embellishment for its own sake would seem out of place in this instance. This stock is fitted with Pachmayr flush sling-sockets, fore, aft, and amidships, to accommodate the CW sling system. There are those who claim that there should be no sling on a rifle for dangerous game, and

I must respect their opinions, but I use one, and I have had occasion to be thankful that I do. On that long walk out, in the flat, shadeless thorn, the carrying mode has proved convenient many times. On two occasions I have used the CW sling on Baby in the shooting mode, and was very glad that it was available. In circumstances where the thickness of the brush makes any sort of sling inadvisable the Pachmayr swivels may be detached in seconds, and the strap thrust through the belt and out of the way.

Baby's sights are of the "ghost-ring" description, with a 1/16″ square post forward and a ¼″ thin-rimmed aperture aft. The front sight is another creation of Georg Hoenig, and is mounted on a broad, ramp base, the shoulders of which extend out far enough on each side of the post to protect it from bumps and jars. This is an excellent design not often found on sporting rifles, where a thin, high blade is particularly subject to outside influence and must be protected either by a hood or by wings, both of which are unsightly and tend to pick up trash on rough duty. The rear sight is the one that came on the action, a feature long since discontinued by the factory. The virtues of the ghost-ring were discovered long ago by such notables as Karamojo Bell and Townsend Whelen. The popular notion that a pin-hole aperture together with a large, blind disk makes for superior precision is open to serious doubt, even in slow-fire target shooting, and such an arrangement certainly makes the system slow. The large aperture, thin-rim rear sight simply fades from view when the eye focuses on the front sight, and the shooter need not do any conscious aligning; he simply puts his front sight where he wants the bullet to strike and squeezes. This system is distinctly faster than the open "express" sight, in addition to being more precise for deliberate shooting and affording a more ample view of the countryside out front. It does seem odd that this excellent sight system, which was discovered by the pioneers and has been verified in each succeeding decade, is unknown on modern sporting arms except those which have been customized. The assumption on the part of the manufacturers must be that everyone is going to use a telescope anyway, so why bother? I maintain that this is an invalid assumption. In the first place, telescopes can fail, and often do at the most unhandy times. Secondly, despite the esteemed opinions of such experienced hands as Ross Seyfried and Finn Aagaard, I can see no reason for a telescope sight on a rifle intended for dangerous game. A scope does not help you shoot, it only helps you see, and any animal that is big enough to kill you is quite easy to see — especially through a ghost-ring. Dangerous animals are normally taken at very short range. In my youth it was customary to set this range at 40 paces or less. This has not changed, and while Baby has taken one buffalo at 117 paces and another at 175, the circumstances were unusual in both cases. On the longer shot the buff had been hit twice, solidly, with a 375, and was getting rapidly to cover. I shot from sitting, using the CW sling in shooting mode, and the buff went on his nose from a dead run. This is not a recommended procedure, but there seemed to be no other way. Six of Baby's nine scores on buffalo have been taken at ranges of 35 yards or less, and the most recent one, nose on, at eight. Baby's sight system (in my opinion, of course) is exactly right.

Hoenig set up Baby's single-stage factory trigger to break clean at 3¼ pounds, and polished the somewhat rough Czech action to glass smoothness. I had occasion recently to fire two shots at maximum speed, rapid-fire, and I do not think I could have done it more quickly with a semi-auto, since the time it took me to get back on target after recoil was no greater than the time necessary to flick the bolt.

Those who feel that intrinsic accuracy is the ultimate measure of a rifle will not be disappointed in Baby. Three-shot groups at 100 yards run around 2¼", and I once had a near cloverleaf at that distance, with two shots touching and the other just barely clear. The sights are set to print 2" high at 100, which brings point-of-aim and point-of-impact into coincidence at about 175. At 200 she prints some 3" low. Thus the weapon shoots effectively dead-on out to distances at which you do not shoot at buffalo. At all useful ranges this rifle prints closer to the exact point-of-aim than the shooter can hold. That is all anyone can ask.

Taken altogether, Baby is a sheer delight — a joy to handle and an amazing inspirer of confidence. On the two blood tracks that I have followed (backing up other hunters), Baby in my hands has given me such a sense of power as almost to dampen the thrill of the occasion (but not quite). Your feeling with Baby in your hands is "If I see him before he sees me, I've got him!"

Baby's combat record does not seem high in comparison to those set by the oldtimers, but in view of the restricted nature of modern hunting, and her perfect score when put to the test, I find it odd that people are willing to make do with less. Certainly placement is critical, and lesser guns can do very well when all goes right. The fact that untold buffalo have been killed with 303 British military rifles does not make it sensible to hunt buffalo with such weapons. The 375, "the king of the mediums," has killed all sorts of buffalo stone dead with one round, but I have personally seen it fail decisively on four occasions, *and with shots apparently perfectly placed.* I have also seen the 458 fail twice. Baby does not fail.

These matters can be discussed, and will be discussed, at great length at conferences and over campfires from one end of the world to the other. No one, no matter how wide his experience, has all the answers, and in the end weapon selection must always come down to opinion. I have my own, of course, but it was corroborated by my Bushman tracker up in the thickets of the Tamafuta country. After he had seen it work on three buffalo, he would greet me in the morning with a grin, gesture at Baby, and shake his head in amazement at there being such an irresistible instrument. He has been hunting a long time, with scores of foreign sportsmen, and he seemed to be saying that there in my hand was the ultimate development of the heavy hunting rifle.

Ideas about what makes a fine rifle "fine" vary a good deal. I recently saw a rifle portrayed in full-color on the cover of a magazine in which the commentator maintained that it was "the finest rifle ever made." This piece was indeed a beautiful artifact, but its beauty consisted primarily of embellishment rather than in utility. It featured an ornately figured walnut stock and enough gold engraving to open a bank account. But it had no sights, and its bolt handle was so sharply checkered as to draw blood if anyone attempted to use it with maximum speed. It was made for hanging on the wall, whereas Baby is made for stopping buffalo — conclusively.

We might wonder if the commercial production of a replica of Baby might be an economically feasible project. It might be, but I rather doubt it. The heavy rifle may be the culmination of an admirable line of endeavor, but we must admit that few people have ever hunted dangerous game, and fewer still may be expected to do so in the future. It would be gratifying if some enterprising manufacturer would step forward to do this, but I doubt if even the most optimistic could expect a large sale. He might indeed be the producer of the Testa Rossa Ferrari among rifles, however, and that would certainly add luster to his name, regardless of whether it put money in the bank.

At this time Baby has three siblings: Baby II belongs to Jacques Dailland of Paris, Baby III (*"Schatzi"*) to Dr. Werner Weissenhofer of Salzburg, and Baby IV to John Gannaway of Phoenix. According to campfire talk this year in Africa, there may be four or five more coming, but Herr Hoenig has rejected the notion of making any more on his own, and the ZKK 602 action appears to have been discontinued. This is a pity, of course, but not to me since I got there first, and I do not see how future copies can ever be made as good as the original. (For the sake of buffalo hunters to come I hope I am wrong.)

THE SPICE OF LIFE

Danger — not variety — is the spice of life. Only when one has glimpsed the imminence of death can one fully appreciate the joy of living. As with the condiments in our food, excess renders the dish unpalatable but absence makes it insipid. Fortunately our tastes differ, and we admit that what is sauce for the goose may certainly not be sauce for the gander, but while the rabbit people may not understand the piquancy of peril, they should know that there are several views on the subject.

Danger, to be appreciated, must be known. Our lives were all forfeit when we were born, but the hour of our peril is not always apparent to us. As you read this you may be seconds away from a fatal heart attack, but you are not in danger — so to speak — since you do not *know* that you are. Danger, in this sense, is the *awareness* of the possibility of imminent death. It is always a shocking experience but it need not be terrifying — and it absolutely must not be allowed to become incapacitating.

"Fear" and "terror" are words too often used in the Age of the Common Man. When I was a lad they were not admissible. Edgar Rice Burroughs' Tarzan, for example, said, "I do not know what you mean by 'fear'. I do not want to die, if that is what you mean, but you speak as if there were something more to it than that." Fear that nullifies a man's ability to cope with the danger which gives rise to the fear is an unacceptable emotion. The awareness of peril, however, is not the same thing at all, because in properly organized personalities it heightens perceptivity, sets the heart and mind to greater activity, and stimulates the entire consciousness in a way not otherwise realized. As Churchill said, "Nothing is so exhilarating as being shot at and missed."

However we may define "sport," man's sports have often been conscious endeavors to achieve the joy that comes from the successful facing of danger. I prefer to define "blood sports" as those voluntarily undertaken activities in which error, failure, incapacity or mistake may well result in the death of the participant. This includes mountain climbing, all forms of motor racing, most forms of water sports, steeplechasing —and the hunting of dangerous game. It does not include coal mining, heavy construction, logging, high-wire show business or any other activity in which the risk of death is great but which is undertaken for pay rather than for joy. (Flying a fighter plane falls between the two.)

The hunting of dangerous game was the first of the blood sports, undertaken both for food and for pleasure. It is obvious that pleasure was involved because it is as easy to kill a harmless beast as a dangerous one, and the food value is the same. Primitive man, however, exulted in his prowess, in his courage and in his skill, and his delight in testing these against a beast which could easily kill him was one of his first human manifestations, differentiating him from a brute beast. Julius Caesar wrote that the killing of an aurochs was the most highly esteemed feat among the early Germans. This thrill is still with us today, though available only to a few. The grass-eaters will never understand it, and there are a great many of those. There are also a great many who have no taste for horseradish, chili, or curry. To the meat-eaters among us such people would seem to lead bland, insipid, pastel lives.

Those of us who know that danger is indeed the spice of life do not wish to convert others to our viewpoint. There is little enough to go around. But we do wish sometimes that people who do not understand would quit trying to tell us to change our attitudes.

Hunting of any sort is viewed askance, even anathematized, by the rabbit people. This is only natural. How should a rabbit understand the mind of the fox? Which beast, however, do you suppose has the more interesting personality? Any sort of hunting revolts the bambiist, but hunting comes in so many different forms that it is difficult for him to focus on any one aspect of it.

To some hunters the prize is what is rare — the bongo, the sitatunga, the snow leopard. To others the prize is what is difficult — the chamois, the mountain sheep, the jaguar. To others, however, the prize is what is deadly — the elephant, the lion, the tiger, the giant bear — but most of all the buffalo.

Danger, like fear, is a subjective concept. No one can say which beast is objectively the "most dangerous" because what is dangerous is what scares *you*. Any man who has ever been caught by anything will tell you that whatever caught him is the most dangerous beast. (Very few have been caught twice by different beasts and lived to tell of it.) The animal which takes the most human lives, year after year, is the crocodile, but he is not a game animal at all. The rhinoceros can certainly kill, and has indeed taken his toll of both hunters and bystanders, but the rhinoceros is not essentially frightening because he is too dimwitted to constitute a respectable adversary. The elephant is smart and his power is irresistible. Many experienced hunters deem him the most dangerous. Lions and tigers are terrifying killing machines, and their frightening speed adds to their image.

But for many of us the pride of place must go to *Syncerus caffer* — the joined-horned infidel. There is something especially frightening about the buffalo. It is a characteristic most often referred to as "vindictiveness." This word cannot properly be applied to any beast, since vengeance is an exclusively human emotion, yet there is something unnaturally demonic in the rage of the buffalo. If you are caught by an elephant, he will tear you to pieces or fling you aside. If you are caught by a rhino, he will toss you and leave. If you are caught by a lion or a bear, he will stop savaging you after you are dead. But not so the buffalo. Once a buffalo has acquired the idea that he is being abused, or even threatened, only death will turn him off. *His* death, not yours. A buffalo may brush aside a man he has not selected, but once he gets to his prime target he does not stop. He hooks and pounds and stamps and, yes, even bites until there is nothing left of his antagonist except shreds. This is not easily explained but it lends to the reputation of the buffalo a glamour which is matched by no other beast.

When I was a lad I saw a photograph from Africa. It depicted a piece of ground about the size of an average living room, and on this ground only three objects were clearly distinguishable. Two were boots with the stubs of feet protruding. The other was a head, resting upside down showing a blond beard and a stump of spine. The rest of the scene consisted of mush, cords and tatters. The buffalo had won. This made a lasting impression upon me.

My hunting partner, Dr. Werner Weissenhofer of Austria, was impressed in a different way. He is a surgeon, and at the time he was attached to a famous hospital noted for its expert treatment of injuries to the lower torso. It had happened that a German hunter had committed the unforgivable error of turning to run from an enraged buffalo. One horn entered between his buttocks and penetrated to the diaphragm while the beast tossed its head in fury, mangling the abdomen. This was its dying act and the hunter was extricated alive by his companions. He was flown immediately to the hospital, where it took him a year and a half to die — with Werner in attendance. This also made a lasting impression.

John A. Hunter, the renowned professional from British East Africa, graphically describes the horrific sound of a buffalo pounding — the savage grunts which accompany each stroke of horn, boss or hoof. There is a weird, frightful joy shown here as the beast seems to exult in an ecstasy of destruction.

This is why the black buffalo is special. That he is also plentiful, prolific, tasty and a magnificent trophy are all extras. What is special about buffalo is *deadliness*.

Just how deadly is he? Certainly one stands a greater risk of being struck by lightning, bitten by a venomous snake, or having his parachute fail to open than of being killed by a buffalo. While many hunters have been so killed the chances are statistically small. But odds are not involved here. The odds are far greater that I, for example, will die of a stroke than of a buffalo charge, yet I do not stand in awe of vascular breakdown but I do stand in awe of the buffalo. That is the difference — a matter of attitude, not statistics. If you are not in awe of the buffalo you cannot enjoy hunting him. One well-known writer who had much experience in the chase asserted that when he was on a buffalo hunt he frequently woke up at night in a cold sweat, anticipating the morrow's adventures. That man obviously got full value out of his buffalo hunting. When asked by his wife why he did it, his simple answer was "Because I'm crazy." She readily agreed with that, as would have any psychiatrist.

If one is a reasonably good shot, thoroughly instructed in bovine anatomy, wielding a weapon of adequate power, and capable of controlling his nerves in an emergency, his chances of coming to grief in a buffalo encounter are low. The glamour of the occasion, however, is no way diminished by this. It is a big experience. I anticipate it, savor it and emphasize it. I turn the volume all the way up. Rabbit people will say that I make entirely too much of it, but I do not mind that. I have little to do with rabbit people — professionally or recreationally.

On my own last buffalo hunt I thought long about my emotions at the moment of contact. I prepared myself in advance to note my sensations. Was I to feel fear? Was my mouth to go dry, my hands shake? Memories of moments of stress are notoriously unreliable, but as I recall it I did not feel these things. When I saw the mighty master bull stand forth from the herd, head high and tail lashing, I was truly awed. I marveled at his colossal strength. I knew his unbelievable resistance to gunfire. I was amazed once again by that appalling stare. "He looked at me as if I owed him money," as Robert Ruark put it. But before anything incapacitating could occur in my emotional condition my concentration shifted to the task at hand, which was shooting — marksmanship. Selection of firing position was the first consideration. It was instantly decided because I had no choice —the shot had to be taken from offhand. Next I remember focussing intently on the front sight, red against black. Lastly I recall putting every ounce of concentration I possessed upon a gentle pressure on the trigger — the "surprise break" of the marksman. My preoccupation with these matters of technique was so great as to blank out any possible feeling of apprehension, excitement — or fear. Perhaps, therefore, I did not enjoy the experience to the fullest. Perhaps if I had been frightened into incapacity and the buff had been killed by my companion —perhaps only then would I have got my money's worth. However I do not think so. I believe I got the full charge. I am immensely impressed by the buffalo, and I will hunt him whenever I can, but at the moment of truth my feelings will probably remain concentrated upon the shot.

Possibly this whole attitude is an affectation — even an obsession. Possibly those of us who love to hunt the buffalo are victims of some sort of mental disease. If so, however, it is a disease we have no desire to cure.

THE SUGGESTION BOX

Consider the African Dung Beetle.

This excellent insect is about the size of an ordinary lemon, cut in half lengthwise. Its abilities are impressive.

(1) It is virtually invulnerable to abuse. Its armor is of high-resistance natural plastic, and it can be run over by a truck without damage, if the ground is soft.

(2) It is a master of vertical take-off and landing.

(3) It can intrench itself in seconds by scooching straight down into the ground.

(4) It repairs and maintains itself without outside aid.

(5) It is not subject to electrical nor hydraulic breakdown.

(6) Its energy intake is modest, and it reproduces itself with minimal labor.

(7) Its primary activity consists in rolling up balls of manure larger than itself in which it incubates its eggs.

My suggestion is that we breed it for size. Suitably magnified, it would be the ideal mount for air cavalry, and if it were stabled in and around Washington, D.C., it would instinctively take over the handling of government forms, thus freeing most of the federal bureaucracy for productive work.

V. THE PAST

SURVIVOR

After the contest, three of us remained at the little range in the gravel pit outside Zürich. The three were Arpad Lucacz, Gerhardt Tauchnitz, and I. As the sun declined, the light rain turned into a fitful sleet, and all the contestants and their families cleared off quickly for the cozy hospitality of the Swiss countryside.

We three — Hungarian, German, and American — built a small fire beneath the lean-to outside the rangehouse and settled down to toast our dinner and tell "sea stories," as old soldiers will. There were thin strips of beef which Arpad coated with paprika, fresh raw onions, and black bread, and there was also a jug of green Hungarian wine. It was not warm enough for us to shed our outer clothing, but the atmosphere around the little fire out of the wind was quite comfortable. The bivouac mood was softened by the knowledge that we were in no danger, and the talk took us back to other times and other places. Infantrymen, like aviators, often feel more in tune with their opposite numbers than with those whom they presumably protect; especially so thirty years after the fact of war.

Gerhardt was a man a little younger than I, of compact build with thinning hair and a cold grey eye. He had been a student in two of my classes in Switzerland, and while not a brilliant shot he had shown solid competence with his P9S. He had been a cooperative, attentive, and intelligent pupil, and since he spoke easy English it was possible to learn directly from him about his war experiences without the handicap of an interpreter. Gerhardt was SS (*Schützstaffel*). To some, that signifies death camps and gas chambers, but Gerhardt was *Waffen SS*, a member of the so-called "elite guard." His division was "Florian Geyer," named after an early Nazi hero whose story I was never able to elicit.

Gerhardt got into the war late because of his age, but immediately found himself on the central Russian front in the

Pripet marshes. He saw plenty of action there, but after the medical staff discovered that he was particularly susceptible to mosquito poisoning he was sent to the Karelian front between Lake Ladoga and the Gulf of Finland. This was an inactive sector, since both sides had come to the understanding that nothing important was to be decided in their zone of operations, and settled down to routine patrolling in dense pine forest. One of the curious aspects of this area was the secret trade carried out between the opposing armies. Soap, tea and sugar were left at crossroads, where they were found and exchanged for similar items in short supply on the other side.

Gerhardt was hospitalized twice with bullet wounds — the first time with three holes in his left shoulder delivered by the 30-caliber Russian pistol cartridge from a Shpagin, and a second time when his right thigh was broken by a Radom pistol. Gerhardt told me that the three wounds in the shoulder had felt like nothing at all, apart from a slight numbness, whereas the 9mm took him off his feet. He mentioned that he had been hit several other times and that if I wanted to know how it felt, I had only to ask him what caliber.

Before the collapse of the German effort, Gerhardt achieved the SS rank equivalent to lieutenant, even though he was not yet 21, and additionally acquired a sort of "kitchen Russian" with which he could communicate with prisoners, after a fashion.

Arpad growled like a bear every time the Russians were mentioned. He had been too young for WWII, but had been driven out of Hungary when the Soviets occupied it. His feeling toward the Russians is akin to that of the Armenians toward the Turks, the Filipinos toward the Japanese, and the Palestinians toward the Jews. Gerhardt, on the other hand, displayed a sort of unemotional neutrality toward races and nations; though, as an indoctrinated Nazi, he thought poorly of the Jews.

These poisonous group enmities are one of the major afflictions of the human race. If we could just bring ourselves to think of human beings as individuals rather than as members of groups, a good portion of the world's sorrow could be averted. In my own case, I saw too much of the Japanese in the Pacific war ever to feel completely friendly again. I know this is wrong, and I try to bury it, but no matter how deep it is thrust, it is still there.

When Germany surrendered, Gerhardt Tauchnitz became a prisoner of the Russians, along with hundreds of thousands of other Germans in uniform. While the Soviets frequently shot any SS men they captured, on general principles, this was not true in his case. Somewhat to his surprise, he found himself in a death camp near Murmansk, where thirty-thousand prisoners of war had been sent to perish of cold, starvation, and despair. The shores of the White Sea form one of the most forbidding landscapes in the world, and there, beyond any means of transportation, the Russians felt that a few guards could hold a very large number of Germans who would quickly become unable to take any vigorous action to save their own lives.

Before privation destroyed his will, Gerhardt found an SS *Hauptsturmführer* (that is equivalent to a captain) with whom he could converse, and the two of them rejected hopelessness. In the captain's view, thirty-thousand Germans, even without weapons, were more than enough to overcome the entire Russian guard force and take over the place. Examining the situation, they agreed that the Russians could use only the very dregs of their military establishment as prison guards on the Arctic Circle when the war was still dying down on the main battlefronts. The people guarding the camp were little more than animals, and the two SS men decided that, with 200 unarmed but well-organized prisoners, they could not only destroy the guard force but set up their own community out of reach of the Russians, who might not have time to pay attention to them until they had consolidated their gains.

So the two set about recruiting the 200 necessary spirits. Gerhardt looked at me keenly and asked, "How many good men are there per hundred, in the world?"

"Allowing for differences in circumstances, condition, and background, I should say perhaps one."

He grinned at me bleakly and said, "Wrong! We thought we could find two hundred out of thirty thousand. How many do you suppose we did find?"

"I don't know," I replied. "That was a pretty grim situation and I dare say the people were more downcast than most."

"We found ten." He held up both hands, fingers spread. "Ten, out of thirty thousand. It seems that a real man is the exception rather than the rule — the very rare exception."

As cold and hunger rapidly reduced the prisoners to zombies, the opportunity came.

A Russian guard entered the stinking hovel in which Gerhardt lay shivering and dreaming of food.

"Any of you swine know anything about typewriters?"

Gerhardt knew about as much about typewriters as he did about television, but since he could make out the question in Russian he immediately announced himself as a typewriter expert. He was in a condition where any change whatever would be an improvement. The guard pointed, "You come!" and Gerhardt tottered to his feet and followed him out into the wind and sleet, through some wire, into a lighted warehouse which was heated at least above the freezing point.

Gerhardt was introduced to a broken typewriter on a desk.

"You fix, piece of bread. You no fix —" and the Russian drew his finger across his throat. "I come back here, one hour."

The lax control, Gerhardt explained, was due to the fact that the guards were armed, the prisoners were not, there was no place to go if anyone crossed the wire, and the Germans were incapacitated by exposure and malnutrition. After the guard left Gerhardt wasted no time on the typewriter, but examined the warehouse as quickly as he could. He found no food, but he did locate a considerable supply of spare Russian uniforms. He found no weapons of any kind, not even a hammer nor a large screwdriver; no rifle, no bayonet, no knife, no crowbar. He was ravenous, but young and fairly healthy still. For lack of a better plan he waited beside the door when the Russian returned and killed him with a chair.

Gerhardt now owned a supply of Russian uniforms, a Mosin-Nagant rifle with five rounds in the magazine, a bayonet, and a knapsack which blessedly contained the end of a loaf of bread.

And there he was on the shores of the White Sea, well clothed and well armed but alone, with seven hundred miles of icy plain between him and the chaos which constituted the Russian rear area after the fall of Berlin.

The wire was no problem, but food desperately was. Gerhardt decided against any attempt to rob the messhall, since someone could be expected to look up the dead guard at any moment. He made his decision and started south, along the single-track railroad connecting Murmansk with Leningrad.

The first leg almost killed him, since his weakened condition was not up to the endless tramp across the tundra, and he had no idea of the intervals between railroad maintenance depots. At length, through the gloom and swirling mist, he made out the dim light of a railroad guard-hut, and his life was saved.

Taking up a prone firing position close enough so that missing was unlikely, he waited like a cat at a mousehole. Eventually the door opened, a man came out to relieve himself in the snow, and Gerhardt killed him with one shot. The second man, stupidly, ran out behind the first and met the same end.

Inside the hut, Gerhardt was warm for the first time he could remember, and he wolfed down more bread than his stomach could hold. Now he had almost fifty rounds of ammunition instead of five.

And then he began to make his way from post to post, drifting in the mist like a wolf, toward a goal which when reached would probably prove even more dangerous than his present condition.

"How many times did you hit a post?" I asked.

"Many times."

"Well, how many? What sort of a guess? A hundred times?"

"Less."

"Ten times?"

"More."

"Twenty?"

"More."

"Fifty?"

"I don't think fifty. I think fewer than fifty."

"And it worked every time?"

"Obviously, since I am here. It was not always as easy, and sometimes I had to wait long, and nearly froze before I could attack."

"But there was always plenty to eat, I imagine."

"Yes, the Russians always have bread with them."

"So you never had to eat a Russian?"

The query did not seem to startle nor upset him.

"No. As I said there was always enough bread."

"Did you ever use anything but the rifle? Say a hammer, or a bayonet, or a strangling cord?"

"No. As we expected, these rear-area Russian troops were of extremely low quality, and even though the authorities must have suspected what was going on they either did not know what to do about it or did not care."

"Were you ever shot at during this trip?"

"Not once. I moved very carefully. Every time I saw them before they saw me."

"That was an excellent piece of tradecraft."

"And some luck. But one is extremely careful when one's life depends upon it."

It took Gerhardt about six weeks to make the trip, and he eventually arrived in the vicinity of Leningrad, where his Russian uniform, Russian rifle, and primitive command of the language seemed sufficient to insure his safety — if he was not too closely questioned. The Russian Army of that period was composed of great numbers of people who were not Russian by culture, and who spoke many different languages. The fact that a Russian soldier could speak only broken Russian was in itself no cause for curiosity.

His instinct was to go home, though he hardly knew why. Germany was a total catastrophe, and though he had no news to this effect he was aware of the predictable results of the massive invasion of his homeland. Still he had no other goal in mind, and decided to take the train. He stood in several chow lines, and answered questions in cheerfully muttered monosyllables. He was able to sleep on the ground under a warm messwagon.

When he arrived at the Leningrad railway station he was in reasonably good condition, all things considered. Like a lion looking over an assortment of possible game animals on the plain before him, Gerhardt considered his options. He had no papers. The Russians did not use them at that time. He had a few rubles, but not enough for any serious bribery. He had no idea what sort of controls might be encountered, nor what sort of record-keeping was involved in a train passage westward. At length, at a street corner outside the station, he discovered an entrepreneur who seemed to be doing a fairly lively business of some financial sort. On investigation it turned out that the fellow was selling forged papers of all types. This was interesting in view of the fact that the Russians had very little use for papers in general. Perhaps only important people needed them.

Gerhardt approached the man and asked what sort of documentation or tickets would be necessary to get him westward to Berlin. The paper-hanger looked at him narrowly and said, "Why do you want to go to Berlin, comrade?"

"Duty, comrade. I must join my regiment."

"What regiment would that be, comrade?"

"What's it to you, Ivan? All I want to know is what it takes to get me there."

Pause.

"I can arrange it. The price will be five-hundred rubles."

"That's high."

"And will be higher. I don't think you are a Russian, friend. I think you are a German. What's more, I don't think you are just a German, I think you are SS."

This statement snapped Gerhardt onto full Red, and as he prepared for action he asked, "And what difference does that make?"

"That means the price is now 1,000 rubles."

"I haven't that much with me, but I can get it. I will be back directly."

Gerhardt turned away, planted his feet, swung the rifle by its muzzle, and caught the man with his full weight on the temple.

The crowd was paralyzed, but every eye was upon him. He made a few incomprehensible statements about military security and treason, and immediately pushed his way back into the train station, since that seemed most likely to give the impression of official business. Through the open door a train was moving westward. He pushed by a couple of people who were asking him questions, jumped aboard, and concealed himself as quickly as he could in a boxcar. The train chuffed out of the station westward for perhaps half-a-mile, stopped, reversed itself, and proceeded southeast toward Orel, deep in the heart of the Soviet Union about midway between Moscow and Kiev.

"That was how it began — my odyssey. It took me a year-and-a-half, and I almost made it."

"You were a year-and-a-half behind the Russian lines without documentation?"

"That's right."

"How did you live? How did you eat?"

"I lived by my wits, and I ate when I could. I stayed nowhere longer than a few hours. By the time people noticed that I was hard to account for I was gone, and they put the matter out of their minds, as people do in Russia."

"Did you do any more fighting?"

"Very little. I had to shoot only twice. The big problem was hunger. The Russians do not eat well in the best of times, and these were not the best of times. You know what hunger is? Hunger is a man stuffing a raw egg into his mouth, shell and all, and crunching it down with enjoyment. You know what cold is? Cold is pouring a kettle of boiling water from shoulder-high and watching it form a stalagmite on the ground. I came to know about that. I don't think you, as an American, would know such things."

Unlike a properly constructed adventure story, Gerhardt Tauchnitz' odyssey included no close contacts whatever. It is doubtful if he spoke 1,000 words in eighteen months. His "profile" was so low as to be practically underground. He had to meet people and to make contacts because he had to eat, but he stole in small amounts when he could, so as to avoid conversation. Similarly he rode very little, because to beg a ride on a truck or on a train was to invite questions. Mainly he walked, and this was complicated by the fact that though he knew the general direction he should take, he had no idea of where he was most of the time.

It is about as far from Orel to Rumania as it is from Murmansk to Leningrad, but the journey zigged and zagged, and took ten times as long.

It was in Rumania that Gerhardt took his last and most serious wound. If you want to know how it feels to be hit high in the back, five inches to the right of the spine, by a major-caliber rifle bullet, Gerhardt said it feels like nothing at all. He was crossing a meadow between two patches of forest — and then he was crawling along by elbows and toes deep amongst the trees.

He was apparently near death for quite a long time, and could remember little except a series of hospitals. That he was cared for at all, at that time and place, seems remarkable testimony to inherent human charity.

At a time when many people are speaking of "survival," Gerhardt's experience can stand as a remarkable example of one sort. The term has acquired rather faddish connotations in the United States in the 1980's, but for Gerhardt Tauchnitz, in the heart of Russia in 1946, its primary aspect became one of almost total isolation. "Survival" means *loneliness*.

I wanted Gerhardt to go on into the night, telling me of incidents and accidents in his long adventure, but the tale was too long for one sitting, and I looked forward to going into it further on other occasions.

As it was, the three of us sat there enjoying slices of sizzling beef paprika, roasted onions, and green Hungarian wine until it became evident that people would begin to wonder where we were. Arpad told of his experiences in escaping from Hungary at the time of the Soviet occupation, and I had a few tales from the South Pacific with which to round out the occasion.

But Gerhardt Tauchnitz' story of his wanderings in the Soviet Union preoccupied me to the extent that I sought him out later with the notion of getting him to write it all down. It was a fantastic story, and certainly deserved telling.

He objected, first on the ground that in de-nazified Germany nobody wanted to hear his tale. I responded that in the first place he might be wrong, and in the second, I would arrange to have the story recorded in America. He said that he could not write in English well enough and that he could not trust a translator. I maintained that it could be translated accurately, and that I, personally, would edit it to make sure that his method of speech and his attitude about the episode would come through directly. He agreed that this was possible, but further insisted that no connection must ever be made between him or his family on this account. I opined that this could be done, and that by means of various cutouts I could insure that upon my own death there would be no possible way of tracing the tale, which would nonetheless become part of the history of the great war.

We agreed to this arrangement, more or less, and on subsequent trips to Europe I met Gerhardt and his wife and attempted to motivate him into writing. He put it off. I wrote him at Christmas two years ago, saying that time was running out for both of us — and just last week it did. Gerhardt Tauchnitz' death notice arrived on my desk, and now the story will never be told.

The anecdotes I have extracted from it are from memory only, and I cannot vouch for their accuracy. A great deal has been lost — and this instance is just one of millions.

How much we would like to know that we can never know, because the people who knew failed to write it down! Some day the world will roll on through space, cold and dark and dead like the moon, and no one and nothing will ever remember Xenophon nor Pericles nor Hannibal nor Charlemagne nor you nor me — nor Gerhardt Tauchnitz. Meanwhile, however, I adjure all and sundry — *if it is worth knowing about, it is worth writing down!*

Arpad Lucacz and Gerhardt Tauchnitz are fictitious names.

SHOCK

I was correcting papers at the kitchen table. The sun was low on a chilly early spring afternoon. Children were home from school on both sides of the street in the little mountain village in Southern California. The ground was wet and bore patches of old snow.

The shot must have been audible, but I do not remember hearing it. However, the sounds coming from the children across the street changed in pitch and tempo. It became apparent that they were now screams — not very loud nor long — but unmistakably screams.

I was so immersed in English sentence structure, and in the best and most concise way to comment upon it, that the idea that something violent might happen had not crossed my mind.

At my wife's call I went to the door and looked across the street. The two houses were situated so that their respective front windows faced each other at a distance of perhaps fifty yards. I could see no one moving, but there was some sort of smudge on the inside of the glass opposite. Short, faint screams seemed to be coming from the far side of the house.

I crossed the street quickly, ran up the front walk and opened the front door, which led directly into the living room. What I saw did not register immediately. To register as a human body a figure must have a head. What was seated in the easy chair facing the door had no head.

Thus unaware of what I was looking at I quickly scanned the living room and noted a curious type of untidiness. The smudge on the inside of the glass was perhaps a foot in diameter and looked like melted vanilla ice cream. On either side of the chair in which my neighbor had been sitting were two white hemispheres about the size of half grapefruit. Above and slightly behind the chair on the Celotex ceiling was a mass of fresh, red blood about three feet in diameter, now dripping back down onto the rug behind the chair. There were smaller unexplained fragments strewn about the living room.

I do not suppose it took as long as it seems in retrospect, but gradually I came to realize that what I was looking at was Harry's headless body sitting in that chair. An empty beer glass was on the table to his left, and against the front of his body, cradled between his legs and in his hands, was a 30-caliber U.S. Model 1917 "Enfield" military rifle. The index finger of his right hand was on the trigger and the muzzle rested where his chin would have been.

The highest part of the body was the tongue. Almost at the same elevation was the cup of the back of the skull, unbloodied and showing a fringe of white hair on the sides and around the back below where the ear lobes had been. As I looked around the room I noted that the forward arch of the mandible, holding intact the two lower canine teeth, was on the stair landing about half way up. In the middle of the living room rug was one detached blue eye. What lay symmetrically on either side of the chair were the two halves of the cerebrum, neatly separated along the median line. Neither of the ears, nor the nose, nor the other eye was immediately visible.

I shouted toward the back of the house to keep the family from returning to the living room. As it happened this was pointless since Harry had made his move in the presence of his family. I went back out the front door and called across the street to my wife to phone the sheriff and the coroner. There was clearly no need for an ambulance.

While waiting for the cars I examined the room gingerly, careful to touch nothing and to watch where I put my feet. I discovered a few small fragments, but nothing large enough to fill a teacup. What had happened was clear enough, but I was puzzled by the absence of a bullet hole in the ceiling.

The first car to arrive was that of the sheriff's deputy, who came in, looked around, and then went quickly outdoors behind the shrubbery. He was evidently new to law enforcement.

Jim, the coroner, arrived shortly thereafter and I called to him to ask his wife, who normally rode with him on official business, to stay in the car.

After examining the scene Jim returned to the front yard and asked Marilyn if she had such a thing as a paper bag in the car. I remember her asking in some puzzlement what he wanted with a paper bag. His response was to tell her not to bother —that he could probably find one in the house.

In a moment the deputy returned, more composed, and he and the coroner commenced doing the things which deputies and coroners are supposed to do on occasions like this. This left me nothing to do but go outside the house to see if I could find an exit hole through the shingles or siding whence the projectile had left the building after the shot. I traced the direction of the barrel as well as I could, but there was no sign of any such thing. I went back in the living room and carefully examined the ceiling, but there was no evidence of any sort of hole in the middle of that blood spot.

As Jim began putting pieces into a paper bag which he had found in the kitchen, we went over to the rifle rack which was affixed to the inner wall of the living room. "What's this?"

On the shelf of the rack, neatly sitting point-up on its base, was a single 30-caliber rifle bullet. We did not touch it, for the photographic crew was on the way, but it was quite obvious that this bullet had recently been subjected to the cramping action of one of two pairs of pliers which lay adjoining it on the gun rack. It seemed that the bullet had been deliberately and carefully separated from the cartridge in which it had been loaded. When, with due precautions, the rifle was opened, the empty case which was extracted from the chamber bore plier marks similar to those on the bullet.

Someone, probably Harry, had taken a live 30-06 cartridge and had removed the bullet, thereafter inserting it into the breech of the rifle in such a way that the powder would not fall out. He had then seated himself, placed the muzzle either in his mouth or under his chin, reached down and pressed the trigger with the index finger of his right hand.

I had seen Nip soldiers in the Pacific who had committed suicide in a similar fashion, but in every case the result was the blowing off of a portion of the top of the skull, never the total demolition of the entire head. What had happened here was the centrifugal diffusion of the explosive power of the propelling charge. What normally would have been used to drive the bullet through the skull, through the house and out into the air, had been momentarily contained within the interior of the head. The effect was as if Harry had taken a mouthful of TNT and fired it.

Now why did Harry do that? I am unprepared to go to hell and ask him — at least not just yet. With or without the bullet in place the result would have been instant death. Why remove the projectile? Someone suggested that possibly he thought that without the bullet the discharge would not hurt him, but I cannot take this seriously. Harry knew a bit about rifles and we had gone to the range together on several occasions. I am convinced that he knew what would happen. The question is where did he learn that? He had spent some time in Misiones Province in Argentina, a turbulent area, and perhaps that form of decapitation is known and practiced there. His decision to perform this shocking act in full view of his wife and children leads to the conclusion that he wanted to make it as spectacular as possible, and that he certainly did.

Personally I never heard of any such thing before or since, but as they used to say on the radio, "Only the Shadow knows what evil lurks in the hearts of men."

After answering all the questions I could I went back across the street, sat down at the kitchen table and got back to work. Perhaps twenty minutes had passed and I wanted to finish those papers before dinner.

THE DAY OF THE MAUSER

Four men roused themselves from an uneasy sleep at dawn on the morning of 28 January, 1904. It was mid-summer at the Etosha Pan, and the night had been hot and unpleasant. Two of the men had been posted atop the unimpressive little mud fort which constituted the northernmost outpost of the German colony of SouthWest Africa. Of the seven who manned the fort, two were on watch and another was ill. Four of them were regular German colonial troops assigned to hold this tiny station at the end of the world for the Kaiser. The three others were German pioneers who had set up little farms a day's march from the fort, and who were trying to make do until their crops and stock might flourish enough to justify the appearance of wives and children and all else necessary for a good life on the frontier.

Two weeks previously the Herero Tribesmen who inhabited the area south of the Etosha Pan had risen in arms against their German overlords, determined upon driving out the white man and seizing his possessions. The alert had gone out immediately, and the various outposts prepared to do what they could to defend themselves. The three farmers had been brought into the fort on the insistence of *Unteroffizier* Fritz Grossman, and they had driven what cattle and horses that they could into a kraal which had been hastily erected adjoining the fort.

With proper Teutonic thoroughness, Grossman, as NCO-in-charge, had drafted the three farmers, Basendowski, Becker and Hartmann, and appointed them temporary soldiers in the German army, granting Basendowski, the senior, the same nominal rank of *Unteroffizier* that he himself held— approximately that of staff sergeant.

Since receiving the alert, Grossman had maintained a two-man watch on the roof of the fort throughout each night.

He was an experienced soldier, and had slept most of the nights through, rousing himself only twice to make sure that the two men on the roof were relieved at proper intervals and that they maintained vigilance. Now, at first light, he stretched, picked up his rifle and moved into the adjoining room to check on the condition of Private Lier, who was raving and tossing with malaria. Grossman felt the man's forehead and muttered to himself.

"He may shake it off, but he sure picked a bad time to go down. He can't shoot in that condition, and by God we need every rifle we can get!"

"*Steht auf,* lads!" the sergeant shouted. "If they're coming today we want to be ready."

"Hey, up there," he called to the roof. "Anything in sight?"

"Nothing that wasn't there yesterday, sarge. Can we come down now?"

"Wait. I'll come up."

Grossman checked his rifle and quickly climbed the ladder to the roof of the building where Becker and Lemke were lying behind the mud crenelations, facing in opposite directions.

"Allright boys, get below and get some coffee. I'll stay up here until everybody is fully awake."

The fort was called Namutoni. It consisted of a rectangular building some thirty-five by seventy-five feet, with a crenelated tower at each end. Its walls were about twelve feet high and its roof was of corrugated iron. Its water supply came from a spring about one hundred twenty paces to the south. The cattle kraal was made of thorn branches and encompassed the northern approach to the fort. The terrain was flat, with intermittent acacia bushes limiting visibility to about one hundred fifty paces in all directions.

Presently Basendowski appeared up the ladder with a mug of coffee in his hand.

"Coffee for you, Fritz. Just the way you like it. Hot, black and tasteless."

"Let's make that '*Unteroffizier* Grossman,' Mr. Basendowski. It is necessary even here to maintain military decorum."

336

"Ja, ja. Sorry, but take your coffee anyway."

"Thanks. Nothing in any direction. I wonder if old Nechale really will join those Herero bastards after all."

Nechale was the Ovambo chief at Ondongwa, some one hundred fifty kilometers north of the Etosha Pan in Ovamboland. The Ovambo and the Herero had never been actually friendly, but when the Herero sent word that they were rising against the Germans, Nechale, alone among the Ovambo leaders, decided that the time was right to pick up some plunder in northern Hereroland before the Herero quit. Word had come back to the outpost at Namutoni that a war party of "many hundreds" of Ovambo had moved out of Ondongwa south toward the Etosha Pan about a week previously. There had been no sign of them at Namutoni, but with a force of only seven men, one of whom was hospitalized, Grossman could spare no one for scouting. The Hottentot servant at the fort, however, had friends outside, and he was quite certain that they would be attacked within a matter of days.

The fort's garrison, if it might be dignified by that term, consisted of its commander, Grossman, Medical Orderly Lassman, and the two privates, Lemke and Lier. These four men were equipped with Mauser M88 bolt action repeating rifles—not quite the latest thing in the Kaiser's armies but good enough for the task. They fired eight millimeter (approximately thirty-two caliber) smokeless cartridges which propelled 227-grain round-nosed jacketed bullets to a velocity of some twenty two hundred feet per second. They were loaded from five-round block clips, and while their repeating mechanism was somewhat imperfect, it could be counted upon—in a clean gun operated by a well-trained soldier. The three farmers all carried Mauser M71 44-caliber, blackpowder single-shots, which fired a 386-grain, soft lead bullet to a velocity of about fourteen hundred fifty foot seconds. The soldiers had the more modern equipment but the farmers were the better shots, having fed themselves with those rifles for many months. One shot, one hit.

Grossman took one more look around. A trio of giraffes ambled southward off to the east against the sunrise. A party of springbok had moved into the waterhole, followed by a pessimistic jackal. From the distance there came the scream of an elephant, but of men there was no sign.

"I'll go down now, and see about breakfast," said Grossman. "I think I'll leave this rifle topside with you, since Lier is in no condition to use it. You know how it works?"

"Ja, sergeant, like you told me, but I would rather use Bertha here. She has a better trigger and I know exactly where she shoots."

"Very well, but if things get hot you may want something that will shoot five times without loading, and trigger-pull be damned."

He swung over the side and disappeared below. Basendowski grinned and sighted carefully at the jackal with his rifle.

"Pow," he said to himself. "Right between the eyes! But we can't spare a shot for you, young fella. It looks like we'll have more important targets any day now."

At ground level Grossman checked with the young medical orderly about the condition of the sick man.

"Can he fight, Lassman? Is he any use at all?"

"Not today, sergeant. Nor, I think, tomorrow. The question is not so much whether he can fight as whether he will live."

"Bad, eh?"

"Well, not good. But perhaps it doesn't matter. If that *Schwarzen* war party is as big as the boy says, no one of us is going to make it."

"That's no way to talk, Lassman! We are German soldiers. We have modern weapons. The Kaiser is counting on us, even way out here. If they show up we will scare them off. If they attack we will drive them off. We are *not* going to die, Lassman! Keep that in mind."

The other three men looked at Grossman without expression, munching their black bread and sausage and sipping their black coffee.

"Here, sarge, have some breakfast. Do you want some more coffee, or would you like a beer?"

"Coffee will do fine for now. I think I will save that beer for later in the day when the sun gets high."

"I've sure got to hand it to you guys in the army," said Becker, one of the farmers. "You people have got enough beer here to stand any sort of siege as long as the ammunition holds out, eh?"

"Like they say, 'With enough biltong, bullets and beer, a man has nothing to fear!' "

"Who says that?" asked Hartmann. "The Bavarians?"

"Sure!" said Lemke. "We Bavarians are the heart and soul of the army."

"But hardly its brains, friend Lemke. My old man always said that a Bavarian was a cross between an Austrian and a human being." Hartmann was from Hanover.

"Just what you would expect from a square-headed Prussian doorstop. You people can't even speak the language!"

"Cut that out!" shouted Grossman. "We are all good Germans here. Save your wisecracks for the *Schwarzen* out there, or the Frogs. Now *there* is a people I could never like. I would actually rather fight the Frogs than the *Schwarzen*."

Just then they heard Basendowski call softly from above, "Sergeant! We have company."

Grossman drained his mug and tossed it into the kitchen bag. He picked up Lier's rifle and barked, "Attention everybody! Hartmann, Becker and Lemke topside, quick. Lassman, see what you can do about getting Lier up there, and bring some sort of shelter for him. Bring all the ammunition. I'll take the west tower with Lassman and Becker. Basendowski, Lemke and Hartmann in the east tower. Move it!"

And he vanished up the ladder.

"Right there, sergeant. Right there the other side of the spring, in the shrubs. Two of them. Dammit, Fritz, they've got rifles!"

"Did you expect they would not have? What do you think those Portuguese traders do for a living? On the other hand I don't think the Dagoes could have taught them how to use them, since they don't know themselves."

"Still, I'd feel better if they were spears."

"So would I, Sergeant Basendowski, so would I. Now get over in the other tower with those two boys. I'll have to see about getting Lier up here and rigging some shade for him."

The six men waited, three in each tower, maintaining sector observation through three hundred sixty degrees. Basendowski and Hartmann exchanged comments in low tones about cattle diseases. Lassman sponged off Lier from time to time. Becker said nothing.

The sun was well clear of the bush, giving promise of yet another hot, humid day, when three figures appeared from the direction of the spring and strode purposely forward, approaching the fort. They were unarmed, not even carrying spears, but they were in full war trappings, and they did not look friendly.

"Lemke, jump down here and cover me while I talk to those people. I don't want them to grab me for a prize."

Grossman spoke some Ovambo, and the couriers spoke some German, imparted to them by the missionaries to the north. With only moderate difficulty they made themselves understood. The message was that Shute, the great captain of the great chief Nechale, was on a hunting trip along the southern edge of the Etosha Pan, and was on his way to pay a visit to the fort at Namutoni. The offer was made to trade a live ox for a bag of rice, but it was obvious that such talk was merely a pretext for examining the nature of the defense and the numbers involved. The kraal behind the fort was nearly full of oxen and horses, and a bag of rice was hardly enough to do much for a full-scale war-party. Grossman told them the equivalent of "Thanks, but no thanks," and they withdrew.

Topside again, Grossman made his estimate of the situation.

"That was a reconnaissance, children. They wanted to see what we had, and how ready we were. At least they know we will not be surprised asleep, but I think what they mainly wanted to find out is whether we have a Gatling. I think they will assume that if we had one we would have shown it to them in order to discourage an attack. I think they will assume that we do not have a Gatling, which is of course the truth. Now they will decide whether it is worth the trouble to try to rub us out, and that will depend upon how many men and how many guns they have.

"Now listen, everybody, I will try to talk them out of attacking if I can, but I don't think I will be successful. If the war party is anything like the size we heard, they will try to run over us. If they do that let us hope that they will attack from one side only, and that they bunch up some. If we have to shoot, and I think we will, for God's sake shoot carefully, children! We have enough ammunition, if we use it well.

"Right now select a firing point on each side of each tower, but we can all fire from the same side if necessary. Place your ammunition on the blanket, where you can reach it easily, and above all let no one shoot until I say so! Then, if I give the order, mark your individual target, hold dead-center and *squeeze*. Do not waste shots on the same man. Try to get two in a row, shoot at that portion of the line directly opposite you, and then work slightly right and left.

"Now get comfortable. Get your breath, and put your faith in God. If you are contrite and righteous men He will not let you fall to the heathen."

II

As the sun rose the heat began to be oppressive. Gradually the acacia scrub to the south beyond the waterhole began to disclose the Ovambo, moving in twos and threes until the brush seemed black with them for a distance of a hundred meters right and left.

Becker swallowed hard and muttered almost to himself, "My God, there must be thousands of them!"

"Not thousands, lad," said Grossman, "but still plenty. Maybe five hundred."

"What difference does it make anyway?" said Lassman. "We are just six. None of us will see the sun go down tonight."

"Steady, my children." The sergeant's voice was surprisingly mellow. "We die when God wills it, and not otherwise. If it is His will that we prevail today, we shall prevail, no matter what their numbers; and if it is not, well, we are the Kaiser's soldiers, and how can we die better than rifle in hand, facing overwhelming numbers? Just don't get excited, boys. Don't worry about sundown. Just worry about that front sight, and squeeze gently."

By this time perhaps one hundred Ovambo had moved to the spring, and were drinking and filling waterskins.

"Look at the bastards," growled Basendowski, "drinking the water my cattle should be drinking. My poor beasts should have been watered long ago."

Grossman called across to him, "Why don't you tell them to begone, Mr. Basendowski? You speak their monkey talk better than I do." Basendowski glanced at the sergeant, grinned and then stood erect. Cupping his hands, he shouted loudly three sentences in Ovambo. The men at the spring looked at the fort, and then with strange docility they began to move back into the shelter of the thorn bush.

"You seem to have a way with them, friend. Maybe you can persuade them to move all the way back to Ondongwa."

"That's what I told them to do, but somehow I don't think they are about to do it. I sure wish we could water the stock, though. God knows how long this standoff is going to continue."

Grossman stood erect and rubbed his chin. He considered his position and swung himself down the ladder to the lower deck. His head reappeared a moment later.

"Lemke and Becker, come on down here and give me a hand."

The three of them went to work, rapidly hauling such stores as they thought they might need up to the roof. All the ammunition, all the explosives and fuses that were available, three full water jugs, twelve bottles of beer, and Lemke's concertina. When they had put the last of the supplies in position Grossman began placing explosive charges at each corner of the two towers, and connecting them with quick fuse. The men looked at these preparations without expression, as the realization finally came through to them that they were in truth unlikely to see the sun go down. As he completed his wiring and crimping Grossman looked up to see everyone staring at him.

"Don't look so solemn, children. Here Lemke, here's your squeeze box. Make yourselves comfortable, and let's have a song. Lassman, let's have a beer all around."

All four of the troopers had provided themselves with musical instruments with which to relieve the monotony of their long, dreary tour at Namutoni. Lemke sat with his back against one of the battlements and commenced to squeeze out the melody of the old traditional song of longing.

"*Ich weiss nicht was soll es bedeuten* . . . ." The three troopers and the three farmers joined in together. Everybody knew both the song and its words. Becker had a surprisingly good voice, and harmonized a third above with his clear tenor.

As the song died away the men drank their beer solemnly, each occupied with his own thoughts. Grossman pointedly ignored the tears on Lemke's bristly cheeks. Lier lay on his cot, shaded by a blanket which had been stretched above his face, and babbled in delirium.

Grossman had placed two M71's and one M88 in the east tower and two 88's and one 71 in the west tower. The spare 88 lay fully loaded by Lier's cot in the west tower. Both rifle types were absolutely deadly at ranges of under two hundred meters, when well handled. The 88's could fire faster, and their smokeless powder did not obscure their view as did the 71's. On the other hand the 71's were probably more likely to hit with each shot under the circumstances. There were two hundred twenty-five rounds per 88, and one hundred forty for each 71. There was ammunition enough, but would there be time enough?

The beer was finished and the sun was higher, when some sort of activity amongst the Ovambo over inside the screen of thorns became apparent to the watchers on the roof. A single voice was raised in a long and ornate chant, punctuated by controlled shouting. Though they could not see clearly through the screen of acacia, it seemed that one man was engaged in a sort of exhortation or war dance. As he moved quickly in a circle they could make out that he was waving a spear in one hand and a rifle in the other. The performance continued for possibly thirty minutes and then ceased sharply. There was no further sound, but the Germans could now see solid ranks of black warriors again taking position facing them at the edge of the thorn.

"Everybody on this side," snapped Grossman, and three men in each tower snuggled into firing position, lying flat behind the battlements.

A single high scream came from the thorn, then suddenly the entire enemy line disappeared in a low haze of white smoke, and immediately afterward came a rolling, crackling crash as three hundred Martinis fired almost together. Nothing struck the building. A mighty shouting began.

"What the hell are they shooting at, Mr. Basendowski?" gasped Hartmann.

"I can't say, my friend, but apparently not at us."

"Look at 'em," said Grossman. "They're shooting those things like bows. They must figure that they get more power the more they elevate the muzzle! That volley must have gone twenty meters over us. God grant they don't learn what they're doing wrong!"

The firing continued, irregularly now, and through the white smoke the crowd of Ovambo came running forward, stopping to fire and then running on as they reloaded. The war cries grew louder.

"Commence firing!" roared Grossman, *"und Gott mit uns!"*

The Mausers opened up on the oncoming mass.

Basendowski squeezed carefully on the center of the chest of a big black who seemed to be leading the effort, and saw him crash forward. He snapped open the bolt and threw a new round in. Hartmann, on the extreme left, fired at the man farthest to his own left, and saw him go thrashing to the ground. Grossman, following his own advice, attempted to take two in column. He saw both go down, but one was immediately up again limping from a leg shot. Becker also scored with his first shot, as did Lemke, but Lassman, the medical corpsman, flinched and placed his round between the feet of his oncoming adversary.

"Damn you, Doc, squeeze that trigger! Don't jerk it, squeeze it. *Squeeze it!*"

It took the attackers about thirty seconds to close the distance between the acacia scrub and the mud walls of the fort. They took a savage pounding, but there were just not enough rifles to stem the tide. Still the rifle fire had an added effect in that it took its toll chiefly among the leaders of the Ovambo. The leaders were in front and those in front were the ones easiest to hit. Thus when the charge reached the walls of the fort there was no one left with any authority to give any direction to the action.

Grossman, who had emptied his first clip and reloaded, leaned over the parapet and fired five shots carefully down into the yelling warriors below him. Then he jumped back, reloaded a second time and reached in despair for the fuse leading to the blasting charges. As he lighted his slow-match the head and shoulders of a black warrior appeared over the wall behind him, just where Lier was stretched out, and the latter, brought around for the moment by the noise of the firing, feebly seized the rifle at his bedside, shoved it into the man's chest and pulled the trigger. A bright gout of blood burst from the entrance wound as the muzzle blast blew it open, and splashed over Lier as he lay. Grossman glimpsed it as he turned. He managed a fleeting grin and said, "Good boy, Albert! We'll make a soldier of you yet." Lier smiled weakly and gasped, "Tell 'em I got one, sarge. Tell 'em!"

The action was now totally confused. A group of unarmed Ovambo rushed around the tower and broke down the kraal, allowing the terrified cattle to stampede. The supporting fire of the attackers who had made it to the fort continued to obscure the scene in smoke. Becker had dropped his 71 and was now using Lier's 88 to good effect, firing at short range down over the wall. The black powder worked to an advantage here since it prevented anyone on either side from seeing clearly, and the Martini fire from outside the fort continued to whistle over the heads of the defenders without damage.

Suddenly the corrugated iron that formed the roof of the west tower erupted upward as three Martinis were fired from the storeroom below.

"So!" shouted Grossman. "What a good idea! But we can do it better, *Schwarzen.* Return it, Lassman, Lemke. Right through the roof, straight down, quickly now!"

And three Germans, firing as fast as they could work their bolts, poured fifteen rounds down into the room below.

No one in the fort was very clear about what happened in the next few minutes. The bedlam of shots and screams and shouts was enhanced by the sound of smashing furniture and storage materials from below. The roof between the towers suddenly went down with a crash and revealed a party of warriors attempting to place ladders they had found against the east wall of the west tower. Basendowski and Hartmann broke down the escalade with back-shots at a range of twenty feet.

Suddenly there was a great screaming, louder and more concerted than before. Through the smoke the defenders could see that the entire attacking party had apparently abandoned the enterprise and was running around the fort and off to the north. Grossman hurled his lighted slow-match over the wall at the fleeing attackers, and picked up his rifle again.

"Now, my children," he roared. "The good God has shown us his favor. Shoot carefully, lads! Oh, for the sake of God shoot carefully! One hit for for each shot! In the Kaiser's name, one hit for each shot!"

Many of the attackers made it, but they left a woeful remnant behind. The grass between the now partially wrecked fort and the thorn was strewn horribly with black and red bodies, some writhing, some stationary. Gulping cries were emitted by those still alive, but there was little of the wailing and moaning that might have been expected. The Bantu people rarely holler when hurt.

There was an exception. One warrior about half way out, apparently shot in the kidney, was shrieking horribly. A kidney shot is too much for even the most stoic. He struggled to his feet, screamed again and fell down, holding his middle. Lemke sighted in on him and commenced trigger pressure. Grossman's hand closed on his shoulder.

"No!" he said.

"But sergeant, he's in agony! Have you no mercy at all?"

"Young man, I have more mercy than he and his friends would have shown us had they carried the place. Hold your fire, and let's see what happens!"

Lassman pressed his face down into his blanket rest, and tried to stop his ears with his fingers.

The nerve-wracking shrieks continued, and through the trees two warriors came running forward, apparently to try to pull their comrade free. Grossman carefully sighted over the top of the parapet and muttered, "Now!"

At the double crack the two would-be rescuers fell and lay still. The screaming diminished and died away.

"There! You see what I had in mind, lads? But we didn't get them all, and you people shot more than you should have. God has saved us for the moment, but who knows what they will do now?"

At that moment there was a vicious crack and a burst of dried mud sprayed the sergeant, who was standing erect. "Everybody down!" he shouted, and followed his own precept. "Either some bird out there has got the range or his flinch compensated for his overhold. We're not out of this yet!"

Basendowski shouted from the east tower, "Anybody hurt over there?"

"Nobody. We're all OK, though I don't think I can believe it. What's the count out there in front?"

"What do you make it? A couple of hundred?"

"No, not that many. We got a good lot but it may not stop them. Among other things they'll be pretty upset with us now. I think some of their best people are lying out there in the grass."

III

It was quiet, except for an occasional moan from the grisly fields on both sides of the fort. The jackal came out of the thorn and lapped at the spring, several degrees more optimistic than before. Jackals have excellent noses.

It was hot, and six of the seven had taken shelter in the wreckage-strewn storeroom beneath the western tower. Lier, still covered with blood, had been laid on a blanket against one wall. Hartmann remained on watch topside. The five bodies they had found in the storeroom had been heaved outside, but the place was a bloody mess, and permeated by a most unpleasant odor. The dead were thickest just outside the walls.

"Eat, children," said Grossman. "Get your strength. You're going to need it."

"I'm not very hungry, sarge," murmured Lemke. "All this excitement has spoiled my appetite."

"Have a beer then, and loosen up, for God's sake! This is just one more day in the Kaiser's army."

"It may well be the last day," said Becker. "Those bastards are not leaving. They're going to come for us again, and what will we do then?"

"We'll do our damnedest. And it will have to do. But somehow I don't think they will be back, at least for a bit. They took a good beating, and they'll have a lot of talk before they decide what to do next."

He turned to Lassman. The boy was staring fixedly at the wall, and shivering slightly despite the heat.

"Come on, lad. You shot pretty well, once you got sorted out. I think you took your full share, especially when they ran away."

" I don't like it, sergeant. I . . . I can't stand it! I can still hear him screaming! I want to go home! I want to be a doctor, not a soldier! I want to go home!"

Basendowski heaved himself to his feet and walked over to the corpsman. He put his hand on his shoulder. "Hang on, son," he said, softly. "None of us likes this, but we've got to do what we must. Hang on!"

The boy looked up and almost shouted, "Hang on for what? We're going to die here! We're all going to die here! We all know that! I want to go home," he wailed.

Grossman stood erect. "Now listen, everybody! We're going to make it. We are *not* going to die. The *Schwarzen* are all over there to the north licking their wounds. When they come back we won't be here. We are going to leave—to the south. We are going to hike out.

"Lassman, you and Lemke rig a litter for Lier. We want two of those poles and a blanket slung between them. Put two spacers at each end, so the center won't sag. Quick now, finish your lunch and let's get going."

"We'll never make it, *Herr Unteroffizier*," said Basendowski. "Those devils will be on us as soon as they know we've moved out. They'll run us down before we've gone a kilometer."

"Maybe they will, Sergeant Basendowski, and then again maybe they won't. If we stay here they will get sensible, and we just don't have enough ammunition left for another party like this morning. We just shot too bloody much! I know we got excited, but we ran through our ammunition like grease through a goose. You know what we've got left? We have just one hundred fifty rounds, for all six of us! Whatever we did this morning, we can't do it again. We've got to move out. We simply have no choice."

"But where will we go, man? Whichever way we move they will track us, and they can move five times as fast as we can when we are carrying a litter. It just won't do!"

"You prefer, perhaps, to wait for them here? When we run dry they can take us alive. You fancy a hot spear threaded up your rectum and out your mouth?"

Grossman stared out the north door toward the thorn. No one was in sight.

"I say we have to take the chance! They just may not see us leave if we move out while they're jabbering. I don't fancy it, children, any more than you do, but it is our only choice.

"We move straight south away from their camp, and then we'll hang a left, and make for your place at Sandhup. From there we'll move on to Grootfontein. God had been good to us so far. I can't believe that He will abandon us now.

"Now everybody load up and prepare to move. Rifles, ammunition, and water. A couple of sticks of biltong apiece. Nothing else. No blankets, no beer, and I regret to say we'll have to leave the musical instruments behind."

He called topside, "Come on down, Hartmann, and get ready to move out. I'll watch from down here."

"Oh my poor cattle," groaned Basendowski. "My beauties. The hope of my future, and now the savages have them all! What a way to end the story! Oh my beauties!"

"The story needn't be over, Mr. Basendowski," said Becker. "The commissioner at Lüderitz will grant us an indemnity and we can make a new start."

"I can't face it, Franz. If we get out of this I'm going home. There may be no land available for a farmer in East Prussia, but maybe I can get a job in a shipyard."

"So that's where he got that Polack name," thought Grossman to himself. "He is *Oberschliesser*. They make good soldiers. No nerves and no imagination." Aloud he said, "Don't take it so hard, Mr. Basendowski. I know it must be terrible to see years of work go up in smoke, but tomorrow is another day. Let's see if we can live through this one."

The sun had begun to decline by the time their preparations were made. Grossman stepped outside and took one last look around on all sides of the fort. There was no one in sight except the dead. He came back, took his place on the right side of the head of the litter, reached down and said, "Allright, lads, up we go!" The six men picked up Lier on his stretcher and set off to the south.

It was not more than yards before the men realized the magnitude of the task they had undertaken. The sun was fearful. The humidity was high. The ground underfoot was mainly sand. Their primary destination was a day's march distant, and any minute they expected to hear a howling behind them as the Ovambo picked up their track. They said nothing. There was nothing to say. They marched.

IV

The Ovambo did not discover the flight, or perhaps they had had enough. The fugitives marched to exhaustion for fourteen hours, without food. They reached Basendowski's farm at dawn and found it wrecked by Bushmen who had taken advantage of the uprising to grab what they could. The only things left were a few chickens and shoats that the Bushmen had not gathered up. This sufficed, however, to stave off starvation. Hindered by the sick man, the troopers were simply not up to the hundred mile march to Grootfontein, but Basendowski and Becker got some rest and a meal and then headed off on foot to report the scene at the military headquarters.

The following day, more or less by coincidence, a relief patrol, which had no knowledge of the fight at Namutoni, arrived and the five men were rescued. Four days later Basendowski and Becker arrived safely at Grootfontein.

Subsequent investigation disclosed that the Ovambo war-party numbered about four hundred, of whom three hundred were armed with Martini-Henry, 45 caliber, single-shot, black-powder rifles. During the attack the Ovambo suffered sixty-eight dead, twenty disabled and forty unaccounted for—presumably wounded too badly to check back in. Thus the six riflemen seemed to have averaged about twenty casualties each. A lot of ammunition was expended and we must assume that some of those riflemen were shooting much better than others. We may surmise that Farmer Basendowski, using a weapon with which he was entirely familiar, and shooting with the proverbially nerveless composure of the *Oberschliesser*, may have accounted for forty or more individual hits.

The Ovambo attacked again on the morning of the second day, only to find that the birds had flown. They then burned the fort to the ground and marched back to Ondongwa, leaving their dead on the field for the hyenas. Shute was thus able to report to Nechale that he had razed the fort and accomplished his mission.

Lier recovered from his bout with malaria, and there were no injuries sustained by any of the Germans.

The bare bones of this action are a matter of record. All dialogue and "corroborative detail" are speculative, though we have photos of beer bottles and musical instruments. We cannot know how it actually was, but this is how it might have been.

The fort was rebuilt, on a larger scale, by the Germans in 1906, but because the land was deemed pacified and because malaria was both prevalent and virulent, the post was neg-lected and fell into ruins. Following WWII, however, the site was declared a national monument and reconstruction was commenced. In 1958 the rebuilt fort was opened for tourist accommodation. Thirty years later we stayed the night in Fort Namutoni—in the "Basendowski Room."

THE CROSSING

In the long view, the watershed of Western civilization was probably World War I. Certainly we have progressed in technology and medicine since then, but hardly in standards —which are more important. Nonetheless, while the *ancien regime* perished in the crucible of European battlefields, important elements of elegance and style persisted all the way up to World War II, lending a certain gloss to a culture which had passed its prime. Among these was the North Atlantic crossing, in the fifteen years between 1925 and the outbreak of World War II. During this short period life on one of the great transatlantic ocean liners reached a level which never had been achieved by anyone before or since. Compared to a first-class passage on one of the great liners, all else pales.

It was my astonishing good fortune to make that crossing no less than twelve times, on the Aquitania, Mauretania, Berengaria, Olympic, Majestic, Rex, Conte di Savoia, Bremen (twice), Europa, Ile de France, and Normandie (twice). I was too young to appreciate the experience fully, but I could observe, and to this day I can recall the wonder of it all.

The thing that made that crossing different from any experience available since was not mere luxury, though that was of the highest order, but rather an electric combination of elegance and excitement. In those days flying was in its infancy, and when important people traveled between the continents they went by ship. Thus on any passage the passenger list included heads of state, artists, philosophers, tycoons, entertainers, bluebloods, and various sorts of adventurers, all dining together, dancing together, playing together, conversing together, and (presumably) sleeping together. (I was too young at the time to understand about the informal game of "musical beds" which seemed to have been widely enjoyed, but I heard about it later in life.)

Looking back half-a-century one naturally forgets the annoyances and frustrations of an experience and remembers only the high points, but those high points soon make up into a brilliant tapestry. What I remember now is a combination of exhilaration and wonder, compared to which a turn in the Concorde is about as exciting as a taxi ride.

In the days of surface transportation one commenced his Atlantic crossing by first making his way to New York. My family lived in Los Angeles, and the run across the continent by train was something of an adventure in itself. Before air-conditioning that train ride had its drawbacks. In order to maintain some semblance of gentility the ladies demanded a stopover of at least a week in New York. New York was quite different then, and that interlude involved a fairly steady round of shopping and theatergoing. Live theater was in full cry, and the streets were safe. As juniormost member of the party I was assigned to zoos, museums, and Central Park. This was no hardship for a West Coast kid.

The real adventure began, however, at embarkation. As fleets of taxis descended upon the piers, armies of baggage-handlers turned out to assemble and account for the party's luggage.

And such luggage! In these latter days it may be impossible to envision the amount of luggage which was deemed adequate in the 20's and 30's. One normally spent five nights aboard ship, and this meant that each lady had to have one very elegant street dress, three dinner dresses and a ball-gown. Each gentleman needed a business suit, a dinner jacket and one full evening dress — "white tie and tails." Beyond that, of course, there had to be clothes for daily wear which varied from business dress to "sporting." And beyond that there was the matter of clothes to be worn in Europe upon arrival, which might or might not coincide with the clothes reserved for the voyage. This regalia was packed into steamer trunks. I do not believe that steamer trunks, as such, are manufactured any more, but they were quite a study at the time. My father's family consisted of five, plus occasional companions, all traveling together. And as I recall it, when all the luggage was stacked on the dock it occupied a space about as large as half a tennis court, though since I started out small I may have an exaggerated memory of this. Let us say, however, that there was a *lot* of luggage. For identification my father had each trunk, box, and case striped with a broad scarlet band bordered with blue and white. He may have been one of the first to employ this system, since I remember that it was remarked upon by pursers and other travelers. Every time the family changed from one mode of travel to another this formidable agglomeration of gear had to be moved, marshalled, counted and moved again, to the accompaniment of appropriate tips. This tipping must have accounted for about 30% of the cost of transportation — perhaps more.

Once everything was in place on the dock my father left his family staring at the cliff-like side of the enormous vessel and went aboard to check with the purser. This man, the purser, was in charge of passenger accommodations and his job was an enormous one. Naturally he could not perform it alone, and his large staff was responsible for the initial impressions of the passengers. As soon as my father had examined the quarters allotted us and found them to his satisfaction, the purser's people took over the task of getting all that luggage aboard, through entrances low in the hull, and transferring it up through the decks to our living quarters. Now it was time for the entire party to go aboard and be introduced to the servants who would be looking out for our comfort throughout the voyage.

In the rather pinched and dreary era we enjoy today, few can remember that one of the amenities of bygone life was personal service. On a first-class ocean voyage each lady was assigned a ladies' maid, and each gentleman a valet. If desired, each "young person" could be assigned an attendant; a sort of nursemaid, baby-sitter or governess, depending upon age.

It was usual for a family group to be allotted a suite of rooms, and to this suite one personal steward was assigned. It was the steward's duty to keep us all happy with any sort of meal or snack we might desire, at any time of day or night. The food in the regular dining facilities was lavish to the point of extravagance, but for those who wished breakfast in bed, or a three a.m. spot of caviar, all was included with the price of the ticket, except for beverages. (This did not apply to beer on the German liners, which was considered part of the food outlay.)

If departure was scheduled after the normal time of the evening meal, the cabin steward set up a full party snack in the family suite, to which all *bon voyage* friends were invited. This was usually composed of champagne, caviar, and paper-thin chicken sandwiches, plus other features such as lobsters and oysters in season. One customarily invited all local friends and well-wishers aboard the vessel for this send-off party. Under Prohibition, of course, nothing alcoholic was served at dockside, but in 1932 this changed and these send-off parties became quite hilarious.

It was somewhat more convenient to schedule a morning departure, since this gave the ladies a chance to hold elaborate conferences with their maids as to the order of precedence of their various evening gowns. Gentlemen could spend that first afternoon exploring the ship, and, if so inclined, enjoying the freedom from the Eighteenth Amendment as soon as the vessel was three miles out. "Dry America" managed to work up a Rabelaisian thirst which has only now begun to taper off. With a daytime departure one did not dress for dinner, but that did not imply informality. Gentlemen wore business suits and ladies wore street dresses.

Dining on the great ocean liners achieved heights which can hardly be understood today, despite the fact that modern restaurants can prepare food that is as good as that then served aboard. Food service was raised to a very high art, and the various liners competed with each other for their reputations as

gourmet heavens. This was before the day of frozen ingre-
dients, and the master chef on each liner made a major effort to
obtain everything just as fresh as possible, right up to the
minute of sailing.

Each passenger family was assigned a table. Each sector of
the dining room was under the supervision of a section *maitre*.
Each table had its own table captain, and there was one waiter for
each two or three passengers. Each section was assigned a *sommelier* to provide the wines for each meal and for each course.

One selected from a menu only on the first night out.
There would be a conference between the head of the family
and the table captain as to menus for the following days. That
is to say, your dinner on both Monday and Tuesday night
would be selected on Monday night. Thereafter all meals
would be planned on the previous day. This gave the table
captain freedom to arrange each meal with the chef some
twenty-four hours in advance. The *sommelier* and the table
captain, in conference with the head of the family, would
indulge in lengthy and meticulous discussions concerning the
exactly appropriate wine to accompany each dish on each day.
There was never any hurry.

Naturally this system resulted in dining of the highest
imaginable quality. Staff employment on the great liners was
highly paid, not easily obtained, and constituted a great
enhancement of the reputation of the individual. Its only
drawback was the possibility of accidentally finding oneself
involved with a customer of low taste. I suppose this had to be
considered an occupational hazard, and a chance that an aspiring waiter just had to risk.

Apart from the glorious food and perfect service, dinner
was always a major event, constituting as it did a celebrity
exhibition, a fashion show and a status display. On the greatest
liners, at the end of the era, the dining hall was usually
approached by a magnificent descending stairway with a landing halfway down. It was expected that each entrant would

descend to the landing and stand there a moment in splendor, accompanied by his lady plus any grown children, aides, secretaries or attendants. There was always, of course, live music, and it became something of a game to time one's entrance to take advantage of just the right selection so that everyone at table could admire and discuss all elements of the procession. This was an age of ostentation, and the whole thing came to a head on the last night out, or Captain's Dinner, at which everyone wore full regalia, including sashes, ribbons, and miniature medals. Ladies of rank wore tiaras at Captain's Dinner.

Quite often a cheerful rapport was established between a table crew and its own particular family. As the voyage proceeded, the floor people would evolve into a sort of cheering section, rooting for their own clients as more attractive, more elegant, or more noteworthy than others. They would not actually cheer, but they could become very complimentary to the ladies. This seemed fully as much spontaneous as it was a method of increasing tips.

But sumptuous dining was hardly the entire purpose of the exercise. Life aboard ship was carefully arranged to provide one delight after another. One generally slept late in the morning and took breakfast in his room. In the early days the most desirable rooms were outside, and were fitted with portholes opening directly to sea, in addition to various sorts of ventilators which could be used when the sea was high or the weather was bad. In nice weather the porthole was open and the salt breeze was a great encouragement to sound sleep. At the end of the period air-conditioning was introduced by the Germans and immediately followed by the other lines. This was a novelty, and produced certain problems of its own. My father, for instance, opted for an inside room just to test the machinery out, and the combination of absolute darkness, bountiful fresh air, and dead silence led some people to sleep the clock around, and thus miss many of the delights which the ship offered in its daily routine. Adolescents are generally great sleepers, and I remember my father having to shake me out with some impatience on several occasions when he thought I might starve to death before I woke up.

Forenoon activities varied with individuals, though almost everyone found occasion to do the required number of laps around the promenade deck. Each vessel's deck was clearly marked with its length so that those who wished to time themselves or spell themselves knew exactly how far they had walked on each turn. The idea was to walk briskly enough to obtain a certain amount of exercise, but this was before the day of jogging, and only children were encouraged to run. A minor problem in etiquette arose here if one happened to be walking clockwise when some acquaintance or friend was walking counter-clockwise at the same time. On first encounter, of course, one could wish a cheery good morning, but on the twelfth or fourteenth such meeting this became mildly annoying. One answer was to reverse one's direction and hope for the best in an attempt to avoid encountering the same problem with somebody else going the same way you had started out.

The boat deck was lined with deck chairs, and it was customary for ladies and gentlemen, after their morning walk, to slip into these and read (people still read for pleasure at that time). At ten o'clock, or thereabouts, the soup cart made it round to the deck chairs, and everyone was offered a cup of hot broth. I discovered this to be somewhat dangerous, since it was so good that I was tempted to drink it before it was cool. I scalded my tongue on one such occasion, which I still remember because it ruined my capacity to enjoy my wonderful meals for most of two days.

But the mornings were certainly not restricted to walking and reading. On every ship there was a complete gymnasium, and as soon as I was big enough I took up the study of the sword. Each gymnasium was manned by a series of trainers who were adept at all sorts of activities from fencing to weightlifting, and could provide expert coaching for those who desired it. From about the age of twelve on I made it a rule to take a brisk workout with the sword for one hour every morning.

There were always the traditional deck games — shuffleboard and deck tennis — for vigorous enjoyment topside in pleasant weather. Also in good weather trapshooting was offered at announced intervals, and when storms sprang up there was a shooting gallery indoors. I remember my astonishment at the elaborate shooting facilities on the Bremen and Europa, which featured forest scenes with running deer and elk on which the film stopped at the moment of the shot and a small white light indicated the placement of the hit. This sort of thing was available in the 1930's, but has only now been rediscovered in shooting circles.

Every ship featured a fully-stocked library complete with librarian, and chess was always offered for those who enjoyed it. Chess struck me as particularly good shipboard entertainment, since all the passengers were relative strangers and had no way of assessing each other's skills. Playing against the same person too often can be dull.

If the morning was spent in sports it was necessary to retire and clean up for lunch, if one chose to dine in the main hall. An assortment of snackbars made this unnecessary, and stewards were always on call in any part of the ship to provide anything from scrambled eggs to a cut of rare roast beef.

After lunch came horse racing, this being one of the four activities in which ladies and gentlemen always indulge when they have the leisure to do so. The racetrack was laid out in one of the main salons, and consisted of an oval ring of six parallel tracks crossed at about ten-foot intervals with prominent stop lines. Each model horse was given a name and a number and the players were encouraged to place their bets. In the center of the oval the director rolled the dice prominently on a green table. At each roll any horse whose number came up moved forward one space. If his number came up two or more times, he was moved forward that number of spaces by the attendants. In steeplechasing it was necessary for a horse to have his number come up twice on the same roll in order to surmount the jump. You might be surprised how exciting this became, especially since fairly large amounts of money were wagered.

Activities continued throughout the day, and were too varied to be enjoyed on each occasion, thus the avid horseracers would never catch up to the trapshooting, and the deck-tennis enthusiasts might never make it to the swimming pool.

Between horse racing and pool time those who wished could be regaled with "high tea" in the British manner —always on British ships and usually on those of other registry. One would not be expected to show up for tea in sporting attire so a change of clothing was in order.

High tea was, of course, a pretty sumptuous repast, including some of the most impressive pastry variations in the world. Restraint was indicated, if not always practiced.

After tea there might be just time for another bout of deck tennis before changing again for swimming.

As I recall it the swimming pool, or pools, were generally enjoyed in the late afternoon, prior to retiring to the cabin in preparation for the evening's great event. These pools were particularly amusing in periods of heavy weather when the water would slosh around at a great rate. It was fun to be knee-deep at one moment and over one's head the next.

I do not recall what the gentlemen did between the swimming pool and the dinner table, but I suspect that they donned their evening clothes considerably earlier than the ladies, and met in one of the various bars for serious conversation about politics, sports and business. The ladies, of course, took several hours of preparation for dinner, and thus were more poised and serene for the great entrance down the stairway. After dinner everyone retired to the smoking room for cognac, cigars, conversation and possibly a bit of cheese. There was always live chamber music in the smoking room, and oddly, by today's standards, almost everyone smoked. To admit that one did not smoke would be rather like admitting that one did not drink. This could only be passed off if one wore brocades and turban, suggesting that he belonged to some exotic religious order. After an hour or so of conversation in the smoking room movies were offered, black and white and silent at first, but this did not detract from the appeal of Clark Gable and Greta Garbo. After movies the married folk usually moved to the ballroom for dancing, while the young folk generally went aloft to the cabaret on the top deck, where jazz and the Charleston were featured.

One of the important attractions of the great days of ocean travel was the character of the guest list. It was rare indeed that the passengers did not include a number of important performing artists, and these people were easily prevailed upon to entertain. I distinctly remember hearing Tito Schipa, Jan Kiepura, Giovanni Martinelli, and Lily Pons sing on shipboard. I do not know what, if any, financial adjustments were made in these cases, but naturally there was no charge for them to the passengers.

At midnight the ship's pool was held. At this gathering the number of miles covered the preceding day was announced, and a selection of numbers approximating that were offered for auction. This was pure gambling, for no one could possibly know the exact number of miles that might be covered between midnight and midnight, and the bidding was furious and prolonged. As each number was sold it was recorded on the board to await the exact determination of mileage covered on the following midnight. Naturally no one ever went hungry or thirsty on these occasions, and I remember that my father's favorite snack was a Welsh rabbit and a pint of Guinness.

What one did after midnight was entirely according to his taste. Dance music in the main ballroom generally wound down about two a.m., but much depended upon the enthusiasm of the performers at the time. In the cabaret topside it frequently continued till dawn, depending entirely upon demand, since there were no binding rules for anything. One could do what he wished whenever he wished. If an activity shut down it was simply because there was no one around to ask for more.

It may be supposed that a passage such as this was restricted to the very wealthy, and in truth it was not cheap. First-class passage, one-way, across the Atlantic, everything included except beverages, ran to three hundred dollars. Today, of course, three-and-a-half hours in a Concorde costs four thousand dollars.

Reminiscing over half-a-century, the thing that puzzles me is the matter of time. Even if such a splendid experience were available now, which of course it is not, and even if I could afford it, which I just might, I see no way that I could take the time. Everyone seems to have become too busy to do anything really interesting. We race madly hither and yon trying to meet airplane schedules, insisting that we have no time. You would think, what with modern communications and transportation, that we could accomplish much more with our lives than those behind us. However we do not seem to. For example, Teddy Roosevelt was limited to surface transportation and he wrote longhand, yet he accomplished more, in more diverse fields, than anyone active today. The same can be said of Winston Churchill. Times have indeed changed, but I am not sure for the better.

One of the interesting things about my recollection of the crossing is the fact that nutrition had not got hold of us by the throat. Nobody gave a thought to cholesterol, salt, butterfat, calories, sugar, booze, tobacco or jogging. There was plenty of exercise available, but it was done for enjoyment rather than for physical condition. On the other hand there were no drugs. We must suppose that certain physicians may have occasionally bombed themselves out on opium, but this was never apparent. All of those people of fifty years ago must have died miserable deaths from various sorts of degenerative diseases, though in general they seem to have lived fully as long as people do now. In any case, they did not allow preoccupation with bad habits to interfere with their enjoyment of life. It is quite possible that a modern health faddist would not be able to enjoy the transatlantic crossing in any case, so perhaps it is just as well that it is no longer available to him.

It is clear from the foregoing that while we have many magnificent cruise ships available today, the cruise experience is in no way comparable to the crossing, mainly because in today's society the people who have both the time and the money for a cruise are not usually very interesting. In the great days of the crossing possibly the most exciting part of the whole experience was the nature of the passenger list. For a few days a passenger could associate on reasonably intimate terms with all the important people in the world, and conversation, of course, was still an art. The transatlantic passenger could live in the lap of luxury in the company of the wise, the great, the rich, the talented and the beautiful.

This was the life of a king, without the Sword of Damocles, and it will never come again.

·KIRCHNER·

MAXIMILIAN I OF HAPSBURG
1459 - 1519
Holy Roman Emperor

Behold the Emperor: Max the First,
　　With his nose of a hawk and his powerful thirst.
He dined right well on his beef and his beer,
　　And the welkin rang with his lordly cheer.

His muscles gleamed like iron bands,
　　He twisted horseshoes in his hands.
He bore his lance on his great black horse,
　　And tilted in many a spirited course.

He rode betimes to dynastic wars,
　　And in days of peace he pursued wild boars.
He laughed and he sang through the livelong day,
　　And never a lady would say him nay.

But grand as he was, he was wistful still,
　　For his heart's desire he might not fulfill.
When never a lady will you deny,
　　You can never be sure of the reason why.

Bold, handsome and powerful though you be,
　　No heart you command can ever be free.
And a heart unfree cannot requite
　　The quest of the soul for pure delight.

Though Max was great yet did he grieve,
　　For he was wise this to perceive.
Let grandeur be its own reward.
　　He knew what he could not afford.

(Based on the emperor's diary, 1510)

367